Praise for L<

"Very few people understand t   DØ372385   : than
Mickey Ibarra. It's the power ι͙͙͙͙ ͙ ͙͙͙ g͙g͙, ͙͙͙p͙͙ ͙͙͙ ͙͙͙ͧͧͧ͘ both
the storyteller and listener by inviting them to take a shared journey,
from the launch of the quest, through times of adversity, to a place
where they can serve as leaders in their community. More than that,
story can help people come together by making them more human
and relatable across political, ethnic and gender divides. Ibarra gathers
prominent Latinos to share their stories with the next generation of
leaders—Latino and non-Latino alike—at a time when shared stories
are so badly needed. *Latino Leaders Speak* belongs in every American
classroom."

—Giovanni Rodriguez, *Forbes* contributor and
founder of The Silicon Valley Story Lab

"'Our stories are powerful and need to be told.' That simple yet seminal statement in *Latino Leaders Speak* is precisely what makes this
book required reading. Many times our stories are not told, or are
told through a stereotypical, negative lens. Many of the contributors
are well known in the Latino community, but their personal stories
are not. Mickey Ibarra's eye-opening personal story itself serves as a
source of inspiration, and these Latino leaders' stories will help
inspire the community to realize that it is possible to achieve one's
dreams and goals despite obstacles."

—Patricia Guadalupe, Contributing Writer, *NBC Latino,*
and Washington Editor, *Latino Magazine*

Latino Leaders Speak

Personal Stories of
Struggle and Triumph

Edited by
Mickey Ibarra & María Pérez-Brown

Arte Público Press
Houston, Texas

Latino Leaders Speak: Personal Stories of Struggle and Triumph is funded in part by a grant from the City of Houston through the Houston Arts Alliance.

Recovering the past, creating the future

Arte Público Press
University of Houston
4902 Gulf Fwy, Bldg 19, Rm 100
Houston, Texas 77204-2004

Cover design by Victoria Castillo

Names: Ibarra, Mickey, editor of compilation. | Perez-Brown, Maria, 1961- editor of compilation.
Title: Latino leaders speak : personal stories of struggle and triumph / Mickey Ibarra and María Pérez-Brown, editors.
Description: Houston, TX : Arte Público Press, [2017]
Identifiers: LCCN 2017003704| ISBN 9781558858435 (alk. paper) | ISBN 9781518501272 (kindle) | ISBN 9781518501289 (pdf)
Subjects: LCSH: Hispanic Americans—Biography. | Success—United States. | Leadership—United States.
Classification: LCC E184.S75 L36232 2010 | DDC 973/.0468—dc 3 LC record available at https://lccn.loc.gov/2017003704

♾ The paper used in this publication meets the requirements of the American National Standard for Information Sciences—Permanence of Paper for Printed Library Materials, ANSI Z39.48-1984.

17 18 19 20   5 4 3 2 1

Table of Contents

INTRODUCTION | MICKEY IBARRA, FOUNDER & CHAIRMAN, LATINO LEADERS NETWORK. ix

Henry Bonilla 1
Congressman, U.S. House of Representatives

Susan Castillo 5
State Superintendent of Schools, State of Oregon

Joaquín Castro 15
Congressman, Texas' 20th District

Francisco G. Cigarroa 19
Physician & Chancellor, The University of Texas System

Henry G. Cisneros 27
U.S. Secretary of Housing & Urban Development

Virgilio P. Elizondo 37
Reverend Father & Professor, The University of Notre Dame

Lily Eskelsen-García 45
President, National Education Association

Alberto R. Gonzales 53
U.S. Attorney General

Carlos Gutiérrez 59
Businessman & U.S. Secretary of Commerce

Luis V. Gutiérrez 67
Congressman, U.S. House of Representatives

José Hernández 77
Astronaut, NASA

Maria Hinojosa 91
Producer, Author & Journalist

Dolores Huerta 105
Civil Rights Activist & President, Dolores Huerta
Foundation

Mel Martínez 113
U.S. Senator & U.S. Secretary of Housing &
Urban Development

Robert "Bob" Menéndez 125
U.S. Senator

Omar Minaya 133
General Manager, NY Mets

Gloria Molina 139
County Supervisor, Los Angeles County

Richard Montañez 149
Author & Executive Vice President, PepsiCo

Janet Murguía 161
President & CEO, National Council of La Raza

Soledad O'Brien 171
Journalist, Producer & Anchor, CNN

Federico Peña 181
Mayor, City of Denver

Thomas E. Pérez 189
Chair of the Democratic National Committee &
U.S. Secretary of Labor

William "Bill" Richardson 195
Governor, New Mexico

Adam Rodríguez 203
Actor & Screenwriter

Ken Salazar 209
U.S. Secretary of the Interior

María Elena Salinas 221
News Anchor, Univision

Ricardo Sánchez 231
Lieutenant General, U.S. Army

Hilda L. Solis 243
U.S. Secretary of Labor

Lionel Sosa 251
Author, Advertising Executive & Artist

Julie Stav 255
Financial Expert & Best-Selling Author

Leticia Van De Putte 261
Texas State Senator

Nydia M. Velázquez 267
Congresswoman, New York's 7th District

Antonio Ramón Villaraigosa 273
Chairman, Democratic National Convention &
Mayor, Los Angeles

Introduction

Mickey Ibarra
Founder & Chairman
Latino Leaders Network

I was an Assistant to the President of the United States and Director of Intergovernmental Affairs at The White House before mustering the courage to publically share my personal story.

President Bill Clinton showed me the way by sharing his story often. First by introducing himself to the American people during the campaign of 1992 using a video biography called "The Man from Hope." This method had never been used before by a presidential candidate and proved to be an effective vehicle for delivering an inspirational message of obstacles overcome to achieve success.

My experience at 1600 Pennsylvania Avenue for nearly four years and observing reactions to the president's story triggered my desire to help others by sharing mine. Our stories are powerful and need to be told; when we do, it gives readers and listeners confidence to achieve their dreams as well.

Now my story: only in America could a Mexican kid who grew up in Utah foster care end-up being a witness to history, working alongside the President of the United States. Thirty-two years after arriving in Washington, I still feel a great deal of gratitude for the lessons learned from the many people who helped me along the way. Please understand that I share my story knowing that every detail may not be accurate but rather, is my best memory and understanding of the facts and sequence of events.

My father, Francisco Nicolás Santiago Ibarra, is a Zapotec Indian who came to this country as a *bracero* from Oaxaca, Mexico in 1945. His first job was picking fruit in Spanish Fork, Utah. Eventually he left the fields and landed a job at Kennecott Copper Mine as a demolition crew member. It was a union job with better pay, benefits and security.

Dad met and married my mother who was younger, white and Mormon. In the early 1950's that was unacceptable for most in Salt Lake City. By the time I was two years old, the predictable happened: my parents divorced causing my father to lose his military draft deferment. He was soon drafted into the United States Army and sent to Germany. Soon after the divorce, my mother, who was 18 years old, relinquished custody of my younger brother David and me to the Children's Service Society of Utah. We were placed together in foster care.

For most of the first fifteen years of my life, we were without traditional parents. As kids, we both wondered about who we were and why we were alone, but we coped with our experience differently. I was the peacemaker and negotiator with a lot to say and always feeling a responsibility to help David make it. But despite my best efforts, David withdrew. He was extremely shy, afraid and angry. David would not talk. I literally talked for him. His teachers at elementary school would come and get me out of class when he was acting-up to settle him down. He often would go to the restroom, hide in the stalls and would not emerge for anyone else.

When I was six years old, we briefly reunited with Dad after he remarried and the State of Utah allowed him to take custody of us. However, when that marriage failed, we were right back in foster care. Although we were very fortunate because of Ila and Cecil Smith in Provo, Utah, a white Mormon family who cared for us for more than seven years at the request of my father.

I talked too much but otherwise was doing fine in school; I got along with everybody. Yet, my brother continued to struggle. This was when I first experienced the impact of skin color. David, who is a shade darker than me, was confronted with discrimination and racism. David was resentful about our life in foster care. Often people would ask David the simple yet hurtful question, "Well, if your name is Ibarra—most often pronounced in Utah as "Eye-Bear-Ah"—how come you're living with the Smith's?" It caused him to fight back with his fists. The same person never asked that question twice, but it dragged David deeper and deeper into trouble.

During the summer of 1966, our father invited us to come and visit him in Sacramento. I was fifteen years old; David was fourteen. By this time my dad had left Utah after using his GI Bill benefits earned during his military service to take night classes at the Hollywood Beauty College in Salt Lake City. He became a hair stylist in Sacramento and was able to achieve his dream of owning a business: The Mona Lisa House of Beauty. Dad operated a successful beauty salon for nearly 30 years.

While vacationing in Sacramento, David pleaded with Dad to let us live with him. He agreed with one condition: we could not split-up. He told us, "You've never been separated before and you're not going to be split-up now." He required that we remain together.

I was not sure about leaving Utah. I had just completed my freshman year at an elite private four-year high school, thanks to the intervention of my foster mom, Ila Smith. Sports were of supreme importance to me, and I had made the junior varsity football team. In the end, I knew David wasn't going to make it in Utah so we decided to reunite with Dad in Sacramento.

Our foster parents were very disappointed. They thought we were making a big mistake. But they realized it was our mistake to make. We packed and shipped all of our belongings by mail, got a bus ticket and off we went to Sacramento in August of 1966.

There are a few crossroads that truly changed my life. The decision to leave Utah was a game changer for David and me. Doing so gave us the opportunity to gain self-awareness and helped us find the identity missing in our lives. We weren't "Eye-Bear-Ah" anymore. We had the opportunity to spend time with our father and learn from him.

I have never been around a harder working man in my life or anyone who is more proud of his Mexican heritage. We were able to meet our family and become more familiar with Mexican culture. It was an amazing and positive experience that for the first time gave us a true sense of belonging.

The biggest change was how many Latinos lived in Sacramento and how much more casual California was about race. We felt immediately more comfortable about our identity; it helped set us on a path to leadership. That path started for me with sports and then continued as senior class president and being voted "Most Likely to Succeed." David joined me in student government as junior class president at Luther Burbank Senior High School. Today he is a successful entrepreneur in Salt Lake City, member of the Latino Leaders Network Board of Directors and founder of the Ibarra Foundation to help Utah Latino students attend college.

Since the early years in Utah and California, I have experienced so many terrific professional leadership opportunities as a teacher, union organizer, White House official and now, some 32 years later, representing my clients. The common thread is advocacy. I am an advocate by profession.

Like reuniting with Dad in Sacramento, my experience advocating for President Clinton at the White House was another pivotal crossroad in my life and career. President Clinton taught me a most valuable lesson about advocacy early on during my time there: "Winning is about addition and multiplication; losing is about subtraction and division." I always try to win by addition and multiplication. It can build a movement, win elections, achieve good policy, fight for a cause and turn-out a crowd. That is the best leadership formula for success in politics and in life.

I realized as we exited the White House on the final day in 2001, it was going to be important for me to figure out how to continue the conversation with so many leaders that I had come to respect during my time there. Nearly four years with a West Wing office made it possible to convene not only hundreds of elected officials but also many non-elected officials, Latino and non-Latino alike. The White House offered a unique platform that most showed up for when invited.

Founding the Latino Leaders Network was in part a strategy for creating a platform to share our personal stories and to help each other succeed. It has embraced a simple yet difficult mission to achieve: "bringing leaders together." To do so, we organize the quarterly Latino Leaders Luncheon Series and the Tribute to Mayors held during the winter and summer meetings of the U.S. Conference of Mayors.

The Latino Leaders Luncheon Series is an opportunity to honor national Latino leaders willing to share their personal stories of overcoming obstacles to achieve success. The gatherings are re-energizing and motivating. They ground us in what leadership requires and how important it is to continue our efforts to help each other succeed.

We honor elected officials and also leaders from all walks of life—entertainment, sports, science, academia and more. We honor a broad cross-section of Latino leaders from different professions and sectors, but also from different ethnicities and backgrounds. We have a diverse Latino leadership community and their stories can help unite us. Yes, we are "stronger together," to borrow a recent campaign slogan.

Since 2004, the Latino Leaders Network has convened 49 luncheon events hosting nearly 11,000 guests. This book, *Latino Leaders Speak: Personal Stories of Struggle and Triumph*, includes 32 keynote addresses delivered at the series as its primary source material. We want to share these stories with everyone in America to learn about our heroes, our role models and our leaders. We especially hope the addresses inspire young people on their paths to success.

While growing up in Utah foster care, I felt different but didn't know why. Reading this book as a young man may have caused me to dream bigger, faster and stronger earlier. We have so much to celebrate and so much to learn from each other.

It is my hope that this book will inspire all readers to dream big, get prepared and get ready to lead.

Henry Bonilla
Congressman
U.S. House of Representatives

September 2, 2008

Henry Bonilla is the founder of The Normandy Group, LLC, a well-respected, bipartisan government relations firm based in Washington, D.C. He is a former congressman who represented Texas' 23rd congressional district in the United States House of Representatives. Bonilla is the first Hispanic Republican ever elected to Congress from the 23rd Congressional District, a district that had been Democrat since its creation in 1967. Before he spent fifteen years in politics, Bonilla spent fifteen years in the television news business as an executive producer and producer of news and public affairs programming in the San Antonio, Austin, New York and Philadelphia markets. Bonilla left his career in television and ran for public office in 1992 after being inspired by then Minority Whip Newt Gingrich.

Born and raised in San Antonio, Texas, Bonilla grew up in a housing project in a Spanish-speaking neighborhood on the West Side of San Antonio. He graduated from South San Antonio High School in 1972 and received his Bachelor of Journalism degree from the University of Texas at Austin in 1976. Today, he uses his life experience to inspire young people to follow their dreams.

I was born in a housing project in a Spanish-speaking neighborhood on the West Side of San Antonio. Later on in life, the family struggled. My grandmother on my mother's side often had to work as a maid at the downtown Baptist Memorial Hospital in San Antonio, taking the bus to work every day for 30 years. It set an example of hard work, doing for yourself and trying to pull yourself up from your bootstraps.

My father was a great example of hard work. But my mother, who was the only one in the family who had a high school degree, understood that if the kids stayed in school, they had a shot at living the American dream. I count my blessings every day that I was so fortunate to be born in a country that allows someone with my background to be successful.

Before I spent fifteen years in federal politics, I spent fifteen years in the television news business as an executive producer and producer of news and public affairs in the television markets of San Antonio, Austin and Philadelphia. At the peak of my career in that line of work, I was responsible for the 11:00 p.m. news on WABC in New York that averaged between 2 and 13 million viewers each night. Back then, I would pinch myself some nights in my New York City apartment talking to my mother. It cost a lot of money to call long distance back to San Antonio but I missed tortillas and chorizo and all of the dishes that she made back home. I had to learn, as I was on the phone with her, how to make and roll tortillas. They didn't come out perfectly round, but at least I had them, a taste of the culture that I grew up in.

Being part of a Hispanic community is something that you always want to hold on to. There are wonderful aspects of the culture regardless of which Hispanic community you come from. But then first and foremost is waking up every day being proud to be an American and proud of what this country has to offer.

As I moved on years later to run for Congress, a lot of people said, "Hey, you can't run for congressional office." This was in 1992. "You've never even run for student council before. How can you run in an area that is 70 percent minority, that has an incumbent congressman who's been in office for eight years, and in politics going on 25 years? You can't possibly win." All I ever had to do is have somebody tell me I couldn't do it, and then I would not be denied.

One of the greatest moments I would have when I was in office is speaking to high school and college students, giving them examples of my life and how they might relate to it so that they could be successful as well. I always walked away thinking that if I just reached one student on any given afternoon or any given night, telling him my story of struggle and, fortunately, of success, they might say, "You know, man, if that guy can do it, coming from his background, maybe I have a shot too."

We owe it to young people, those of us who have been successful, to let them know the story of struggle and success, of meeting failures and getting up again, getting knocked down and continuing to move forward. We owe it to them to provide that opportunity for them as well to be successful.

Sometimes, you never know when it's going to come back to you. I'd be in a crowd later on and a young college student would tap me on the shoulder and say, "Mr. Bonilla, I remember what you told me a couple of years ago. Now, I'm attending MIT. I never thought I had a chance to do that." Or, "I'm attending a local college. I never thought I really was college material." You walk away thinking, *wow, you've made a difference.*

As I moved on in Congress, some days I'd say to myself, "I can't believe I'm getting to do what I do." I co-chaired the last two conventions. I got to be a chairman on the Appropriations Committee that decided funding for the entire federal government for my entire fourteen years in office. And then I think back to those days when we had to live in a little metal mobile home in my grandmother's backyard for a while, just because we didn't have a place to live in between homes growing up on the South Side of San Antonio. Then I would think of how far I had come.

I want to leave the legacy of opportunity for my children and their grandchildren in the future. I don't want them to wake up someday and say, "what happened to my country? How has it become so different from what my dad grew up in that gave him that opportunity?" So, every day while I was in office and what I to do today as well, I work for those principles, and will continue until the day I die, to preserve the environment that this country has provided for many of you and me to prosper and to grow—if you're willing to work hard, stay out of trouble, continue working and apply yourself. That is what I'm committed to doing until my last day on this earth.

Susan Castillo

State Superintendent of Schools
State of Oregon

May 16, 2007

Susan Castillo is an Oregon politician who served as the Superintendent of Public Instruction from 2003 to 2012. A Democrat, she also served as a senator in the Oregon legislature from 1997 to 2003. Before entering politics, she pursued a career in broadcast journalism, first for Oregon Public Broadcasting and later for KVAL-TV in Eugene. Upon her resignation as superintendent to pursue an opportunity in the private sector, the position was eliminated as an elected office.

Castillo was born in 1951 in East Los Angeles and grew up in southern California with her large extended family. Her grandparents were first-generation immigrants to the United States from Mexico. Her father became a deputy sheriff. Castillo's mother dropped out of school in the eighth grade and spent much of her life working in a factory, an example that Castillo later cited as primary in her own advocacy of education as a route to opportunity.

Castillo's journey from a self-described "mediocre student" and college drop-out to becoming the chief administrator of public education, overseeing more than half a million students in 1,200 schools, proves that it is never too late to pursue your passion and be highly successful. Like many first-generation Latino students whose parents can't really provide the guidance they need to pursue higher education, Castillo found an amazing mentor in a woman who was her boss and saw something in her and encouraged her to achieve success.

I was a mediocre student. I was unmotivated and a daydreamer. I doubt many of my teachers would even remember Susan Castillo. But today, I'm Oregon's Superintendent of Public Instruction. I oversee a public-school system with well over half a million students and 1,200 schools with an education budget topping $6 billion. America, what a country, huh?

I'm a West Coast Latina, born in East L.A., the grandchild of Mexican immigrants. My dad was a sheriff's deputy. My mother worked in a factory. She left school in the eighth grade. She always encouraged me and my brothers to earn a living with our brains rather than with our backs, as she did. When I was a toddler, we moved to a mostly white middle-class suburb because my parents wanted us to have opportunities that we would probably not get in the Los Angeles neighborhoods that they grew up in. I went to high school in the late '60s, a pretty crazy time to be a teenager. But I wasn't a big rebel because my dad was a police officer so I couldn't get into much trouble.

The one demonstration that I did take part in was a little sit-down at school to protest the school administration's objections to the rock group Steppenwolf performing at our school. Remember *Born to be Wild*? That was us. Anyway, that was pretty much the extent of my radical student activism: one sit-down strike.

After I graduated, I didn't really believe that college was for me. My parents made sure, of course, that my brothers and I did complete our high school education. But in my household as I was growing up, we didn't have conversations about what university I was going to be going on to. No one in my high school talked to me about going to college or even about the possibility of college. I did, however, enroll in a junior college. I took a few classes and dropped out. I lacked clear direction like a lot of people in their late teens and early twenties. A few years later, I moved to Oregon and was working in the secretarial pool at Oregon State University. I was what you'd call a late bloomer. Then my life took a sharp turn when I got assigned to work as secretary to an amazing woman named Pearl Spears Gray, who at the time was the head of the university's affirmative action program.

Pearl was a wonderfully dynamic, outspoken African-American woman. She was a fearless and tireless advocate for justice. She moved people and institutions with her courage and intelligence. I was pretty much in awe of her every day. Pearl saw something in me that most of my teachers probably missed. She saw potential. Pearl was my mentor. She encouraged me to go to school and earn my degree. During a time in my life when I didn't know what I wanted to do or be, Pearl believed in me. At that point, that was all that I needed.

I want to emphasize the important role that we play as leaders in mentoring others and how powerful those words, "you have potential," are when you say them to someone else. "Let me help you set high goals for yourself. You can be successful in college." Those words can change someone's life. Pearl's words certainly changed mine.

As a student at Oregon State, everything changed. I was motivated to hit the books—eager to learn. I loved it. I was like a sponge. I earned my degree and started my journalism career as a news reporter for a local television station in Eugene, Oregon. I was feeling quite content with my broadcasting career, covering the State Legislature, state government and education issues, when I was approached about becoming a state senator. I spent so many years covering politics from the outside with a reporter's objectivity, but I also wanted to try to make a difference in the public policy arena.

When I decided to do it, I can remember sitting at home in front of my computer, writing my first political speech about the major issues and where I stood on them, as well as telling my story of family and background. As I looked at the first draft, I could barely get through it because I became very emotional. I was sitting there in front of my computer and just crying. I was just sobbing, and I didn't understand why I was so emotional.

And then it hit me at that moment: I was fulfilling the dream of my grandparents. They came to this country with very little. They worked. They struggled. They strived to make a living and to raise families. They really believed that this is the land of opportunity.

Here I was getting to live that dream. I have to tell you that that was a powerful, profound moment in my life. It is at the core of what drives me in the public service work that I do today, because everyone should have an opportunity to live the dream. That's what motivates me.

As the first Hispanic woman elected to the legislature in Oregon, I had something to prove. I worked very hard, diving into issues spanning policy, farm worker rights and environmental protection. I served on the Senate Education Committee and felt a strong connection to helping our schools. A few years later when Democrats were looking for someone to run for school superintendent, which is a state-wide elected position in Oregon, I went after it and won. I'm now in my fifth year on the job after winning re-election. I've tackled all sorts of issues and have had my share of arguments and controversies. But from the start, my top priority has always been closing the achievement gap for poor and minority students.

Across this country, you see poor students, you see minority students—millions of them—lagging behind in reading and math, failing and dropping out of school and missing out on that dream. For too long, society and schools wrote off these kids as unable to learn or as unreachable. There have been plenty of excuses. There was plenty of blame to go around: poverty, crime, drugs, dysfunctional families. Well, I don't believe in making excuses, especially when it comes to our kids. I believe in taking responsibility, and that is the work of closing the achievement gap. That's what it's all about: taking responsibility for our children.

By far, the biggest, fastest growing demographic of kids is Hispanic. More than one out of five school children in this country is Hispanic. That's more than a 50 percent increase since the early 90s. Now, Oregon is not California or Texas or Florida, but like many states, we are experiencing a boom too. Today, Latinos represent 15 percent of our students in Oregon. We're expected to double our numbers by 2020. Nationally, Latino students are more likely to come from poverty. Three out of four Latino kids qualify for free or reduced school lunch. Latinos don't do as well on reading and math tests. They're more likely to drop out and less likely to go to college. When you add the number of other English-language learners, about five million kids across this country, it's plain to see that we've got our work cut out for us in America's schools.

But here is the good news. Nationally and in Oregon, we are beginning to narrow the achievement gap. Make no mistake, we have a long way to go. We're not where we need to be. But we are making slow, steady progress. We need to approach this work with a sense of urgency all across this country.

The most amazing thing, at least in Oregon, is that we did make progress on this issue during a time when our state budget was in a serious downturn and schools were being forced to make devastating cuts, eliminating programs and increasing class sizes. Now money isn't everything, or else we wouldn't have been able to make the progress that we have been making. But adequate funding is very important. We have to make sure that our schools in Oregon have reasonable class sizes and can offer our kids quality art and music programs, as well as those twenty-first-century skills that they need to be successful.

So how is it getting done? Well, there isn't a magic formula. There is no textbook with step by step instructions about how you close the gap. But I can tell you what's working in Oregon, at least when we look at our successful schools and the work that they're doing. Everything begins with high expectations for what students can achieve—all students. Just because a child lives in poverty or his parents are too tired from working three jobs to help with homework, it doesn't mean he's not smart or that she can't learn. Do you do everything you can to help that child cope with the challenges he faces outside of school? Absolutely. But do you lower your standards because you feel sorry for that child? No way.

Let me tell you about one of our wonderful principals in Oregon. Her name is Endelia Schofield. She's the principal of W. L. Henry Elementary School where three out of four kids are Latino and most come from poverty. She has this call and response thing that she does when she visits with her students. She asks them, "What's your job?" The kids call back, "To learn." Then she asks, "So when you grow up, you can go where?" And all these beautiful kids answer, "College." I just love that because most of these kids' parents never graduated from high school. These kids are already thinking about going to college. That is the American dream right there.

Next, you invest in early childhood education. I believe that public education is vastly underfunded in this country from preschool all the way to higher education. If you want to make a smart long-term investment with a big payoff in the future, you spend on preschool, full-day kindergarten and extra help for our first graders so that these kids, when their brains are still developing, learn how to be learners and get their schooling off to the strongest possible start.

Schools also need to do a better job getting parents and communities involved. You sometimes hear that culture and language throw up barriers that are difficult to overcome. A lot of parents don't have much schooling themselves or the experience with the system has left them feeling wary and burned. That all may be true, but we cannot give up, because all parents at heart want what's best for their children.

Schools need to get more creative about reaching out, offering afterschool programs, night classes and social events. We need more training so that our teachers know how best to educate kids from diverse backgrounds. All teachers want their students to succeed. We need to help them do that. I also believe that schools need to be more entrepreneurial about coordinating what they do with local governments, nonprofits and businesses, big and small. There are resources out there. We just need to do a better job of tapping into them.

Finally, you need accountability. I talked about teachers holding high expectations for kids. Well, we need to have high expectations for our schools too. We have so much data now to track how students are doing. We need to press for progress. Not everything that goes on in a classroom can be captured on a spreadsheet, but you do need to know how you're doing, whether you're a school, a teacher or a student.

When a school is underperforming, we need to understand why and address those issues swiftly, whether that means shoring up leadership or changing the curriculum. And we don't play the blame game. When we see a school that's excelling, that's really reaching for the stars with all of their students, we need to understand what's going on there, too, so we can make that happen in more schools.

In Oregon, I started the Celebrating Student Success event. It's a conference and a banquet to honor schools that are making a difference. I have to tell you that that evening has become the highlight of my year. We've recognized schools from the inner city and from tiny farm towns, and, more importantly, everybody gets together to share on strategies that really work for our kids, getting down to real specifics like how to organize schedules to boost literacy or how to improve attendance. There is so much amazing, innovative work going on in our schools. Too often, we focus on the failures when we have so much to learn from the successes.

I hope everyone in this room will join me, if you aren't already getting involved in what's happening in our public schools, whether that means raising money or awareness, volunteering in classrooms or just being an advocate, because I know what it feels like to be a kid who isn't connecting with school. But I also know the thrill of finally getting it, of discovering a love of learning and how education can transform your life.

Since 9/11 and the Iraq War, education has been set aside nationally. If we really care about this country's future, we need to think big about our schools. Education absolutely needs to be put back at the top of our nation's priority list. Now, insiders talk about education and No Child Left Behind. There's lots of that talk going on right here in D.C., but I can't believe that in both recent presidential candidate debates, whether it was the Democrats or the Republicans, there was no mention of education. That needs to change.

I see three key areas where we need to get to work right away. One of them is calling out a national agenda to build an education workforce that is the best in the world. I have seen it time and again: a great textbook doesn't make a great education. You need quality teachers making that one-on-one connection with students. So, let's get them the quality training and the support that they need to help every student succeed in this 21st century global economy. Let's develop strong leadership in our schools so that those leaders have the skills to create successful learning environments for our students.

Two, let's make sure that our children start school ready to learn. The achievement gap begins before children enter school. So, we need quality preschool programs and parent training to ensure that when kids start kindergarten, they hit the ground running. If not, they're already behind. It's much easier to do well in a race when you're not playing catch-up from the very start.

Three, let's make some targeted investments in our middle schools and high schools to help our struggling students. We can help students struggling in secondary school and get them on course to success, if we make the right investments in our secondary schools. I believe that we as a nation can do better by our children than we're doing. I believe all children, no matter what color they are, what language they speak at home or how much money their parents make, are entitled to the very best education, because every child is entitled to the dream.

We can do better, and working together with intelligence, dedication and passion, we will. There are so many students who are late bloomers like me who need that inspiration, who need to believe in themselves and have someone show them the way. It's up to us to provide support to their school and their teachers so that they all have an opportunity to live the dream.

Joaquín Castro

Congressman
Texas' 20th District

March 20, 2015

Congressman Joaquín Castro was keenly aware of his place in history when he was elected to represent Texas' 20th Congressional District. He follows the long legacy of two Latino legends elected into that position—Henry B. González, who represented the district for more than thirty years, and his son, Charlie González, who represented the district for fourteen more years. Born in San Antonio, Texas in 1974, Castro is a second-generation Mexican American who was raised on the city's West Side and is a proud product of the San Antonio public school system. The Castro family's history in the United States began nearly one hundred years ago when his grandmother, Victoria Castro, came to Texas as a young orphan. In the spirit of the American Dream, she often worked two and three jobs at a time to be able to give her only daughter (Joaquín's mother, Rosie) and her grandchildren a better life.

After high school, Castro attended Stanford University and went on to earn his Juris Doctorate from Harvard Law School in 2000. At twenty-eight years old, Castro returned to San Antonio, joined a private law practice and was elected into the Texas Legislature. He served five terms as state representative for District 125, and in 2012 was elected to serve Texas Congressional District 20 in the U.S House of Representatives. Joaquín's identical twin brother, Julián Castro, was elected in 2013 to his third term as Mayor of San Antonio. On July 28, 2014, Julián Castro was sworn in as Secretary of the U.S. Department of Housing and Urban Development (HUD).

Castro credits his parents with instilling in him and his brother a passion for politics and an appreciation for the democratic process. Now in his second term in the U.S. House of Representatives, he serves on the House Armed Services Committee, as well as the House Foreign Affairs Committee. On his office coffee table, Castro keeps a book of Hispanic Americans in Congress with Henry B. González on its cover, a reminder that he stands on the shoulders of legendary leaders.

The American dream is not a sprint or even a marathon; it is a relay. Our families don't always make it there in a span of one generation, but each family passes on its successes to the next generation. We believe that. The reason my brother, Julián Castro, said that when he spoke at the 2012 Democratic National Convention is because it was true in our family.

My grandmother, Victoria Castro, was the first in our family to come to the United States from Coahuila, México. She was from a very small town called San Pedro. My grandmother was six years old when she came to this country. She came with her younger sister, Trinidad, not because they wanted to but because both their parents had died around the time of the Mexican Revolution. My grandmother came because the closest relatives who could take her in were not in Mexico but in San Antonio, Texas. That's how my family ended up settling there.

It was a lot easier to come to United States then, even for people coming from México, believe it or not. In fact, tracing our lineage was something my family had never done. But right before my brother spoke at the DNC in 2012, there was a genealogist, I believe from the *Huffington Post*, who went back and traced my grandmother's history and found the document that allowed her to come into this country. She crossed the border at Eagle Pass, Texas. There is a line in that document that asks the purpose for which she was coming; written into that line, it says, "to live." She was coming to live.

My grandmother worked as a maid, a babysitter and a cook. Her entire career, her entire adult life and even as a child she did everything she could to give her only child, my mom, the best of life that she could possibly have. My parents were the first in their families to go to college, and they did the same thing for my brother and me. The reason why Julián told that story back then, and why I tell it to you now, is not because I think that story is special, but because that is the story of so many of our families who worked so hard over the years to do everything they could to give their kids and their grandkids a better chance in life than they had.

My mom was the first in our family to get involved in politics. My brother was elected to the San Antonio City Council at 26 years old. I was elected to the state legislature at 28, but it was my mom who ran for the San Antonio City Council as a young woman of 23. She ran under a party that was called the Raza Unida Party. Back then in Texas, believe it or not, everybody was a Democrat. And in the Texas legislature, there were literally, out of a 150 state reps, less than ten Republicans. My mom ran for city council at a time when cities had still not created single-member districts; so you were still running at-large elections and in a place system. My mom came in second, I think, out of six or eight candidates back then. And as a young woman, it was a big step for her because not only were there very few Latinos on the city council, but there were also very few women who dared to run for office, who dared to challenge the system back then and take a chance at running. So, I felt like an old man at 28 because my mom ran at 23. But she did so because back then, the place where we grew up, the West Side of San Antonio, like so many places in this country, never received its fair share.

My mom was born into a time when in Texas there were still signs that read "No dogs or Mexicans allowed;" she was working to change that. And the people that she worked with in the party were working to change that. My mom eventually became a Democrat again. She continued to be active, not only in Democratic Party politics in helping women candidates and Latinas, but also in doing things like supporting efforts to combat domestic violence, in building up libraries and all of these wonderful things that she's been able to do over the years. My dad worked as a teacher in the Edgewood Independent School District for twenty-six years. And before that, he was part of a group that started a small school, called Jacinto Treviño College, dedicated to educating Mexican-Americans in Texas. It lasted several years and then finally succumbed in the 1970s to a lack of funding.

That was the household we grew up in; a household that believed that when a government works right, through public service you can do great things in people's lives. I still believe that today. And when people ask each of us who are involved in government or in our communities what we believe about the role of government in American life, I believe this based on my experience. I believe that what makes our country special is that together as Americans, in my grandmother's generation, in my mom's generation and even in this generation, we have come together to build what I call an infrastructure of opportunity in this country.

Just as there is an infrastructure of streets and roads and highways that help all of us to get where we want to go, the beauty of America is that there is an infrastructure of opportunity that helps people get where they want to go in life. And that includes great public schools and universities, a strong healthcare system and an economy that's built around well-paying jobs so people who work hard can support themselves and their family members. That is the America that we have sought to build over the years. That is the reason that people have come from México and Latin America and Europe and Asia and all over the world: because we are the preeminent nation of opportunity. And so, the call to all of us, not only in Congress or as elected officials, but as Americans, is to do every single thing that we can to build that infrastructure of opportunity, to preserve it, to grow it and to make sure that just as my grandmother and my parents made sure the infrastructure of opportunity was there for my brother and me, that we all make sure it is there for the next generation of Americans.

Francisco G. Cigarroa
Physician & Chancellor
The University of Texas System

June 30, 2009

Dr. Francisco Cigarroa is a nationally renowned pediatric and transplant surgeon. He received his bachelor's degree in biology from Yale University and his medical degree from The University of Texas Southwestern Medical Center at Dallas. He completed fellowships in pediatric surgery and transplant surgery at Johns Hopkins Hospital. Dr. Cigarroa became a faculty member at The University of Texas Health Science Center San Antonio in 1995. He was part of a surgical team that performed the first split liver donor transplant between two recipients in Texas.

In 2009, Dr. Cigarroa became the first Hispanic to be named Chancellor of The University of Texas System. Chancellor Cigarroa oversaw one of the largest public systems of higher education in the nation, with nine universities and six health institutions, an annual operating budget of $13 billion, more than 215,000 students, 19,000 faculty members and 68,000 staff members, at that time. After five years, he returned full-time to his passion for patient care.

I am one of ten children—five sisters and four brothers—and I'm proud to say that during my growing up, the fundamental joy in our family was the love and respect for each other, the importance of education and giving back to our communities.

My grandmother, Abuelita, would get us together every Sunday for *comidas*. We were 36 grandchildren all together. Abuelita would give each of us a dollar and just as we were thinking about buying super bubbles and candy, she'd take it back, and say "M'i-jito, this is for your college education. This is a savings and I'm saving it for you." She kept her word. I went through the public school systems of Laredo, Texas, a small border city where I grew up. But when we graduated from high school, she'd give us a check to pay for part of our college tuition. All 36 of her grandchildren received a college education. All nine of my brothers and sisters not only received a college education, but also received professional degrees. To this day, that's what gives my parents the most joy.

I left Laredo, Texas and I embarked upon a higher education degree at Yale. The most difficult transition in my life was that transition from Laredo to Yale. That first year, every time I received a grade, I thought that the next day would be my last day at Yale. But my parents and grandparents, individuals who loved me, said, "Don't give up. Continue to focus. And if you love medicine, you still have an opportunity to do that."

Yale gave me a tremendous work ethic because I really had to catch up. I never let up my work ethic of trying to do better. And by the time I got to medical school, it ended up being a relatively easy road. Although after the third time of taking biochemistry, I decided maybe economics was for me. I remember being in the library at The University of Texas Southwestern Medical Center, closing my book and saying, "I quit. I'm going back to Laredo and I'm going to talk to Dad." So, I arrived in Laredo about 10:30 that night. Dad had about 100 patients in his clinic that day, and it was probably about eleven o'clock at night before he got out of the clinic. I stepped down from the hill where the hospital was, and Dad was there and it was dark. He said, "Carlos, what are you doing here?" I said, "No, Dad. It's Francisco." He was confused because there were ten of us and it was kind of dark. He said, "Oh my goodness, Francisco, I thought you were in medical school."

"Well, Dad," I said. "I need to talk to you." We had about a 45-minute conversation. Dad is somebody who always wants the best for his children. He said, "Well, son, I completely understand. Let's go talk to Mother."

It was midnight by the time I got to the house in Laredo, and Mother was asleep. When we got to the master bedroom where she was, Dad said, "Look who's here!" Mother asked, "Well, what are you doing here? I thought you were taking a biochemistry exam in about four days?" She knew this because we'd always ask her to say a prayer before every exam. That started at Yale because I thought I'd flunk every test. When I told her what my new plans were, she said, "Nothing of it." She scolded the both of us—me for trying to quit and Dad for agreeing. The following morning, we took the six a.m. Texas International flight out of Laredo back to Dallas. She made Dad stay in class with me for three or four days. We both agreed that the wrath of Mother was not worth it. We did not want to experience that again and thought that medical school would be a lot easier.

Now, Mother, as you can imagine, was a disciplinarian. I still have a couple of scars on my back. Some recent, I may add. She always demanded one thing of her children and that was an A in conduct. She felt that if we received an A in conduct, we would be respectful of each other, we would listen and we would turn in our homework on time. She realized that not everybody could get an A-plus in calculus or math, but an A in conduct was extremely important to her because it was within our control. One day, three Cigarroas—two cousins and myself—got a C in conduct. We were terrified. My entrepreneur cousin felt that it was easy to convert a C to an A. That's when I learned the lesson of honesty and integrity: that day never to be forgotten in the Cigarroa household.

I ended up having a glorious time at Southwestern Medical School. I was exposed to what I believe were some of the greatest faculty that I've had the opportunity to work with. There, I met Dr. Michael Brown, a faculty member who eventually became a

Nobel laureate. After meeting him I realize the power that a faculty member has to influence a young student in choosing a career path. He asked me, "What are your plans?" I said, "Well, my plans are to go back to Laredo and join my father's practice." He responded, "Well, have you ever thought about pursuing a career in academic medicine?" He was already thinking about how important it is to identify a young, bright, talented student to become the future pipeline of faculty members in academic health centers. So, Dr. Michael Brown was the one who encouraged me to pursue a career in academic surgery and wrote my letter of recommendation to Mass General. When I got accepted to Massachusetts General Hospital, I ran back to Michael Brown and told him how ecstatic I was. He said, "Don't disappoint me." I often go back to him and ask him, "Have I disappointed you yet, Dr. Brown?" To which he responds, "No. But there's still time."

At Massachusetts General Hospital, I was exposed to incredible physicians and physician scientists, and I fell in love with the field of pediatric surgery. From Massachusetts General Hospital, I went to Johns Hopkins and did a fellowship in both pediatric surgery and transplantation surgery, because I took care of so many children with some terrible hepatic insufficiency problems. At the end of my fellowship at Johns Hopkins, I was offered a wonderful opportunity to join their faculty as the director of their pediatric transplant program. I was about to sign on the dotted line when I came running home to my wife, Graciela, and my two children, María Cristina and Barbara. I told Graciela about this great opportunity. She said "Well, that sounds wonderful. I think I'll come and visit you and the children every other weekend." She had other goals in mind: going back to Texas.

She asked me a very important question, "Who have been the most important people in your life?" I answered, "Well, my parents, my grandparents, my cousins, my brothers and sisters, and also being in that enriched region of South Texas." She continued asking me fundamental questions about what really mattered. "Don't you want your children to be exposed to that environment? Don't you want your children to be exposed to the beautiful Mexican-American culture that we were a part of? Don't you have a responsibility to give back to a region that has given so much to you?"

I recalled that growing up along the Texas-Mexico border region gave us great joy as kids. We really learned and lived the best of both worlds, the United States and Mexico. My grandfather was a rancher in Mexico, and that's where I learned the love of the land. My father, my uncle and my grandfather were physicians in that border town. I had the opportunity to make house calls with my father, seeing firsthand the healthcare disparities because those patients did not have access to healthcare unless the physicians went to their homes. As a fifteen year old, I got to see my very first operation with my uncle, Leo, a general surgeon who would have to travel sometimes hundreds of miles, because that region of Texas did not have a general surgeon.

I was a little confused, so I talked to my Dad about it, and he made it crystal clear. Dad reminded me that he was still a practicing physician in Laredo, Texas, 52 years after he started practicing. He asked me, "Are you concerned that you need to be at a very large academic health center? Because if you are, I think you're missing the point. The point is that the relationship between a physician and a patient is just as powerful and just as important in Cotulla, Texas as it is in Baltimore or in Boston. So, if that's what you're thinking about, I would ask you to re-assess." I had my answer. We went back to San Antonio, where I joined the faculty of the University of Texas Health Science Center in San Antonio.

When I told a colleague of mine at Johns Hopkins Hospital that I declined the offer to become the director of their pediatric transplantation program, he said, "You know, Francisco, I'm really concerned that you're committing academic suicide." They had a little problem imagining what the opportunities were in South Texas.

No other university, I believe, would've given a young assistant professor the opportunity that the University of Texas gave me. They had the confidence to allow me to establish a pediatric transplant program in San Antonio. Within five years, we built one of the largest pediatric transplant programs in Texas. And it was that university that also allowed me one day to take care of the nanny who actually changed our diapers in Laredo. One weekend when I was on-call, our nanny came in with fulminant hepatic failure, and I ended up doing her transplant one week later. What are the chances of that happening? It goes back to coming back to the region that gave me so much. It was the University of Texas that gave me the opportunity to become the president of the University of Texas Health Science Center in San Antonio. Five years after I started, I called my Johns Hopkins colleague again to ask if he could write a letter of recommendation for me. "Well, of course, Francisco. You must be being promoted to associate professor." And I said, "Well, that happened last week. But I'm asking whether you'd write a letter of recommendation for me to become President of the Health Science Center." And there was a pause and he said, "My goodness, things are going well for you."

My growing up in Laredo gave me a roadmap for what works on the border in terms of education and the delivery of healthcare. But pediatric surgery was the ideal background for leading an academic health center, because it exposed me to one of the most demanding surgical fellowships in the world under the mentorship of outstanding clinician scientists. My surgical training provided me the strong foundation that I continue to rely on today. I learned that a surgeon needs to lead, be decisive and inspire a team of professionals to do their very best. As a leader in surgery, a surgeon must hold himself or herself, along with members of the team, accountable when the expected patient outcome is not achieved. It's a microcosm of what goes on in real life in regards to organizations, especially universities. And I may add there were many times that we were dealt incredible challenges.

I recall when I was two months into my fellowship in transplantation surgery, I was involved with a liver transplant of an adult patient with severe portal hypertension. I was being guided through this operation by the master surgeon. I remember that as I gently placed the clamp on the inferior vena cava, the vein tore like wet tissue paper and the patient exsanguinated and died on the O.R. table. There is nothing more unsettling, more defeating for a surgeon. You can imagine how badly I felt having to speak to the patient's family. Well, I thought I'd have a couple of days to recover from that, but four hours later, I was back in the operating room doing another emergency liver transplant with the same master surgeon. I told this master surgeon, "Please, you proceed and I'll assist." He said, "No. You must do the operation. You must learn from the past, but now your total attention is on this patient, and here is the scalpel." If that was not a growing experience for me, nothing was. You must be able to pick yourself up, remain focused and move ahead.

After several years, I realized that I had met all my objectives as president of the Health Science Center. I had fixed the practice plan, enhanced philanthropy and really changed the culture of the university. I believed it was time for me to go back to something I loved to do every day, which was pediatric and transplant surgery. So, I announced in public that I was going back to surgery. It was completely unexpected that the Board of Regents would ask me to consider leading the University of Texas System, this time as the Chancellor of the University of Texas System. This was a very competitive process: I had to interview, I had to compete, but they wanted me not to close that door. So, again, another road: should I do this or should I go back to pediatric surgery?

The great poet Robert Frost's famous line from The Road Not Taken, "Two roads diverged in a wood and I took the one less traveled by, and that has made all the difference," is what I turn to today when pondering our life choices. And those roads, those divergent roads were very important for me as I was asked to consider the daily life of a wonderful profession, pediatric surgery, or the daily life of a key administrative leader in higher education.

Without all of my experiences I would not have had the choices so beautifully described by Robert Frost as two diverging roads—whether to practice medicine exclusively as a pediatric and transplant surgeon or lead an academic health center as president and then as chancellor of the University of Texas System. In considering my choices, I came to the conclusion that higher education saves lives. Literacy improves public health. It improves the economic vibrancy of this nation. It improves national security, not only of this nation but the world. And if I could have a part in enhancing the University of Texas System's success, then I felt I wasn't far from the Hippocratic oath of improving the quality of life for others.

I realized that every step of my collective educational life experience had provided me with the attributes necessary to lead a university system with both academic and health institutions and to acquire the trust of faculty, students and staff so that I could carry out the mission of the University. I am forever grateful to that board of regents who realized that despite Francisco Cigarroa not having any administrative background or experience, they felt that I could lead a university.

As part of the interview process, I had to provide a couple of letters of recommendation. I couldn't help myself. I called this distinguished surgeon from Johns Hopkins and asked him, "Could you write me a letter of recommendation?" He asked, "What are you up to?" I said, "Well, I've been asked to interview for the chancellorship of the University of Texas System, one of the greatest institutions of higher education in the world." And he said, "Oh, my goodness. Can I get a job with you?" I said, "I don't know. You could be committing academic suicide."

Henry G. Cisneros
U.S. Secretary of Housing & Urban Development

September 8, 2011

Henry Gabriel Cisneros has devoted his life to public service on the local and national levels. He served as Secretary of Housing and Urban Development in President Bill Clinton's administration from 1993 to 1997. Previously, he was the first Latino to serve as mayor of San Antonio, Texas in contemporary times for four terms, from 1981 to 1989. To Mayor Cisneros' credit is his having increased the city's economic base, attracting high tech industries, developing tourism, all of which created many more jobs for San Antonio citizens. At HUD, Cisneros worked on revitalizing and increasing public housing as well as furthering policies that were successful in achieving the nation's highest ever rate of home ownership. After serving in the presidential cabinet, Cisneros became the president and COO for the Univision network from 1997 to 2000. He later founded American City Vista (later named CityView), a corporation dedicated to building homes for low and moderate income families. Cisneros remains actively involved in politics, especially as a Democrat and in support of minority candidates to hold office.

Mickey, thank you for this honor. Mickey Ibarra has done many noteworthy things in his life, such as creating the Latino Leaders Network and bringing it to Los Angeles. What a wonderful assemblage of friends and associates and acquaintances from across many years. Thank for being here. And Mickey, thank you for pulling us all together.

Mickey asked me to share some personal insights today. I promise to do that. But first, let me say that Mickey's personal story is inspiring. He and his brother grew up in Utah in foster homes. Mickey was the older brother by eleven months. They struggled rough through life and worked their way through high school and football and college. In time, Mickey became Assistant to the President of the United States when Bill Clinton named him to that position in the White House. His brother has been very successful in business. They never quit. So, ladies and gentlemen, let us recognize Mickey Ibarra for all that he has done in his time.

Mickey was an assistant to the president at the same time that Janet Murguía was in the White House, and when María Echaveste was the Deputy Chief of Staff. President Clinton did a good job of naming some very capable people to staff the White House. I want to recognize Gloria Molina. Gloria, thank you so much for your years of service. Gloria is an exemplar of honesty and conviction and determination. She has made special contributions in every position she has held: the California State Assembly, the Los Angeles City Council and as a path-breaking County Supervisor. No one will be able to match what she has done over these years. I speak literally the truth. No one will be able to match her because all future supervisors will have term limits, and Gloria has served for almost twenty years and will leave a tremendous legacy.

I want to recognize Mayor Villaraigosa, who could not be here. One of my memories of public life in Los Angeles involves Mayor Villaraigosa and Gloria Molina. When Mayor Villaraigosa and Xavier Becerra were coming up together, it looked like they were on a collision course, because both intended to run for mayor of Los Angeles. We met at Gloria's home in an effort to try, as friends, to explore how a damaging fight could be averted. Gloria brought me into that discussion. We met on Sunday mornings, around 7:30 a.m. over *pan dulce* in her home. And it is amazing the way things sorted out. Today, as we speak, that Super Committee is meeting in Washington composed of six senators and six congress persons, working together to address a question that is right at the heart of the future of our country: "How are we going to deal with the scale of national debt and deficit?" And, tonight in Washington, in the audience for President Obama's address on the deficit and debt, on the economy and jobs, is Mayor of Los Angeles Antonio Villaraigosa, who is the president of the U.S. Conference of Mayors and who was invited tonight as a guest of the President of the United States. So it's an uplifting thing, Gloria, that all those years ago we were working to avoid a destructive political collision and both of you made major contributions, a story of our community and our progress.

I want to thank, in a very sincere way for her years of help and partnership, my wife, Mary Alice, who for the last four years has served on the City Council in San Antonio. She has held the same seat that I held from 1975 to 1981 and has done a great job of providing constituency services and improving our community. She is now president of a nonprofit we created in our home neighborhood about ten years ago—American Sunrise.

We live in the home that my grandparents owned. Our West Side barrio in San Antonio is the equivalent of East Los Angeles. We wanted to do something about the fact that the children in our neighborhood have fewer chances in life. We bought an adjacent house and set it up as an afterschool learning center. It has become the base for a nonprofit that operates in a one square mile area of the West Side of San Antonio. We have children come every afternoon after school for additional instruction in math, science and reading. And we're going on from there to middle school children and high school kids, offering SAT prep that they can't get elsewhere. We can improve their SAT scores to get them into college as well as involve their parents in literacy and citizenship. We call our program American Sunrise, and the driving force is Mary Alice Cisneros. I want to recognize her and thank her for her work.

Also here today is my daughter, Teresa, and her husband, Sean Burton. Friends, please meet my daughter Teresa and Sean Burton, who live here in L.A. Teresa is a lawyer who has worked in the city attorney's office and the mother of two of our four grandchildren. Sean is the president of CityView, the company of which I am the chairman, and where Sean is doing a great job.

I will try to be succinct in my remarks, but I do want to comply with Mickey's admonition to offer a few words of personal reflection which fit into the larger picture of the progress of our people, of our community.

I grew up in San Antonio. My grandfather was exiled among the shifting factions of Mexico. He arrived in San Antonio in 1926, under threat of execution in Mexico. He set up a business, a very successful printing shop. My mother was one of seven children. My father was a soldier who went to World War II from New Mexico and spent four years in New Guinea in the Pacific combat zone. There, he contracted malaria and was sent to San Antonio to recover. He roomed with a soldier who had a sister and that sister became my mother; the rest is history. My grandfather, who was an old Mexican-style patriarch, said to my dad, "You can marry her, but you can't take her out of San Antonio." That is why we're from San Antonio and not from some other place in the country. My dad made a commitment.

We grew up in a neighborhood in which all of the people were *mejicanos*. As I said, envision East L.A.'s Boyle Heights. Most of the men were World War II veterans. We lived in an idyllic lower-middle-class setting. I have sometimes said it was like a Norman Rockwell painting, except all the faces were brown. I went outside the house and whistled and sixteen guys, roughly between my age and my brother's age, five years younger, would come out and we'd start football games and baseball games in the street at any hour of the day. We grew up in a cocoon of family and friends. We were protected from the discrimination and the segregation that continued to plague Texas in that era.

San Antonio was insulated more than most Texas cities from the type of virulent segregation and discrimination against *meji-canos*. We lived among people who were proud of their heritage and they were not going to be kept down. They were very hard-working, and combined ethnic pride with a sense of social justice.

Among the people who came out of our neighborhood was one of the founders of the Mexican American Legal Defense and Education Fund (MALDEF), Gregory Luna, and the founder of the Southwest Voter Registration Education Project, Willie Velásquez. The first Spanish radio station in the United States, KCOR, was established by San Antonio's Cortez family. KWX television, the building block of Univision, was founded in San Antonio. The Association of Hispanic Colleges and Universities and Avance were established there. Here today is Sonia Rodríguez, who was the president of a seminal organization named Communities Organized for Public Service, a predecessor of UNO in Los Angeles, both created by Ernie Cortés, himself from a Latino neighborhood of San Antonio.

I grew up with a mother who had a keen social conscience. I remember going to the doctor with her as a small boy, maybe seven, in 1955, on a bus with no air conditioning. In those days, the politicians in Texas all wore white suits. The first time I saw the mayor, we were on a bus and my mother said, "Look out the window. That's the mayor over in the plaza." She said that he should be ashamed that on that same plaza were water fountains that were identified as white and colored. And the Woolworth store beside the plaza had bathrooms that said white and colored. African Americans couldn't use the counter there.

So under my mother's tutelage it has been impossible for me over my life not to relate to people who are marginalized, who haven't had opportunities. My mother imbued a deep sense of what's fair and what's unfair. I share that with you because I think it is also true of many of you in this room and many of our people. I believe that our community is unusually attuned to fairness for a variety of reasons. Perhaps it's our religion. Perhaps it's the remembrance of family, extended family. I know this: that no matter what other successes we achieve, we remember our roots. So I want not only to highlight that attribute, but also encourage it. You see, our community needs that sense of connection from its leaders and from those who've been fortunate. We need that sense of remembrance in order for all of us to progress.

The year 1968, when I graduated from college, was one of the most tumultuous years in American history. In March, President Johnson decided not to run for reelection because of the national divisions over the Vietnam War. In April, Dr. King was assassinated. I remember the night. In June, Senator Kennedy was killed here in Los Angeles at the Ambassador Hotel. By that summer, America's cities were burning, including Chicago during the Democratic Convention which became a police riot.

It was in that year that I concluded that what I wanted to do with my life was in the realm of public service—to try to make the country better. I knew I wanted to serve but I didn't know in what capacity. And then the prospect of improving the nation's cities was opened to me. I had the opportunity as a college student to travel to the East Coast as a delegate to a conference at West Point. I saw that New York City had Mayor John Lindsay trying to make the city work for all of its residents, black, white and brown, so that New York wouldn't burn like Cleveland, Detroit, Washington and so many other cities had.

I came back to Texas and listened like never before to the messages of Julian Bond and Andrew Young. And in our community, to the ideas of Raúl Yzaguirre, who was just starting out at that time, and César Chávez, of course. I concluded what I wanted to do was in the realm of community building, of city building. So that's what I studied. I went home and was elected to the city council and served on an at-large city council, citywide, for two terms. When the MALDEF brought a suit, the Justice Department intervened to change the election system. There were two Latinos out of nine in a city that was 60 percent Latino. The seven people who were not

Latino lived within a mile of each other in the wealthiest part of town.

MALDEF sued to create single-member districts. We had a referendum to change the system and barely won it, the equivalent of ten votes per precinct citywide. But we won it. And in the next election we had an eleven-member city council in which six were minorities. The city thought a revolution had occurred. Civic leaders thought the city was going to melt down with six minorities: five Latinos and an African-American on the city council. All of us were young and under 35 years of age. I was a college professor. Another council member was a social worker. We had a junior college professor. We were a very different group from the traditional chamber of commerce: sixty-year-old business people who had served on the city council. The city began to take a different path.

I must say that I think that the intervening years have been the most progressive San Antonio has ever had. I use that word "progressive" not just in the way we think of center-left politics, but in terms of job creation and inclusion of all San Antonians in the resulting prosperity. The organization that Sonia was president of, COPS, was very much a part of that process.

I developed a mindset which has served me well through the rest of my life, including the time I spent with President Clinton in his cabinet, which is a formulation of how cities work. To put it as simply as possible, I used to say to the people of San Antonio, "a good boxer has to have two punches. You can't just have a right hand; you've got to have a left as well." In my formulation, a city has to have two punches. First, we have to grow jobs. We have to raise incomes. We have to support the practical things to create economic momentum.

The second punch is we have to harness that economic momentum and make it work for the people who are at the margins. That means everything from job training and community college and universities made accessible, with the help of COPS-type community organizations to corporate jobs programs and striving for major public infrastructure projects. That's what it takes to create the jobs. That's what it takes to expand economic opportunity. That's been the model that has served San Antonio well.

It's also what I shared to President Clinton while I was Secretary of HUD. I'm very proud to have been part of the administration that produced the longest economic expansion in American history, generated the lowest unemployment rates, resulted in the lowest poverty rates and fueled the highest formation of jobs and small businesses. We made it work for people.

I remember the morning we were in the Rose Garden at the White House when we were to have an announcement on another subject. As I left HUD to go to the White House, my staff handed me a piece of paper that showed, for the first time since records on the distribution of incomes were kept, that income distribution was narrowing. One of the hardest challenges in American economics is to move the actual distribution of income and wealth. It is always the top percent that has the vast bulk of the resources and the people in the bottom quintile have one or two percent of the total wealth. On President Clinton's watch, we actually were beginning to move that hardest of hardest of economic metrics. I showed the data that had been given to me to President Clinton, and he was elated.

That has been motivation. It has also been the practical goal of my public work. And it has been for me a philosophy of life. That is why the present economic setback we are enduring is so disheartening, because we have seen the squandering of the surplus that was amassed. We have seen world forces on a collision course with unwise responses. We have seen new forms of implacable opposition, including the present Tea Party rhetoric. It's hard for me to understand. We are seeing programs that work to help people being dismantled. Unfortunately, it is impossible to escape the conclusion that a good measure of the motivation is anti-minority, including the anti-immigrant sentiment that we saw last summer in Arizona, and that we see today in communities in Pennsylvania, in Nebraska, in too many places all across our country. Thank God for MALDEF and the other advocates among us who fight the battle.

But what it says to me is that we have to continue to fight with the tools we have, and that includes pride in our community and in our people and belief in what we can contribute in our country. We will be an integral part of a better American future. That is the task that lies ahead.

So let me close by saying that as I think about that future, I am personally committed to three things. The first is to act on my belief that the places where we live, our communities, our cities, are the platforms by which we are going to create a better life for people. That's why I am in the housing business. At CityView we are building homes, taking institutional capital and building homes for working families across the nation. However, we must go beyond that. We must build green. We must build affordable. We must build for emerging communities of striving new Americans. We must utilize capital in new ways. We must make our community stronger.

Secondly, I believe that my best expenditure of time in the years that remain to me—I'm 64 years old now and, though God willing, I hope to work until at least 90, a short 26 years from now—is in helping our people, our community, the largest minority in the country, integrate successfully into the American mainstream. If there's going to be a durable American middle class, it's going to be the passage of people who are poor into the middle class.

The numbers say it clearly. If we're going to have academic excellence in America, it's going to be children who are presently dropping out who become the workforce talent that the country is going to need. If we're going to compete economically with China and India, it's going to be people like those in Los Angeles and San Antonio, minorities of all heritages who will shoulder the load.

We must take our best practices in education and economic empowerment to scale. This is an effort which cannot fail. As the NASA flight director said in the movie *Apollo 13*, "Failure is not an option." Because we love our country, we must not fail. This is not a matter only for the people left behind; compassion is not a matter only of humanitarian instincts; this is a matter of the future of the country we are preparing for our children. Thank God we are a people who are hungry, who are hungry to advance, who are committed to work, who understand sacrifice today to do better for their families tomorrow. America is fortunate to have our Latino brothers and sisters to help build its future. And the best is yet to come.

The final personal commitment I make is to family. In the immediate sense, of course, it's my immediate family—my wife, my daughters and son, to their husbands, to my grandchildren. But I'm doubly blessed. I am blessed to have a broad extended family. That is you. Antonio Villaraigosa is like a younger brother to me. He is a better-looking younger brother. The other day, I was walking by a newsstand at the airport and I spotted a magazine cover. I said, "Whoa, that's a good picture of Antonio." But it was Mark Sánchez, the quarterback of the New York Jets. Don't tell Antonio I told you that. He is good-looking, but not that good-looking.

I have had the good fortune of interfacing with a lot of young talent. Councilman Cárdenas, who is over here, running for Congress—what a great thing that is. I have watched him since he started in elective office. I have watched Julián Castro, the present mayor of San Antonio, blossom into a national figure. So at this point in my life, I cherish a rich extended family: men and women, people in business, people in politics, younger and older. My heart overflows with good will and hopes as I watch our Latino community earn its place of honor in this blessed land, the United States of America.

Virgilio P. Elizondo

Reverend Father & Professor
The University of Notre Dame

September 6, 2006

Virgilio P. Elizondo (August 28, 1935–March 14, 2016) was a
Mexican-American, Roman Catholic priest, community activist and a
leading scholar of Liberation and Hispanic Theology. He was widely
regarded as "the father of U.S. Latino religious thought." Elizondo was
the founder of the Pastoral Institute at the University of the Incarnate
Word. He was also a co-founder of the Mexican-American Cultural Center, a think tank for scholars and religious leaders to develop pastoral
ministry and theology from a Hispanic perspective. He was well known
for his book, Galilean Journey: The Mexican-American Promise,
which examined the similarities between Jesus' Galilean background
and the mestizo experience.

Elizondo was born in San Antonio, Texas in 1935 to Mexican immigrants who ran a grocery store. He grew up in a society where the Mexican-American community was barred from many segments of the city
and speaking Spanish was not welcome. Never hearing English spoken,
he himself was unable to speak it fluently until he had reached the sixth
grade.

I was born and raised in the West Side of San Antonio, Texas.
My parents were immigrants. Mother came from Mexico City,
Daddy came from Chihuahua, and they both came for the same

reason: economic poverty and need. They came as young persons; mother was twelve, father was thirteen, didn't know any English, made their way, struggled, and met at San Fernando Cathedral where I later became the priest.

San Fernando is very special because it was founded in 1731. George Washington was not born yet. A *viejita* told me once she was a descendant of the originals. My parents had immigrated. La viejita's parents had come with the Canary Islanders in the 1700s. She said, "Our family was here when the Spanish people first arrived. It became New Spain. Then our family was still here when this became Mexico. Then our family was still here when this became the Republic of Texas. Then our family was still here when it became the United States. Our family was still here when it became the Confederacy of the South. And our family is still here now that it's the United States. *Padrecito,* we don't know what country we'll become next, but we'll still be here." Some of us have a sense of roots, of profound roots. Our profound roots have been there and started to make San Antonio.

San Antonio has ancient roots, if you can imagine this, of 10,000 years of life, of continuous life that's been coming together and mingling and providing for the people. I was born in that beautiful portion of San Antonio where the only language, the only tradition, the only customs, was *español.* We didn't know any other language. We had our *panaderías,* we had our *tortillerías,* we had our movie stars and our theaters, the *Nacional* and the *Alameda.* Everything was Mexico in the United States. I think I grew up in paradise—people loved each other, our music, our songs and our traditions—until I went to school. That was the most traumatic moment that I can remember in my life.

When I went to school, I didn't know what all those foreigners were speaking. They were speaking English. I had never heard English. So, I flunked the first grade. That was my first experience, and I hated school. I was daydreaming. I was looking out the window. I wanted to quit. But my parents, who had little to no education, said education's a must. I'll never forget that, and

I will always be grateful. They had not had the privilege of an education, but they knew for my sister and me that education was an unquestioned fact. And so, my mother stayed on me. I was so creative in making excuses. I could create any excuse you would imagine for not going to school but they never worked, because mother said, "No. A la escuela. ¡Vámonos! Aguántate." This is where the aguántate becomes a virtue. I tell our young people today that's an important virtue. If you don't like school, you have boring teachers, you have bad food, you have boring textbooks—aguántate and go for it. I learned that from my parents.

Finally, I had a teacher in the fifth grade who made all the difference in the world. She was a German nun, but she took a personal interest in me. She took a personal interest and, all of a sudden, everything started to change. Rather than hating school, I learned to love school. I got excited and wanted to study more. From then, I started to move from just barely passing to making good grades to making excellent grades. One person made a difference. One person that was not a Mexican-American, was not a Latina, but believed in me. She believed in me as I was and started to give me a strong sense of who I am.

And by the way, it was at that time that my name was changed. You know, in those days, you didn't question teachers. The teachers could not pronounce "Virgilio." That was just too big for them. So, they named me "Virgil." At school I was Virgil and at home I was Virgilio. I was reminded of this father that didn't want his son to go through all the trauma of the teachers not understanding Mexican names, so he told his son, "Son, when you go to school, this is the way you pronounce your name in English." He wrote it down very carefully for his son on a piece of paper. So, the son got to school, the teachers called the role, and the teacher said, "Son, what's your name?" "My name is Pretty Near See the War." The teacher said, "What?" "Yes. My name is Pretty Near See the War." So, the teacher asked him to bring his birth certificate in. Well, his name was Casimiro Guerra. So, you know, that poor kid lived with that name afterwards.

I realized that going to school and going to college in those days was a privilege. There were very few Latinos in college. I was going to study science. I wanted to be a scientist. I actually have my first degree in chemistry and mathematics. So, those of you going for science, go for it. I started to realize that as a Latino in college, I had an obligation to my community. Those were the days when segregation wasn't questioned, when low wages weren't questioned—all the evils were there.

In San Antonio, we had the fortune of having an archbishop, Archbishop Robert E. Lucey, who was totally committed to the social agenda. He desegregated schools way before the country did; he really pushed for just wages and he pushed for Mexican-Americans to get educated. He said he refused to believe that we're inferior to everybody else. I was very inspired by him. He was the one person from "the establishment" who was really speaking something I could understand, making sense to me as a Mexican-American and seeing the suffering, segregation, exploitation that was rampant. I saw an archbishop that was taking a stand. That was so marvelous that he inspired me to go from science to the priesthood.

I realized that the Church could make a difference, because God believes in equality, because God believes in equal opportunity and that was the basic tenet of the Bible: every man and woman—not black, white, Japanese, Mexican— is created in the image and likeness of God. Every man and woman is sacred, and there's no one that's less than others. I went to the seminary and became a priest precisely the time when the civil rights movement was going strong, when all the Chicano movements were beginning, where LULAC was going very strong. By the way, my father, had been a member of LULAC, and I had worked for the first election of Henry B. González to city councilman. I worked the neighborhood organizing bingos to raise money to get him elected.

I became a priest when all these things were in motion. Even for us in the church, the Vatican was in motion too. God called us as a Church to be concerned about the poor, to develop a pride in the culture of the people, that a culture of people was to give, develop a pride in the music and the art and everything that made people, people. This should be part of the Church. The Church should not be something European; it should come out of the people, out of the soul of the people. The Vatican had a tremendous impact on me as a young priest just beginning. At that time, we actually founded an organization called PADRES to confront the Catholic Church from within. We wanted to challenge the Catholic Church to open its doors to Latinos and get involved in education, political education, community organizing, labor organizing and to bring Latino culture into the Church.

At that time, I had the privilege of attending an international Church meeting; my first contact with the international community was in Medellin, Colombia in 1968. It was a crucial year for the Church in Latin America, when the Church had us re-read the Bible as a book of the failures and sufferings and struggles of people who didn't give up, people who amid their suffering and struggle developed a new hope and a new vision and became even greater than before.

It was fascinating for me to read the Bible from that perspective. I read of the prophets of the Old Testament, that when the people were in exile, they developed their most beautiful, fascinating thoughts. That's when they started thinking of a new heaven and a new earth and a new humanity. When they were suffering the most, they thought their most fascinating thoughts. This was the way we had to go: not just do patch-up work, but do something new and exciting not just for us but for everyone.

I found out about a center in Asia, the East Asian Pastoral Institute, that was studying the encounter of cultures, the encounter of the East and the West. I went and spent two years working the institute and studying anthropology. It was a fascinating two years, living with Chinese, Japanese, Malaysians and Africans. For the first time, I had stepped totally outside my comfort zone and saw myself from another perspective. It gave me insights into our own Latino struggles that I never suspected. I had to step out to see in and gain insight. I had to take distance to gain perspective. This was a fascinating time that really marked my life.

On the way back, I stopped in Mexico City where I realized that the great border between Latin America and the United States wasn't just a geographical or political frontier. It was really a *frontera*, not a line of division, but the cradle of a new humanity, the birth for a new humanity that's being enriched by the sources that come into it. We founded the Mexican American Cultural Center in San Antonio, Texas, to begin to look deeper into the dynamics, where there could be mutual enrichment and we could all be winners and not losers. We'd all contribute the best and be enriched by the beauty of the United States, but not at the cost of losing the beauty that we bring with us from Mexico, Colombia, Ecuador and Brazil.

Then I was asked by a friend to go study in France and live with his family. I think the fascination of going to France for a while was more exciting than the doctorate. I took up the challenge, spent the summer learning French and I went and did my doctoral studies in France. I had the chance to really go deeper into our European roots, our Spanish roots, which I never fully had appreciated. I saw the beauty of Spain that had been kind of the bucket of Europe, the Spain that had been the recipient of all the great civilizations of Europe. The Spaniards had pulled it together about the time of the encounter with America, and that was us, the rich, indigenous cultures.

I started to discover the African influence in Mexico. I never had known, for instance, that the second president of Mexico was an Afro-Mexican. I never had known that a couple of states in Mexico are named after African leaders. I had never known that José Morelos was an African Mexican; he was the leader of the Mexican War for Independence. I started to see that we weren't just Europe and Native America, with its Asian roots, but also Afro-American together within our bodies, within our bloods and in our systems. I started to pull all that together into a doctorate degree, through that, I was invited to work in the International Theological Commission, which includes theologians from Europe, Africa and Asia. We would meet once a year, and each one of us would publish a book once a year that was translated into seven different languages. This had a tremendous worldwide impact.

At that time, we also started the Ecumenical Association of Third World Theologians to bring Asian thinkers together with Latin American thinkers, African thinkers and the minorities of the United States—African Americans, Latin Americans and Native Americans. It was fascinating to bring these people together. We'd meet in a different continent each year, sometimes in Asia, sometimes Latin America, sometimes in India with the common theme of bringing people together. And finally, we started to realize the importance of teaching.

I went to San Fernando Cathedral and I started televised Mass with Telemundo. At one time, we had the most popular program in Chicago and in Los Angeles. It was amazing and it was simple. We brought our folklore into it. We brought our *canción*, our *danzas* and our beauty, and people loved it. It was a Catholic Mass but with *sabor latino*. I mean it had real flavor.

San Fernando really taught me the importance of enriching our religion. And our religion enriched our movement. The basis is that God says, "don't give up." God says because you've suffered, you can create new vision and new dreams that others have not thought about. And that's the work I've been doing in Notre Dame since I started teaching six years ago. I'm trying to create a new vision and new dreams where Latinos can be a part of it, not just at the undergraduate level but at the Master's and the Ph.D. levels. We need to get into psychology, sociology, history and every field—that's our challenge.

I'm so grateful to God, my parents, my family, my friends, the people I learned so much from—they've been my greatest teachers. I could never thank God enough. We need to create a new vision for humanity. I think somewhere in our body and blood, we carry the genes and the chromosomes of all the people in the world already. We have to externalize this and come up with a sense of vision and dreams. I dare to dream and I do dream that someday we'll have a real, new world. We'll have a new world where people of all backgrounds can really come together and enrich each other, where people can enjoy a hemisphere without borders. If Europe can have a common Europe, why can't we have a common America someday? I know it's not easy. I know I may not see it in my lifetime, but for those who trust in God, nothing is impossible.

Lily Eskelsen-García

President
National Education Association

March 13, 2012

Lily Eskelsen-García is president of the National Education Association, the nation's largest labor union. Eskelsen-García began her career in education as a school lunch lady and now leads a professional association of three million educators. She is the first Latina to lead the NEA and one of the country's most influential Hispanic educators. Her passion for and dedication to children's education has been the driving force that has propelled her throughout her career and her life. Eskelsen-García believes in the sacred duty of all educators to be professionals and to care for the whole student—mind, body and character—no matter how students arrive and no matter their learning conditions, their home conditions or their health conditions. She also believes that professionalism carries the responsibility to take action, individually and collectively, toward making the promise of public education a reality and preparing the whole and happy child to succeed in becoming a whole and happy adult.

Eskelsen-García graduated magna cum laude in elementary education from the University of Utah and later earned a Master's degree in instructional technology.

My grandfather was born in Nicaragua. He never spoke a word of English. My mother grew up in Colón, Panama. She met my father when he was a soldier in the Canal Zone. They raised six noisy kids and moved every two or three years, the way military families do. I was born in Fort Hood, Texas, and lived in El Paso; Robins Air Base in Warner Robins, Georgia; Fort Wainwright, Alaska; and Ft. Lawton in Seattle. Then, my parents decided, when they retired, to take their little Catholic family and move, of course, to Brigham City, Utah, where diversity means you found a Presbyterian. I was seventeen years old and in high school when my husband asked me to marry him. He was much, much older; he was eighteen. We got married a week after I graduated from high school.

Of course, I had to work. All I knew was I wanted to work around children. And so, I applied to be a teacher's aide at all these schools and daycare centers. Finally I got to a Head Start Program. They said, "Well, we only have an opening in the cafeteria, in the kitchen." "A job's a job. I'll take it."

I have to tell you, I was an incredible lunch lady. But I will admit that calling myself 'The Lunch Lady' is actually padding my résumé. I was the 'Salad Girl.' I was not up to hot food yet, but I loved being around the kids. I would just make up names when they came through my line, like, "Hey, boyfriend, you're going to eat those peas"; "All right, cutie-poo, let's finish that milk." They'd laugh and they liked going through my line. And when there was an opening as a teacher's aide in the kindergarten, the principal asked me if I wanted it.

I have got to tell you, I was an incredible teacher's aide. I would bring my guitar. I taught five year olds how to sing all the words to the classic, "Don't stick your finger up your nose because your nose knows it's not the place it goes," and we sang it with dignity. After I did that for a year, the kindergarten teacher said, "Lily, you're really good with kids. Have you ever thought about going to college and maybe becoming a teacher?" I was almost twenty years old. That was the first time in my life anyone had suggested that I might want to go to college. So, there was this little seed planted and a Redwood forest grew out of my head. I said to myself, "I would be an incredible teacher.

I'm going to college! I wonder how you do that. How do you actually go to college?" No one had talked to me about it because it wasn't in my parents' experience. They weren't against me going to college but my mother hadn't gone to college; my father never finished eighth grade. When I told them that I was going to go to college, they were so excited, but I was on my own to figure out how to do it.

By that time, my husband and I had a six-month-old baby, and we figured we could do this college thing with his G.I. Bill and folk singing on weekends in every bar in Salt Lake City: both of them. I'd have Jeremy in his stroller and be pushing him around the campus of the University of Utah while Ruel was in his biology class. Then I'd shove the stroller over there and I'd run to my political science class. We just went back and forth for four years. So, we both went to college. And actually, our little baby at the end of four years had gone through four years of college—what a gifted child.

I started teaching at Orchard Elementary fourth grade and, I've got to tell you, I was an incredible teacher. I truly was. I believed in project-based learning. I had my kids do all the work, which was the secret to my success. They set up the science fair. They organized the blood drive. They wrote the pen pal letters to the Golden Living Center residents asking them for their memories of World War II.

And they solved real problems. The closest I ever came to violating that church-state thing was my bulletin board that read, "Though shalt not whine." All right? In my class, if you were going to complain about something, the next words out of your mouth had to be: " . . . and here is what I'm going to do about it."

Once, when one of my friends, Miss Trautmann who taught next door, told me about how hard it was for her husband, Dave, who used a wheel chair to compete with able-bodied shoppers for the handicapped parking spaces, my kids decided to do something about it.

We held a class meeting. After some debate, they voted unanimously to form little vigilante committees and systematically egg the illegally parked cars. Well, as a point of information, I threw in some new vocabulary words, like "bail," and they voted, I think wisely, to reconsider. They instead decided to make the public more aware of why they should leave those parking spaces for the folks they were meant for. They wrote a public service announcement in the form of a handicap rap from Dave's point of view (Park in my Space/ If you dare /And I'll run you over/ With my wheelchair). We got it published in newspapers; we sent it to radio stations and they played it; the local TV station had it produced as a public service announcement staring Dave and with all my kids making a citizen's arrest of the villain (played by our school custodian) who parks in the handicap space. High art.

I taught at Orchard for twelve years and decided that I wanted a change. I asked for a special assignment at the Salt Lake Homeless Shelter, which ran a one-room school for students whose parents would not let them leave the shelter for security reasons. It was the best gig in the whole wide world, because it was an entire loving community that cared about that whole child: healthcare, counselors, people working with parents, a dentist, a doctor who would come in. The world of a teacher can be a very isolated world. At the shelter, we were a big family of professionals caring for families who needed us.

It was at this shelter school that I began to truly understand the gift of a second language. Many of my students and their parents spoke only Spanish. My mother had not raised us speaking Spanish. *Mi español es muy malo, pero la culpa de mi madre.* Once, I scolded her, "Ma, how could you not teach me Spanish when my brain worked?" She said something I didn't understand. She said, "I didn't think it would be good for you." And I pressed her, "What are you talking about? The principal would be waxing my car if I were bilingual! Bilingual teachers are gold! How could that not be good for me?" She started to cry. "You don't know what it was like. When I came here and people heard you speaking Spanish, they didn't like it. They would stare at you. I didn't want people to stare at my children like that, so I decided not to teach you. I know it was a mistake." Then she scolded me, "But you know that you can learn! You can take lessons. You should take classes at night."

I am not an incredible student. I'm really bad at doing my homework. I blame the teacher for not motivating me, of course. But I signed up for classes. I shamelessly used all of my students at the homeless shelter to practice my Spanish. I used Julio. Julio was eight years old, one of my older students. He was the angriest human being I've ever met in my life. He hated his parents for their poverty. He hated that they were making him live in a homeless shelter. He hated the other kids for being younger than he was. He hated me for making him pretend this was a real school.

One day I was sitting in the playground at recess, pretending to watch the kids, but I was actually doing my Spanish homework that was due that night. Then I heard Julio yell something across the playground in Spanish. Right then, I got the best teacher idea I've ever had in my life. I said, "*Julio, ven, te necesito ayudarme,*" which I really hope means, "Come over here, I need you to help me." He was intrigued. "Julio, my mom is going be so mad at me if I can't pass this class. You have to help me do my homework." He sat down next to me. I started reading my work. He started correcting me. He kept saying helpful, encouraging things like, "*Estúpida maestra loca,*" which he told me means, "Good job."

So, I started calling him, "*Maestro.*" I said, "*Maestro,* recess is over. Get the kids lined up." He got the kids lined up. I said, "*Maestro,* I'm going to get the second-graders on the computer. You take the kindergarteners over to the reading rug and start the story." And he'd take the kindergarteners over to the reading rug and start the story. By the end of the week, he would pop into the room and he wouldn't even ask if I needed help. He'd just come in and he'd go, "Okay, I'm here." And I'd say, "Oh, *buenos días, maestro*. Can you do the color flashcards with Chester?" He'd grab the cards and he'd say, "Man, she can't do nothing without me." Then, he'd do the color flash cards with Chester.

I said, "Oh, *maestro*, you're such a good teacher. You should go to college, come back here and be a teacher with me." He laughed and said, "I ain't going to be no teacher." He said, "When I go to college, I'm going to be a wrestler with the World Wrestling Federation. ¡*Lucha Libre!*"

He said, "When."

"When I go to college." This is my seed. Maybe a little Redwood forest will pop out of his head. Maybe not, *pero creo que sí*.

My work has been a big part of my life, but so is my family. My family is a very big part of my story. It's a made-for-TV *Lifetime* original movie waiting to be. My sons, my two boys, they are incredible human beings. They are young men who won their struggle with drugs and who are today strong and healthy and happy with families of their own. I was married to that eighteen-year-old boy for 36 years until he died last year. He lost his lifelong struggle with depression and took his life.

Mickey did a very dangerous thing asking me to come and tell my story, because it's a very long story. It's a story within other stories. But it's an incredible story, like your incredible story. I have never met another human being that doesn't have an incredible story inside of them. Our stories are just the funny, touching, tragic things that happen to us while we go about the business of living. My story is no more important than your story, really.

The most boring things about people's stories are usually their résumés and their titles. You could have read my bio, but then you wouldn't have known anything about me. You wouldn't have known what's in my heart and makes me get up in the morning. My life is full of the stories of children—my children, other people's children—and caring about their lives is more than my job. Children are my cause.

A big part of my story is my union, my National Education Association. My beloved NEA. My NEA is the best chance I have to fight for something better for students, for the children I have loved, *para todos los niños, todos nuestros niños,* for all our children. Education is *el camino.* It is that path that will lead them to their own incredible lives.

For me and for my colleagues, over three million educators in this country working in America, pre-school to graduate school, it's a mission that we live. It's not a mission on our website. It's a mission that's written across our hearts, like it's written in my favorite poem, "Give me your hungry children, your sick children, your homeless, your abused children. Give me your children who need love as badly as they need learning. Give me your children who have talents and gifts and skills. And give me those that have none. Give them all to me, in whatever shape they come, whatever color their skin, whatever language they speak, wherever they find God, give them all to me. Because this is a public school. We will give you the doctors and the scientists and the carpenters. We'll give you the lawyers and the ministers and the teachers of tomorrow. We will give you the mothers and the fathers and the thinkers and the builders and the artists and the dreamers. We will give you the American dream. We will give you the future."

And that future is that every blessed child will have an incredible story to tell every day of their lives.

Alberto R. Gonzales

U.S. Attorney General

November 2, 2005

Alberto R. Gonzales was born in San Antonio, Texas and raised in Houston. He is a graduate of Texas public schools, Rice University and Harvard Law School. Gonzales served in the United States Air Force between 1973 and 1975, and attended the United States Air Force Academy between 1975 and 1977.

Gonzales was nominated by President George W. Bush and confirmed by the United States Senate as the 80th Attorney General of the United States on February 3, 2005 and served in that capacity until September 2007. He has worked as a partner at a major Houston law firm (Vinson & Elkins) and held positions as Justice on the Texas Supreme Court, Texas Secretary of State, General Counsel to the Governor of Texas and Counsel to the President of the United States. Judge Gonzales has also served as a Visiting Professor and minority/veteran recruitment consultant at Texas Tech University.

I love my family. I believe in God and I am grateful for my country, the United States of America, which has allowed me to live the American dream. I served in our Armed Forces because I believe the freedoms and opportunities available in America are worth defending and, ultimately, worth dying for.

I am proud of our beautiful culture, the language, the foods and the traditions. We all want to pursue prosperity and opportunity for all Hispanics. We all want to see our kids get an education. We want everyone to be able to own a home or business. We all want an equal opportunity to pursue a dream.

We may differ, of course, on how best to achieve these broad objectives. We may have a different history or heritage due to geography. We may have different tastes in food, dialects, religion or politics, but in the end, there is more that binds us. We can all agree, for example, that too many of our children are getting into trouble and dropping out of school. We can all agree that the future leadership of our communities is at risk. The key is to focus our energy, to direct our priorities and to engage in a meaningful debate with clarity of purpose, but a discussion that is respectful and tolerant of dissenting views. We may be from different ends of a political spectrum, but we enjoy a cultural tie that cannot be broken.

I'm often asked what it is like to be the first Hispanic attorney general. I tell them that I am a son of a poor cotton picker and construction worker, that my parents never finished grade school. I tell them that I know what it's like to face a life with few opportunities, with nothing more than a heart full of hope, a mind full of dreams and a willingness to work hard. I tell them that I am the Attorney General for all Americans, but I take great pride in the fact that the son of an American migrant worker serves as the chief law enforcement officer of the United States.

President Bush also takes great pride in that fact, and I am not the only Hispanic leader in this administration. When President Bush looks around the table at a cabinet meeting, he also sees Carlos Gutiérrez, our commerce secretary. When he surveys the federal agencies, he sees names like Richard Carmona, Gary Vásquez, Hector Barreto, Anna Cabral, Cari Domínguez and many others. The president surrounded himself with public servants who are qualified and represented the diversity of the American people. He also applied these principles in making nominations to federal judicial appointments, a task that I worked on personally with him as White House counsel. I know the president well. Diversity at all levels of government is as important to him as it is to you. It was a great privilege to help the president select a diverse group of qualified nominees to share his judicial philosophy.

Let me talk a little bit about our recent Supreme Court nominee, Judge Sam Alito. Judge Alito understands that there is no Hispanic Constitution, there is no African American Constitution, and there is no White Constitution. There is just one Constitution for all Americans. Judge Alito has been on the bench for fifteen years and has argued in front of the Supreme Court twelve times. He is well known for his fairness in his character and his commitment to the rule of law. During his 30 years of public service, much of which was spent with Department of Justice, Judge Alito has earned the reputation for excellence that, quite frankly, few in this country can equal.

One of the great things about this process is that you don't have to take my word for this. Listen to his words as he responds to questions in his confirmation hearings. The Senate and the American public will learn more about Judge Alito's qualifications and his approach to judging. So, I ask you and others to reserve judgment and give him an opportunity to show why he would be good for the Court and for the country. Judge Alito, like many of you, is the product of the immigrant dream. He will bring his unique experiences and background to the Supreme Court just as I have brought mine to my time as attorney general.

I have noticed over the course of my first month as attorney general that my family's personal story has given me a unique appreciation for the challenges faced by many Americans. I recently spoke to a group of Latino law enforcement officers. I told them a story about a veteran deputy from the Los Angeles Police Department's anti-gang unit. It was the story of a man, Deputy Ortiz, who went to work early on Friday, June 23rd, as he often did in order to get a jump on a street gang investigation.

The thirty-five-year-old deputy had been with the Los Angeles Sheriff's Department for fifteen years. He was a five-year veteran with his department's Anti-Gang Task Force and had just returned from his honeymoon.

Deputy Ortiz was going door-to-door conducting interviews in a gang-plagued neighborhood. At 3 p.m., he knocked on the door of a house and was checking IDs when someone shot him in the head from point-blank range. As L.A. Sheriff Lee Baca described it, this was an assassination of a deputy. It was a sudden attack that gave the deputy no chance. The alleged gunman was José Luis Orozco, a suspected gang member. When Sheriff Baca spoke to the press about the murder, he printed out Orozco's rap sheet; it was five feet long.

The investigation that Deputy Ortiz was conducting on the day that he died was part of a broader effort to reclaim the small community of Hawaiian Gardens from intimidation, drug sales and violence. Deputy Ortiz sacrificed his life to do his duty. It struck me that everyone involved was Hispanic: a brave Hispanic deputy, a positive Hispanic leader in Sheriff Baca and, unfortunately, a young Hispanic already lost to the dangerous life of guns, drugs and gangs.

It's a telling example both of the progress we've made and the long distance we have yet to travel. Gangs are a growing problem for the Hispanic community—we all know it. Gangs wipe out the dreams of our children; they cost us future leaders. I have directed my U.S. attorneys around the country to work with partners at the federal, state and local levels to stop the spread of gangs and curb the rampant violence from gang activities.

As the chief law enforcement officer of the country, my official role in responding to gangs and troubled youth is to lead investigations and promote prosecutions. But as a father, that is not where I want to be. We need to get to these kids, our kids, before they join gangs, before they drop out of school, before they get into trouble. Education and prevention are as important as enforcement, and the department works to share necessary resources and training so that the hopes of our kids are not extinguished. That American dream, preserving that dream, is a reason that so many immigrants, millions every year, come to this country in search of a better life for their families.

Now, recently, the President reiterated his vision for a comprehensive immigration reform program. He outlined a number of steps to strengthen security along our borders and to provide real options for people who want to stay in the United States to work temporarily.

Like many of you, I am a product of the immigrant dream. I understand how important it can be for people looking to provide for their families. The President understands that too. He knows that family values, for example, do not stop at the Rio Grande River. He knows that immigrants have formed an important part of the American fabric of our society, that America has a wonderful and long tradition of having open arms and welcoming people from other countries hoping to come to America simply to pursue a dream.

The President also knows that the security of our citizens depends in part on our ability to control the border. We need to know who's coming into this country and why they are coming here. With the temporary worker program, fewer people will try to sneak in unlawfully to work. That means that our enforcement efforts can focus on catching drug smugglers, terrorists and gunrunners. Today, Homeland Security Secretary Mike Chertoff is announcing a new Secure Borders Initiative. The Secure Borders Initiative is going to increase our ability to gain what Secretary Chertoff calls "operational control" on our borders. This is a new program which will provide additional resources and technology at our borders. It will make our country safer from the threat of terrorism. The Secure Borders Initiative will also work hand in hand with the temporary worker program, again, with the goal of curbing illegal criminal activity and clearing a path for legal work in the United States.

This is a very complicated issue that has generated a great deal of passion here in Washington, around our communities and, quite frankly, among our state leaders who are struggling to provide services to folks in their communities. We need your reasoned voices as leaders in this debate about immigration. On this issue and many, many others that confront our community, we need your leadership. As we work to ensure the hope and the opportunity of America for every citizen, I appreciate your ongoing efforts to nurture the Hispanic community, especially as role models for young Hispanics.

Carlos Gutiérrez

CEO & Chairman of the Board of Kellogg & U.S. Secretary of Commerce

March 21, 2013

Carlos Gutiérrez is Chair of Albright Stonebridge Group (ASG). Secretary Gutiérrez served as U.S. Secretary of Commerce from 2005 to 2009 under President George W. Bush, working with foreign government and business leaders to advance economic relationships, enhance trade and promote U.S. exports. Secretary Gutiérrez also played a key role in the passage of landmark free trade agreements that removed trade barriers, expanded export opportunities and boosted global investment. Previously, Secretary Gutiérrez spent nearly 30 years with Kellogg Company, a global manufacturer and marketer of well-known food brands. After assignments in Latin America, Canada, Asia and the United States, he became president and chief executive officer of Kellogg in 1999–the youngest CEO in the company's hundred-year history. In April 2000, he was named chairman of the board of the company.

Secretary Gutiérrez was born in Havana, Cuba in 1963, the son of a pineapple plantation owner whose property was expropriated after the Cuban Revolution. The Gutiérrez family fled to the United States in 1960, when Gutiérrez was six years old. Then Gutiérrez' father moved the family to Mexico after he got a job with the H. J. Heinz Company. Gutiérrez studied business administration at the Monterrey Institute of Technology and joined Kellogg in Mexico in 1975 at the age of 22 as a sales representative and management trainee. One of his early assign-

ments was driving a delivery-truck route to local stores. As he rose through the ranks from sales representative to president and CEO, Gutiérrez had to overcome many prejudices, proving that a Latino leader can in fact lead non-Latinos.

After working at Kellogg for about five years, I was given the chance to run Kellogg de México. I'll never forget a conversation I had with my then boss, who was the president of Kellogg International. I said, "I have been here for five years. I think we've done a pretty good job, and I would like to be transferred to another country." He said, "Oh, of course. We can think about a new transfer for you." I said, "I'd like to go to one of the big Anglo markets." With cereal, the per capita consumption in markets like the United States, Canada, Great Britain, Ireland and Australia was bigger. I didn't understand the question he asked me after this. He said, "Are you sure you want to do that? You want to go to Canada instead of, say, being the president of Latin America? You know, you can lead Latins." And he kept insisting on that, "Do you want to go and be a leader in Canada or do you want to stay and lead Latins?"

This was 1988, and we've come a long way since. I think what the president was asking was can a Latin lead non-Latins? I didn't realize that that was the question. And I thought about it and thought about it. As I moved on in my career, I thought about it some more. I thought about it every day. Why is it that he had this perception that a Latin can be a good leader as long as he's leading Latins? This is a very difficult obstacle for Latins to combat, and probably, unfortunately, still is a perception in some people's minds. But, again, we've come a long way. I'm sure that that question was once asked about African Americans. Can an African American lead non-African Americans? Well, we've got an African American president, so we've answered that question!

I started observing leadership at that time. And by the way, I did get the transfer to Canada. As I look back now, I've had the opportunity to observe some great leaders. I've met leaders who are tall and who are short, some who are thin and some who are heavyset, some are extroverts, some are painfully shy. There is no such thing as a profile for a leader. In the business world ten years ago, people thought it was Jack Welch. So, I guess, that means if you want to be a great leader, you had to be this little Irish guy who ran around screaming at everybody. But that was his style.

Every leader I've observed who has been great has had his or her own style. So, there is no such thing as a profile of a leader that people are born with. Everyone has a shot at it. But I have observed four simple traits about great leaders. One is they have the will to lead. They have to want to lead. Leadership is risky business, because you tell people, "Follow me, and I'm going to take you to a good place." If it doesn't work out, you're responsible.

Some people love that. Some people love the idea of getting up in the morning and solving an insurmountable problem. Some people love the idea of having a terrible problem in their company, because they can get in there and exert leadership and do what they have to do to make it right. Not everybody does. I know a lot of people who like to be the boss; that doesn't mean that they are people who have the will to lead. Every leader I have observed tends to have the will to lead.

The second trait is that great leaders believe in something that's bigger than them. If your people observe that you believe only in yourself, they're going to follow you because they have to. Because they're probably working for you and they're getting paid. But they're not going to follow you to the end. They're going to tolerate you. For great leaders that I've observed, it's the team that is bigger than they are, or it's the institution, it's the organization, it's the project, or it's whatever it is, but every day they display that they are smaller than that, that the objective is the biggest thing in their lives. Once people see that, they'll follow them wherever. People can see when a person is always looking up—when they are looking to see how they can get promoted and how they can get recognition and how they can become the guy who gets all the credit. That is a real trap.

The third trait is that great leaders are self-aware. They know what they're good at and what they're not good at. I wish I knew this 25 years ago. Twenty years ago, as a thirty-year-old leader, I thought the job of the leader was to know everything. I had to have every answer; I had to ask every good question, I had to do all the talking. That's why I was leader. And, for my people, it was miserable. We have all probably worked for someone who had to be right because they were the leader. As I observed growing leaders and more mature leaders, I found that they had the self-confidence to say, "Hey, this is who I am. I'm good at this stuff, but I'm not very good at this. So, I'm going to surround myself with people who are good at what I'm not good at." It takes a lot of self-confidence, but the sooner you get there, the sooner you are self-aware and very comfortable with who you are, the quicker you will get to great leadership. People love that. They love vulnerability. They love a leader who isn't afraid to be vulnerable. They love someone who understands that you cannot be good at everything. That's where the diversity comes in, as you surround yourself with people who are different. And that takes you to diversity.

We have all seen companies where the senior management was the same. They play golf on weekends together, take breaks together and finish each other's sentences. That's not a team where new ideas are going to come from. It just isn't. It has been proven. So, when people ask, "Is diversity just a program? What is it for?" I say diversity is about everything. If you have a leader leading the team who's an introvert, he probably wants to surround himself with some extroverts. Imagine a team of introverts and extroverts, or people who have different cultural backgrounds, who are born in different countries, who have a different gender, who have different sexual orientation; people who are different. And that makes a tremendous difference.

Finally, the last trait I have noticed in great leaders is that you can understand when they talk. I had the opportunity to spend time in Baghdad with General David Petraeus, and the first thing he said to me was, "Mr. Gutiérrez, you work in business, so you probably know that all great strategies start with a simple idea." He said, "Our simple idea was that we'd go into a town and we'd clear it out of the bad guys and then we'd go back to camp, and the bad guys would come back in. So, the insight, the simple insight that led to what we call the surge was we have to sleep where we fight. That's it. That led to the strategy. But it was a simple idea."

Too often, people confuse complexity with sophistication. We've all seen the leader who walks into a room with a one-hour PowerPoint presentation and charts that nobody understands. People walk away questioning whether it's their fault they don't understand. "Oh, I probably don't understand it because it's me. But no wonder he's a senior VP because he understands these things. The circles and arrows and thousands of numbers on one page, it's just an amazing thing." Great leaders understand that their job is to communicate, not to impress. So, if you walk out of a room with a leader and you're not really sure what it is he or she wants, it is not your fault. It's the idea that they mistook complexity for sophistication.

I had a secret weapon when I was coming up the corporate ladder, it was a role model who I never met, by the way, and I still regret to this day that I never met him. I may have been the second Hispanic CEO, but the person who I admired and followed was, I think, the first Hispanic CEO. The man's name was Roberto Goizueta. He was a Cuban American. I was sitting in my office in Mexico when I got *Fortune* magazine and started reading I said, "My God, it's a Cuban-American CEO of the Coca-Cola Company." This was 1984.

As of that day, I became a fanatic about Coca-Cola. I read their annual reports. I read any article that had his name. I read anything about what he was like. And I'll tell you, it helped me. It helped me. It's a great thing to have someone you admire. It's a great thing to have role models. It requires a little bit of humility, because some people think, "Hey, I'm not going to admire anybody. I'm just going to admire my father and my mother and my brother, and that's all there is." But it's actually very, very healthy. I'll tell you a little bit about this man who I came to know through reading. By the way, he had the reputation of answering every single letter that was written to him. So, I wrote him a letter, saying, "Hey, I'm a general manager of Kellogg Mexico. I'm also Cuban American. It's amazing that you've gone to the top, and I admire you." He never answered. So, he answered almost every letter.

I always asked everyone from Coke I talked to, "Talk about Roberto. Talk about Roberto." He was very shy, some would say painfully shy, which is rare for a Cuban American. He had a very strong Cuban accent, very strong. So he didn't like to do a lot of public speaking. It didn't suit him. It just wasn't what he loved. His passion was financial strategy. He was a genius. He knew how to make money. He would stay in Atlanta and surround himself with his finance folks and think through how to move the company forward strategically.

And speaking about self-awareness and believing in something bigger than yourself, he did one of the gutsiest things I've ever seen in the world of business: he named as his president, his number two, a man by the name of Don Keough. Don Keough was a *backslapping* Irish man who just loved people. He loved the sales force. He loved customers. He loved the employees. Roberto said, "You go out and you run this company. I'm going to give you the strategy, but you go out and do whatever you need to do. Because the kind of stuff that you're good at is not the stuff that I'm good at."

The amazing thing is that Don Keough was Roberto's competition for the top job, but Roberto had the foresight, the self-awareness, the sense that, "This isn't about me, this is about the Coca-Cola Company." He had the guts to appoint him. They were together for about fifteen years. You go back and look at that performance of that company. It's one of the most amazing things I've seen in my life.

I was lucky to have someone like that, someone who paved the way and made it easier for me. I could follow him, see how he was doing it and see how he was leading other people. Don't ever think that it's wrong or bad to admire someone. I think it's actually a very, very noble and a very courageous thing to do.

I was at an offsite one time at my old company, and we were talking about diversity—a pretty big group, about 50 senior people in the company; it was in the 1990s. The president of the North American business, which was the biggest business in the company, was kind of like my competitor for the top job. He was saying, "You know, on work-life balance, it's not just the company's responsibility. It's also the employee's responsibility. The employee has to take charge and has to also tell us that he or she needs some work-life balance. For example, if you have a little league game and you want to go see your son play little league at two o'clock in the afternoon, you should be able to tell your boss, 'Hey, my son's playing little league this afternoon. I won't be here.'"

Now, by that time, I had been in the company for almost 25 years, and it occurred to me that I had missed a lot of my son's little league games. I used to go to the ones that were at seven o'clock at night, but I don't ever remember in my whole career leaving at two o'clock in the afternoon to go to a little league game. And maybe it was a little bit of an immigrant's insecurity. Maybe I was just a little bit too concerned about stereotypes. So, if I asked my boss, say, "It's two o'clock in the afternoon. I want to go to a little league game," I thought what they would think is, "Of course, these Cubans, all they think about is baseball."

I didn't push it. If somebody worked ten hours a day, I'd work fourteen. If others went to the little league game, I would stay and work. I don't regret it. I think that the burden that every generation of immigrants has had is the burden that we've got to prove ourselves. You can say, "Heck, no. I don't have to prove myself to anyone." But we're doing this because we believe in something bigger than ourselves. We believe in our community. And if we have to do that because there are people who are suspicious, people who don't understand, do it. Do it. It'll help you and it'll work.

I believe that this generation of immigrants . . . Our job is to prove that because of Hispanic immigration that this country has had, whether they came in undocumented or whether they came in through the front door with a passport and a visa, this country will be better because we are all here. This country will be a better country because of our community. I would not have gotten to the CEO job if it weren't for the workers who worked on the shop floor in that factory in Mexico. Many of them didn't have a first- or second-grade education, but the way they worked when we, as a leadership team, finally got their confidence, made us look so good—I'll never forget those folks. I see them. I still see their faces, and I see them all over the place in D.C. I still see them around the country, I still see them in New York, and I know what our people can do. I know what they can do for this country. We've got this incredible opportunity in our hands to improve their lives and to improve the prosperity of this country by finally, finally having the foresight, the courage to pass immigration reform.

It's great when we hear, "Hey, fourteen percent of our company is Hispanic," or "We're shooting for thirteen," or "We've got eight percent of our directors on the board that are Hispanic"— we've been through that, that's the past. We want leadership. Shoot for the top. Yes, shoot to lead Anglo Americans. Shoot to step out of the community. Shoot for the mainstream. You've got it, you deserve it and you've got it in your blood. Don't let anyone try to box you in a corner that says you can only manage Latin people, you're going to be the Latin American guy, you're okay but stay in your community. No way. Get into the mainstream. Get into the middle of things. Lead and shoot for the top, and you'll be surprised. You'll be surprised how dreams come true and magic does happen in this incredible country.

Luis V. Gutiérrez

Congressman
U.S. House of Representatives

June 15, 2011

Now in his twelfth term, Congressman Luis V. Gutiérrez is the sen-
ior member of the Illinois delegation in the U.S. House of Representa-
tives. Elected in 1992, he is an experienced legislator and energetic
spokesman on behalf of his constituents in Illinois' Fourth District in the
heart of Chicago. Congressman Gutiérrez is nationally recognized for his
tireless leadership on Latino and immigrant community issues. Gutié-
rrez played an instrumental role in advocating for executive action by
President Obama to provide deportation relief to certain long-term
undocumented immigrants and their families through the Deferred
Action for Childhood Arrivals.

Married and both a father and grandfather, Representative Gutié-
rrez was born and raised in Chicago to parents who had themselves
migrated to Chicago from Puerto Rico in the early 1950s. He previously
served as an Alderman in the City of Chicago and has been a teacher, a
social worker and a cab driver, among other diverse experiences. After an
African-American congressman won the primary for mayor of Chicago,
it was while driving a cab that he decided that if he wanted to change
things in his Democratic party, the best thing to do was run for office.

In 1984 I ran for Democratic committeeman so that I could
become part of that Democratic Cook County machine. I ran

against Dan Rostenkowski, chairman of the Ways and Means Committee, because he made a decision that Harold Washington, a Democratic congressman, would win the primary, and he and other Democrats decided that a Republican would do better than he would. They started a campaign in '83 that was called, "Epton: Before It's Too Late." I kind of responded viscerally to that kind of prejudice within my own Democratic Party. The next year I decided that the best way to deal with this is to take them out. I was driving a cab back then, and it was a little difficult driving a cab and running against the chairman of the Ways and Means Committee. But I got a whopping 24.8 percent of the vote.

I still remember, it was seven o'clock on that election night on March 15th. The radio was playing a little music and announced the polls had closed. I remember my wife looking at me, because a tear came down from my eye. She said, "But don't cry. You don't even know how badly you've done yet." I said, "Honey, seriously, I'm just happy it's over." You know, I didn't quite understand what I was getting into. I was tired of knocking on people's doors. I was tired of asking people for money. I was tired of them putting up my poster, taking down my poster. Dan Rostenkowski was very good at politics; he got all my neighbors to put up his poster, and it was difficult to drive home. I told her I was really crying because I was happy that I would never do this again. Of course, I didn't keep that promise. I did it again.

But there was someone who reached out to me and did see some promise, in spite of the dismal election results. Someone did see some promise in me and said, "You know, you really shouldn't be driving a cab. You should be doing something else. You should be organizing and you should be helping people register to vote and galvanizing the community and empowering that community." He told me growing numbers doesn't mean growing influence unless we organize. That was Juan Andrade, who hired me after that devastating defeat. I want to thank him very much. We're all here because somebody at some point extended a helping hand, gave us encouragement at the points in our lives when it seemed most unlikely that we would succeed.

My mom and dad came to the United States of America from Puerto Rico in 1952. They didn't speak English. They didn't even have warm coats so they could get through the winter. They came here with a determination and a desire to do better for themselves, and with an understanding that back in Puerto Rico there wasn't much of a future for them. My father was 21 years old and my mother was nineteen, he had never passed ninth grade. They came here to forge a better future for themselves. I still remember as I research and look at how they were received. There were articles in the venerable New York Times about how there were too many Puerto Ricans in New York City and how they were bringing diseases, tropical diseases, over-running our welfare system and our housing system, and how they were a blight on the city of New York.

There's a famous story about a New York Times photographer being sent out to a Puerto Rican neighborhood in New York City on a Sunday. He was looking for a picture, except, he said, "I can't take just any picture back to the paper. They asked me to take this picture." I said, "What's the problem?" He answered, "Well, it's Sunday and all these kids have their little suits on and their ties and their shoes and they're all . . . " "That's the way we dress up when we go to church." He couldn't find a picture that would fit the stereotype of what it was supposedly to be Puerto Rican in the urban area. I know that from a personal experience.

My mom and dad worked really, really hard. They didn't have a financial adviser but they saved their money. You know, I'm a big supporter of reproductive rights and women's rights, but since my mom came from nine and my dad came from fourteen, they only had two of us because they were pretty smart about planning. They learned to live on one check and save the other. They learned that maybe two kids—Luisito and Nala—were enough so that they could move on. They worked really hard, and so, in 1969, they fulfilled their dream. The dream of many Puerto Ricans is always to get back to Puerto Rico.

They bought their Chevy, and their French provincial furniture; they got Luna plastic covers to cover their furniture so that nobody would mess with them, and they moved back. They really didn't let my sister and me speak English, because we lived in a bilingual household. We spoke to my mom and dad in English and they spoke to us in Spanish, and we understood each other perfectly well. I still remember getting off the airplane when we arrived in San Juan, Puerto Rico. Of course, I'd prefer Chicago, it gets warm there, but it was like July in Puerto Rico. I said, "Papi, can you buy me a Coke?" He looked at me sternly and said, "*Hijo, estamos en Puerto Rico. Aquí se habla español.*" Back then you didn't share with your parents your most intimate thoughts. I didn't say anything like, "You've had fifteen years to let me in on this, right?" So, I kind of said, "Okay, I guess it's time to speak Spanish." I tell you that because it was a wonderful experience, and yet it was such a terrifying experience for me. It really helped to define who I am today.

They sent me to school in Puerto Rico, where you start high school in 10th grade. I was a freshman all over again. I remember filling out the form to enroll myself in my homeroom, and where it says to write in your name, I put Luis Gutiérrez, right? The teacher took the card and said, "*Para un momentito, hombre.*" I stood up and he was like, "*¿Cuál es tu nombre?*" I thought, *I've had so many pronunciations of my last name*—because I was in public school in Chicago, every year I get a new teacher, it was Guterez, and every year it was a kind of different pronunciation. I was good with it. I'm not claiming discrimination or anything here today. It's just different. I told the teacher, "I have variety of ways." I wasn't quite sure which one to pick, so I said, "Luis Gutiérrez," and the whole classroom started laughing.

Now, you have to remember that I'm fifteen years old. This is adolescence. *¿Ustedes han estudiado la palabra adolescencia?* You know that it's made up of two words, right? "*Adolescencia*" is made up of two words, right? *Dolor y ciencia*—*la ciencia del dolor*. No, I'm serious. I'm fifteen years old and I'm really going to understand what adolescence is all about: the pain. So, he said, "I don't know what it's like in Chicago, but here a minimum requirement is that you know your complete name." He was very, very mean and very, very tough, and very unfair to me. He said, "You need to go home." I left, and I went home crying. I said to my mom, "They won't let me enroll in school, they say I don't know my name, and they keep bringing up this thing, *que si yo no tengo madre*." You had to have your mother's maiden name because that's your full name in any Latin American country, and Puerto Rico—I don't want to cause a political stir here—is a Latin American country, populated by 3.7 million American citizens.

That night, I learned something wonderful for the first time in my life: my name. I kept saying it: "Luis Vicente Gutiérrez Olmedo. Luis Vicente Gutiérrez Olmedo." I really liked it. I kept saying, "*Tú sabes*, maybe I can write the next best novel *or tú sabes, porque sonaba como un nombre interesante*." I practiced all night, and I went back to school the next day. I filled out the card and, before the teacher started the class, I said to myself, "I'm going to make sure I practice this in front of a small group before the big group." I went up to a young girl and simply said to her, "*Hola. Mi nombre es Luis Vicente Gutiérrez Olmedo. ¿Cómo te llamas tú?*" It's something you do when you're a sophomore in high school. She raised up her hand and said, "Mister, mister . . . "—that's what they call teachers in Puerto Rico. "Mister, mister. *El gringo me está molestando*."

I can't think of a time that I felt more alone and more isolated and smaller in my whole life than being an adolescent at that age. I knew what it was truly to be an immigrant, a foreigner, the person who was different; this person who was laughed at; this person who didn't understand the language and the mores and the idiosyncrasies; the kid that didn't fit in. I've got to tell you something: it drives me every day when I see new immigrants that come to this country and they're laughed about and they're ridiculed and they're exploited and nobody stands up for them.

Nevertheless, I made some really good friends in that high school in Puerto Rico. They didn't laugh. They extended me a warm hand and taught me the language and accepted me. They embraced me, made me feel human again. They made me feel powerful because of their friendship. That's all I try to do every day: to say to the immigrants in this country, "You have a friend that is going to make you feel powerful and whole and human, too, in spite of the fact that you may be exploited." I'm going to continue to go from city to city, create event after event, hear the testimonies of those who are affected by our broken immigration system until we fix it, because it is necessary to fix the kind of destructive force that our broken immigration system has.

I remember when I was with Bob Menéndez and Albio Sires in Elizabeth, New Jersey, and this Puerto Rican man gets up there and says, "I'm a Puerto Rican veteran. I served this country. They want to deport my wife because they say she's here illegally. Although I'm an American citizen and served this country, she has to go back to where she came from for ten years, Congressman. I served this country. I paid the highest tax any citizen can pay: the risk of their limbs and their life and their blood. Can you do something, because I've got three months to live before I die of cancer? Can I please leave her with my children?"

I went to the Napa Valley, and a woman came up and said, "You know what, I was deported after I got married to my American citizen husband. They deported me. They said I had to stay ten more years in Mexico before I could come back. I was pregnant, Congressman. I'd like to read you the letter that my husband wrote me." It was a beautiful, beautiful love letter from her husband, obviously heartbroken that they were separated as he was in California and she was stuck because of our broken immigration system. She read the letter and said, "I was pregnant at the time he wrote it. This is my three-year-old son." I asked, "Why'd you say my three-year-old son?" She said, "I just want you to know my husband couldn't deal with the separation. He committed suicide."

In our immigration system, there are four million American citizen children, four million who have one or two parents who are undocumented. Those four million American citizen children fear that the government of the United States of America is going to come and knock on their door one day and take away their mother or their father. There's something fundamentally wrong when you have four million American citizen children who are going to be four million American citizen adults, and the first thing they learn about their government is to fear their government because it will destroy their family. That's wrong.

We have 65,000 kids—the estimated number of undocumented children who graduate from U.S. high schools each year. They graduate from high school class valedictorians. They're admitted to Princeton and Harvard. They're the best and the brightest. Given the rate of kids dropping out of school, just think about all the adversity they face. They're smart and they're as American as our own children that were born here. They pledge allegiance to the only flag they know, the one of the United States of America. And what do we do? We want to deport them. They want to go on to college and succeed. Clearly, you don't have to be a lawyer to know that a three or four year old cannot premeditatedly violate a law, a law that he cannot understand. They are truly innocent, and we should do something about that; allow those young men and women to integrate themselves fully into the fabric of our society, go to college, serve in the military and help us grow and create a better, stronger economic nation of the United States of America.

If you want to use the immigration system so that you can ratchet up the deportation of gang bangers and drug dealers and rapists and murderers who prey upon my community and your community, then I'm with you. But there are certain people who are working very hard and who have deep roots in this country. There are people who work and sweat and toil at some of the toughest jobs in America, and they only want to raise their children and become part of the American fabric. Don't deport them. Let's find a system that will integrate them. That's the American way.

I'm so proud to be a member of the Hispanic Congressional Caucus. I can't wait until we have more members so that we can be more powerful and more influential. I'm going around the country saying I know that the Congress failed to pass and enact Comprehensive Immigration Reform. I know that the President of the United States is not a king, and I know that he can't rule by edict. But I also know that within the framework of our laws, the President of the United States has immense prosecutorial discretion. He should use that discretion in the same manner as this administration did when it saw the devastating impact of the earthquake in Haiti and said, "We will not send anyone back to Haiti, regardless of their immigration status until a society is established there that can receive them, nurture them and keep them safe." And we've done that. That's the right thing to do. We shouldn't deport a million young men and women who are going to school and to college who came here through no fault of their own.

The Hispanic Congressional Caucus is engaged in a conversation and a dialogue with the President of the United States, asking him, "Mr. President, won't you use that prosecutorial discretion that's conferred to you? You don't need a new law. You just need to use the one we have." I've heard the administration say to me, "Oh, Luis, if we do that, then the Republicans will take it away." Well, if you use a law to keep people from discrimination, are you worried that you're going to allow them to continue to be discriminated? If you're going to use a law to keep people safe in the workplace protected by labor laws, do you think they'll to take it away and let people die? Change takes courage. And this is a very particular time.

My hope is that the President goes to Puerto Rico and drinks a piña colada, wears a guayabera, goes out to El Paso and gives a great speech. I want the president of the United States to understand; that's my task. Let me tell you, I would prefer to get invitations to the balls and the dinners at the White House and I would prefer to be on Air Force One. But you want to know something? I have to tell you that this is too important, because I never forget that fifteen-year-old kid that everybody laughed at in his classroom. I know there are people just like me today.

There was a wonderful gift that I was given one day in Chicago. I was in Back of the Yards over on 47th and Ashland, when this tall man came up to me. He must've been, I don't know, like 250 pounds, 6'3", 6'4", big guy, Mexican. He stretched out his hand and said, "Hola, Gutiérrez." So I shook his hand, right? He said, "*Te quiero felicitar por el trabajo que haces en el congreso.*" And I kept thinking, I *hope you let go of my hand really soon*, because he was very enthusiastic. Then he said, "*Pero quiero decirte una cosa más.*" I said, "*Dime.*" He said, "*Tu español ha mejorado muchísimo.*" I thought to myself, *it's all those times repeating those words in front of the mirror.* So I said, "*Gracias, ¿pero sabes por qué mi español ha mejorado?*" He said something very interesting: "*Porque cuando te escucho suenas más y más como mexicano.*"

Now, for those of us who all know there is no such language as Mexican or Puerto Rican—it's all Spanish—what was his message to me? That I speak for him, right? That the values that I uphold, the fight that I fight, are his values, is his fight. That he sees a compatriot, someone just like him.

I'm going to tell you something. It's true that 500,000 Latinos turn eighteen every year. There are 50 million of us. Seventy-five percent of all Latinos, in spite of everything you've heard on the news, are actually citizens of the United States of America. And 93 percent of all Latinos under eighteen are citizens of the United States of America; that other 25 percent aren't. And 20 percent of those are permanent residents, eight million of whom can become citizens tomorrow. You know how we're going to turn them into citizens and turn them into power, so that if he comes from Bolivia, and a Colombian doesn't hear a Bolivian, he hears a fellow

Colombian? *Cuando el boricua habla, el dominicano escucha a otro dominicano, y cuando un mexicano habla, el guatemalteco escucha a un paisano de él, y no un mexicano. ¿Y cuándo nosotros aprendemos a hablar con una voz clara y sencilla y única como nosotros podemos? Cuando usemos lo que yo he venido a aprender es el vernáculo de Dios, el español de una manera en la cual nosotros podemos transformar este país.*

So, I just figured, there was a reason my mom and dad took me back to Puerto Rico: it was to learn about the idiosyncrasies and to learn the language and the mores, so that one day I could stand up for those who didn't have a voice. And to everyone here who's Puerto Rican, I want to say to you, remember what it was like when no one would stand up for us, when there were no voices of power to defend us? You know what, we've been blessed with a powerful presence here and a powerful history of fight in this country. I'm proud of the history of Puerto Ricans here in this country. We're not going to allow it to happen to anyone else while we're on our watch.

José Hernández

Astronaut
NASA

March 1, 2010

Raised in a migrant farm working family, José Hernández grew up making the grueling trek with his family from Mexico up through the Central Valley of California, picking strawberries and beets, and to Northern California, where they picked cucumbers, cherries and peaches. As his parents and four siblings moved from town to town, they would live in a two-bedroom shack, sending the kids to the local schools during the week and having the kids join them at work in the fields on weekends.

In spite of having just a third-grade education, his parents understood the importance of school and demanded José and his siblings work just as hard in the classroom as they did in the fields. Hernández considers his father a great motivator and recalls one day when he and his four siblings were especially tired from working. His father asked how they felt and said, "Good, remember this feeling because this is your future if you don't go to school."

Hernández was about eight years old when he first saw the astronauts walk on the moon on his grainy black and white television. This image of astronauts floating in slow motion as they walked on the moon inspired the little boy who was holding the antenna to get the best reception possible. That's when the dream was born. He told his father and mother that that's what he wanted to do, to be an astronaut!

In 2004, Hernández was accepted into NASA's astronaut candidate class. In 2009, aboard the Space Shuttle Discovery, his dream became a reality.

There are leaders in every aspect of our lives who basically help us along the way, *porque* this journey of becoming an astronaut and going to space was not a journey of one man but a journey of a *familia*, a journey of teachers, a journey of professionals who helped me along the way to achieve a dream. A lot of people always ask, "Okay. How did you become an astronaut? What was the process and how did it happen? *¿Cómo pasó, mexicano del barrio?* You grew up in Stockton, California. I mean, how did you go from there to become an astronaut?"

As most of you know, I come from a typical migrant farm-working family from La Piedad, Michoacán. People ask, "So, what's a typical migrant farm-working family like?" Well, let me just paint the scenery for you. A lot of you are going to be able to resonate with my story because a lot of you have very similar experiences.

What we did was every year around February we would be in La Piedad, Michoacán, and my father would load up the kids, the four of us, in the car with my mom and we would make a two-day trek up to Southern California. We would start off in Ontario and we'd start working, picking strawberries. From there, we would work our way up to the Central Valley, up to Salinas, working *la lechuga y el betabel con el azadón*, hoeing lettuce and sugar beets. Then we would spend the bulk of our time up in Northern California, in Stockton, Modesto and Lodi, where we would pick cucumbers, cherries and peaches. Then we would end the journey with the grapes during the grape season. This would take us to about November.

In November, my parents would say, "Okay. We're going to go back to Mexico. It's *tiempo de las fiestas navideñas*, Christmas season, so it's not worth it to put you guys in school in Mexico. We want you to get three or four months' worth of homework from the teachers and you take it to La Piedad with you." Then we would study by ourselves there. Come February or March, that whole process would repeat itself.

You can see how difficult our education process was in the early days. This happened all the way until I was about twelve years old. We would go to three or four different school districts throughout the school year, and we would miss three or four months of school. So what happened to me was that it was tough for me to learn the English language because we were a Spanish-speaking family. Even though I was born in the States, I was speaking Spanish *en la casa, y eso sí en la escuela: español derecho.* It wasn't formal Spanish. I think what made us different from a typical migrant farm-working family was the fact that my parents, in spite of their third-grade education, gave a lot of importance to education. What made them different was that Monday through Friday they always saw to it that we went to school. Wherever we went, three or four different school districts, we enrolled in school. But we were working in the field Saturday and Sunday. While every kid loves summer vacation, you can imagine how we dreaded it, because that meant we were going to be out there seven days a week as opposed to two days a week.

My dad was a master at getting us motivated. Every day after working in the fields, we would get in the car with our crusted Levi's—because in the morning the ground is soggy and wet and you get mud on your Levi's; by the end of the day, it dries and it's caked and baked so it's stiff. You get in the car and you're all dusty and sweaty. Every day before my dad started the car, he would look at us in the back seat and say, "*¿Cómo se sienten?*" We said we were tired. And he'd say, "Remember this feeling . . . because if you don't go to school, *es lo que van a hacer toda su vida.* This is your future if you don't go to school." It was a very powerful message that stuck to us.

I think if my mom had gone to college, she would have been a great psychologist because mothers have the ability to put the burden on you, to challenge you. She'd say, "Ay, *m'ijo, ustedes van a tener una mucho mejor vida que nosotros y ojalá nos puedan ayudar cuando estén grandes"*—You are going to have a better life than us and I hope you will help us when you're older. There they are. Putting the guilt trip on you, right? But the important thing was that she would always talk about college. Whenever we'd go to a nice clean office, she would see *el señor con corbata* and she'd say, *"Mira, así quiero verlos a ustedes, trabajando en una oficina, no en el campo como nosotros"*—That's how I want to see you, working in an office and not in the fields like us. She would sit us at the bench and always talk of when we went to college, when we went to the university. She would never say, "If you go." She expected us to go, and that set the bit right away. Those were the very powerful messages they gave us.

The other thing that they did, which I think was very different from typical migrant farm-working families, was they sat down with us every day at home while we did the homework in the kitchen. She would give us something to eat and say, *"No se levanten hasta que terminen la tarea"*—Don't get up until you finish your homework. And for first, second and third grade, that worked fine because they could help us with homework. But for the fifth, sixth, seventh grades, *ya ni papás que la entendieran.* They were still smart enough to realize if we finished the homework. I guess my point here is that as parents, because I'm a parent of five kids, we need to spend time with our kids during the homework process. It's not just a matter of telling the kids, *"Oye, m'ijo,* finish your homework and let me watch my *novela."* It doesn't suffice for the fathers to go out *con los amigos y tomar unas cervazas.* The whole thing is you've got to engage, you've got to be a family, and you've got to be together.

A lot of times, we put the burden on the public-school system, but you know what, it starts with the family. If the family has started the process, then we can then point to the school system: "Okay, why isn't my kid doing this?" Once you answer the question that you're doing everything at home to make sure your son or daughter succeeds, then I think we can hold the public-school system accountable. But it starts at home.

The other thing that happened during my education, as we would go up and down California, what I call the "California circuit," was a visit by my second-grade teacher. It was amazing. It was November and it was time to go back to Mexico. I went to my second-grade teacher—a very young, beautiful and tall *chinita*, fresh off of college—and I told her, "We're going to go to Mexico. Can I have three or four months' worth of homework?" She had been through that with my other three siblings, as I was the youngest. I saw her roll her eyes and say, "You know what, José? Tell your parents I'm going to be in your home tonight. I'm going to go visit your house." I said, "Okay." Of course, I went running home that day to tell my parents, trying to give them as much notice as possible. We lived about a mile, a mile and a half, from the school. Back then you could walk to school for a mile and a half. Now, we'll get arrested if we have our child walk a mile to school, right? But back then we would go through tracks and everything as we ran home from the school.

When I got home, I got two different reactions from my parents. The first thing my dad said was "*¿Qué hiciste, muchacho? What did you do?* What kind of trouble did you get into now?" I said, "No. She's coming because I told her we were moving to Mexico." The other reaction was completely opposite. My mother said, "*Va a venir la maestra, vamos a limpiar la casa y a hacer tortillas de harina. Para darle de comer a la maestra*"—We have to clean the house and make tortillas to give the teacher something to eat. You know how mothers are, especially Mexican mothers. They want to be as hospitable as possible and they prepare dinner and everything for the guest.

So, the teacher came and spoke to my parents in her broken Spanish, and my parents answered in their broken English, but they got the message together in a language that my parents could understand. I remember her saying, "*Han de plantar raíces en un lugar*, set roots in one place, *porque tienen hijos que son muy inteligentes y les gusta la escuela. Dénles una chanza para estudiar*—give them a chance so they can study." To my parents' credit, they took that advice and started making Stockton our home. *Eso sí*, for a migrant farm worker to stay in one place, that's tough because farm work is not available year-round in one particular place. I remember *mi pobre papá* used to go out in the fog in the middle of winter when it was cold and freezing and he would go and work pruning cherry trees, peach trees and all that, just to make ends meet. It wasn't an easy life after that, but it was a sacrifice that he made and one we realized that he was making.

Unfortunately, I have to confess that I'm old enough to remember the tail end of the Apollo program. I was about seven or eight years old when the Apollo program was going on. Everybody during that time saw the astronauts on TV as they walked on the moon. We were no different. Our only difference is we had the old TV with integrated speakers, with four legs, you know, *blanca y negra*, and a very fuzzy snowy picture. Sometimes you got that horizontal bar that you would have to go slap the TV so that it stopped.

Satellite didn't exist at that time, and we couldn't afford cable, so we had rabbit ear antennas. Whenever something happened that was very important—first of all, we didn't have a remote, so guess who the remote was: the youngest in the family, yours truly—*cambiar el canal y subirle el volumen y todo eso*. I would do it all. And then, of course, when something important happened, my dad would ask, "*Muchacho, ajusta la antena para verlo mejor*"—to get better reception. Then, what happened when you grabbed the antenna? You got a good ground, right? I'm an electrical engineer. I know that you get a good ground. And so, what did my dad tell me? "Get up there, get up there. *Ahí, quédate*. Now stay there." So, I'd try to look at the image as I was adjusting the TV to make sure I'd get a glimpse of the astronauts as well. Now I kid with my siblings, I say, "*¿Ya ven?* It was through osmosis that the signals went through my brain, and that's how I became an astronaut. The astronauts came through me." That's why I became an astronaut.

But that's really and truly when the dream was born. I was about eight years old when I first saw the astronauts walking on the moon. The images I saw . . . you heard them talking and you heard that beep, one-sixth of gravity, so they were kind of like floating, in slow motion, and then I would run outside and see the full moon. I'd run inside and see the astronauts walking on the moon. I'd do the same thing again and again. I'm sure every eight and nine year old at that time was fascinated and wanted to be an astronaut as well. What happened with me was I got hooked on that and said, "You know, I'm going to be an astronaut." I shared that dream with my parents, and to their credit, they allowed me to dream.

That's the other thing that we don't do. We don't allow our kids to dream. Sometimes we put our own barriers in front of them and don't allow our kids to dream. My parents were very supportive and said, "You see, *hijo*, just study hard *y lo puedes lograr*." I'm sure in the back of their minds though: "*Pobrecito*. He doesn't stand a chance, but let's not bust his bubble." I was naïve enough to think that I could get selected. It was not an impossible dream, and I kept working towards that. I kept saying that's what I'm going to do.

Here's another thing: the power of mentors, even if you don't know the mentors and they are just role models. I was a senior in high school getting ready to graduate. I knew I was going to the University of the Pacific to major in engineering because English was not my strongest suit; it was math. Because of the inability to learn English in the early years, I migrated to math, and two plus two is four in any language. So, I knew I was going to major in engineering.

Then I heard some astounding news: Dr. Franklin Chang Díaz got selected as an astronaut. The name Chang *no me pareció. Chang, ¿qué onda?* But then I heard "Díaz." I said, "Wow. That sounds like Hernández: Díaz. I wonder if he's Latino." I started looking at his bio and noticed that he was the first Latino-American astronaut to get selected by NASA. He had a PhD and came from humble beginnings, just like me. But he came from Costa Rica. Then I was jealous. *Pero, envidia de la buena,* a good type of jealousy.

I said, "*Si este vato pudo, ¿por qué yo no?*" If he was able to do it, why can't I? I mean, he seemed like a homie, like me. That's when I promised myself that I was going to do everything in my power to get selected as an astronaut. If that meant going to graduate school and getting advanced degrees, that's what I was going to do. Of course, that's where I had the blessing of meeting my good friend, Tony Cárdenas.

I went ahead and finished graduate school and started working at Lawrence Livermore National Laboratory. I worked on three major projects there. I worked in the *Star Wars* project, the development of the X-ray laser, which meant electronic equipment being deployed up in space. That allowed me to learn orbital mechanics.

Second was working on a mammography project, developing the first full-field digital mammography project for the early detection of breast cancer. This opened up a whole new field of study in developing cancer detection algorithms for images in digital and imaging processing. We worked with a company in Denver, Colorado, Fischer Imaging, and helped them develop the first full-field digital mammography system.

The third was full circle. I worked with the Russians. I spent two years in Washington at the Department of Energy working on nuclear non-proliferation, where we basically helped the Russians dispose of nuclear material. In that process, I was able to learn a little bit of Russian.

The reason why I did that was that during this whole time, I was applying to NASA for the astronaut program. Every year I would ask myself, "José, what have you done differently to make yourself more attractive, more marketable to NASA to become an astronaut?" If I couldn't answer that question, I'd say, "You're slacking, dude. You've got to do something different. You've got to improve yourself." That's why it wasn't an accident that I started working on the *Star Wars* project, because that was space-related, medical. The more you know about your body and medicine, the better NASA likes it, because there's a lot of self-care, self-management, self-medication up in space when you don't have a doctor.

Then, I worked on the nuclear non-proliferation project because it was during that time that the United States and Russia had signed an agreement to develop an international space station. I put two and two together right away. When this project came up to work with the Russians and learn the Russian language and culture, I jumped on it because I said, "That's what's going to make me more attractive to NASA." I applied for six straight years, and I would always get a formal letter saying, "Hey, don't call us. We'll call you." It wasn't until the sixth year that I got interviewed.

The way the process works is that more than 4,000 people applied to the NASA program for astronauts. Out of those 4000, they selected 300. They checked their references. Out of those 300, they selected 100 lucky ones to get interviewed for one whole week at NASA. These 100 people took a battery of psychological and physical exams where you get poked and prodded everywhere—those males over 40 know what I'm talking about. Then a committee interviews you. Finally, everybody goes home and waits to hear the results. I sort of got cocky because I was in the final 40. Of course, then I got the news that I didn't get selected.

The next two years went by for the next selection, and I got interviewed again. Year eight, and the same thing happened: I made the 40 finalists, and *ni mangos*, I didn't get anything. I was finishing up my two-year rotation here, getting ready to go back to California to Lawrence Livermore Lab, when I got the news that I didn't get selected in year eight. But I did get the invitation to go work for NASA as a civil servant. But it came with some caveats. They said, "Well, you need to come back. You need to come work for us as an engineer. There are no guarantees that we'll even interview you again. We just want to have a better look at you; so, we're making it clear that we're not even going to guarantee that we're going to interview you. By the way, you've got to take a pay cut and you've got to move to Houston."

Well, you can imagine how well that went over with my wife. It was like, "Hey, honey, we're not going to have nice weather California. We're going to hot and muggy Houston. By the way, you can't spend more money. You've got to tighten the belt." In all honesty, though, she was actually the one that encouraged me, because I always looked out for the family first. I had thirteen years at Lawrence Livermore Lab, and a nice career going with a nice trajectory, which is why they brought me to the Department of Energy, so I could go back and manage a program. I had to give all that up.

My wife told me something that I would never forget: "*Siempre vas a tener el gusanito.*" You're always going to have that little worm inside you that's always going to be asking you, gnawing at you, saying, "What if? What if you didn't take that job? What would have happened?" It was obvious that if I didn't take that job, they weren't going to consider me in the future. That sort of stuck with me. She said, "Don't disqualify yourself. Let them disqualify you. Don't make that decision of not going. Let's go. We'll make ends meet. We're going to be all right in Houston. If you don't like it, then we'll go back to California."

I took that risk in year eight. In the year 2000, we moved the family to Houston with the understanding that there was going to be a selection in 2002. Well, they cancelled that selection and there wasn't another selection until 2004. What started as a two-year experiment was a four-year experiment. I put in four good years there and ended up being the branch chief of the Materials and Processes branch. We actually had the Columbia shuttle accident; because we do non-destructive testing, we do forensics, my group was instrumental in the reconstruction of the accident and finding the root cause. It sort of gave me visibility at the management level and, when the new selections came up in

2004, I was actually selected. It was twelve years after I started applying and three interviews before I finally got selected as a NASA astronaut, in 2004.

Obviously, when you first get selected as an astronaut, you're not eligible for flight assignment because you're just coming off the street. You are an "astronaut candidate" and have to train for two years. It wasn't until 2006 that we graduated and became what we call a card-carrying astronaut eligible for flight assignment.

In 2008 I got my first assignment, which was STS-128 to fly onboard the Discovery; the date for the flight was last year. We trained for about fourteen months as a crew of seven and we actually executed the 128th mission of the space shuttles; ours was Discovery, which was the 32nd mission, and flew from August 28 to September 11. During those fourteen days, we were up in space and went around the Earth 217 times at approximately 17,500 miles an hour, and travelled a total of 5.7 million miles. There are two things I always say about that: 1) I wish there was a Frequent Flyer program for that and 2) for the ladies, I have a lot of mileage, but don't worry about that.

The experience of going up in space is . . . you just cannot put it into words. It's just one of the most awesome feelings in the world. Let me just lay the groundwork for the launch. You dress up in your orange pumpkin pressurized suit, you get strapped into the seat and then there's about three hours of nice, quiet time that you can even take catnaps before the launch counts down to zero. You're down there and you have time to make peace with your Maker, if you will, and start reflecting. One of the best feelings I had while I was sitting there was looking at my partners and thinking, "When I was my son's age, fifteen, I was out picking cucumbers during the summers. Now, I'm here representing the United States as an astronaut. How cool is that?" It truly is a great country, where you can make your dreams a reality.

As the count progresses to zero, you go from dead silence to everything rattling and rolling—a lot of noise. I'm the flight engineer sitting right behind the two pilots. I have the best seat in the house, but I'm also the busiest during those eight-and-a-half minutes of the most dynamic phase of flight, taking off and thrusting into space. I feel the thrust and *me persigno*, I cross myself. I'm a religious man, and for that millisecond that I feel scared, yes, I do for that millisecond. I say to myself, "What did I get myself into?" But then after that, we're off the ground and see the launch pad to the side and the tower, and our training takes over. It's amazing. I start hawking all the instruments and making sure I'm making the milestones, turning those eight-and-a-half minutes into dynamic flight. I call it the best Disneyland ticket ride ever. We reach space in those eight-and-a-half minutes, and, all of a sudden, we're floating, things are just floating; everything quiets down, and now we're going 17,500 miles an hour around the Earth, which is truly amazing, truly amazing.

We joined with the International Space Station. It took us one day to get close to it and dock. We performed three main objectives: we traded one of our crewmembers, Nicole Stott, a woman engineer, for Tom Kopra, who had been up there for four months. We conducted three space walks. We also transferred seven tons of material and equipment, including exercise equipment for the crew that was going to stay in the International Space Station.

During that dock time, there were seven of us from the shuttle and six from the station; a total of thirteen astronauts up there in a space equal to a five-bedroom home. Thirteen of us representing five different countries. I say six countries, if I include Mexico—I always include a plug for Mexico. We conducted our mission for those fourteen days, undocked, came home and had a flawless landing. We ended up landing at Edwards Air Force Base. Our preference was to land in Florida at the Kennedy Space Center, but the weather didn't allow it, so we went over there. Three hours later, I took the whole crew to a restaurant called Domingo's *para comida mexicana con una cerveza*. They had Mexican food and a beer. Life was good.

A lot of people ask me, "Well, what are you going to do now, José? How can you top that?" Well, I'm going to be moving down here to Houston for a six-month to one-year assignment at NASA headquarters to work out of the Office of Legislative Affairs. I'll be working with our lawmakers to spread the good word about what NASA does with respect to our mission and objectives.

As you know, President Obama changed the mission objectives of NASA just recently. We're actually pretty excited about it. A lot of people think that the budget got cut. On the contrary, I think the budget got increased. The International Space Station, which was slated to close in 2015, got extended to 2020. We're going to be conducting much more scientific research. What did get changed was the constellation program, an Apollo-like architecture with a capsule that was going to take us to the International Space Station and, from there, to the moon. We were going to set up a long-duration base outpost and learn how to live on the moon for long durations in hopes of developing the technology that would eventually allow us to go to Mars. That got scrapped. Instead, what the President is doing is spreading the resources for that program among private companies, so that we can stimulate the technology to get commercialized. These companies can develop their own vehicles, and we would have access to those vehicles. The hope is that things will move a lot faster and be cheaper to develop. So, we're pretty excited about that.

Finally, I'd like to say, I take my role as a mentor very seriously. I'd like to be the mentor that Franklin Chang Díaz was for me. To close the story with Franklin Chang Díaz: when I got interviewed the third time in 2004, he was on the committee and I was able to meet him for the first time. During the interview, I told him the story of how he inspired me. I certainly do take my role as a mentor very seriously, talking to kids and encouraging them to stay in school. I have a foundation called José Hernández Reaching for the Stars. What we try to do with that foundation is very simple. We're trying to increase the number of kids going into science, technology, engineering and mathematics (STEM). It behooves us to increase those numbers because if we're going to be number one and stay at the number one position, from a technical perspective, we need to increase the kids going into science and engineering, especially Hispanics and other minorities. If we're going to continue to be competitive in this world, we have to engage all segments of society in getting a good education. That includes our Latino kids. We have to engage them. Specifically, we have to engage them in the STEM areas. We need to get them involved in science, because that's what makes our country great. That's what is able to make us go to the moon and come back; that's what will enable us to go to Mars. We have to keep motivating our kids to move forward and get a good education.

There is basically a simple recipe for success. First of all, you have to have a strong foundation, which starts at home. You have to have a dream. You have to encourage your kids to dream and then convert that dream into a plan. And then, provide a good education for them. Add perseverance, *ganas y corazón*. You put all those ingredients together and "the sky is not the limit, *son las estrellas.*"

Maria Hinojosa
Producer, Author & Journalist

November 6, 2007

Maria Hinojosa is an award-winning news anchor and reporter who covers America's untold stories and highlights today's critical issues. In 2010, Hinojosa created the Futuro Media Group, an independent, nonprofit organization producing multimedia journalism that explores and gives a critical voice to the diversity of the American experience. As the anchor and executive producer of the Peabody Award-winning show Latino USA, which is distributed by NPR, and anchor and executive producer of the PBS show America by the Numbers with Maria Hinojosa, both produced by Futuro Media, she has informed millions about the changing cultural and political landscape in the United States and abroad.

Hinojosa's twenty-eight-year history as an award-winning journalist includes reporting for PBS, CBS, WNBC, CNN, NPR and CBS Radio and anchoring the Emmy Award-winning talk show Maria Hinojosa: One-on-One. She is the author of two books and has won dozens of awards, including four Emmys, the John Chancellor Award, the Studs Terkel Community Media Award, the Robert F. Kennedy Award and the Edward R. Murrow Award.

Hinojosa's life story, as well as her parents' experience coming to America, have served to inspire her mission as a journalist—"you must own the power of your own voice."

As a journalist, we have a responsibility. That's why I'm going to share some stories of what I've seen on the frontline. The first story I'm going to tell is about crossing the border for the very first time. My dad is a medical doctor, a research doctor in oto-laryngology. He was in Mexico. I was the kind of surprise fourth kid. My dad had been promised a job at a hospital that was being built by the Mexican government. It was going to be a research hospital. But there was a change of government and the hospital never got built. My father essentially was a man who needed a job. The University of Chicago knew about my father and, so, asked him to please come and work at the University of Chicago. My dad left six months later.

Then, my mom got on an airplane from Mexico City to Dallas, because there were no direct flights at that time. Just the thought of my mother getting on an airplane with four kids under the age of seven and not speaking perfect English . . . I was about a year and a half old in the early 1960s and had some kind of a rash on my body. When we got to the immigration point at Dallas airport, a very large immigration official said to my mother, "Well, you know what? Everybody else can go, but this little baby's got to go into quarantine." My mother was like, "I don't understand. Say that again?" He said, "You all are fine, but the little baby has got to go into quarantine." My mother, who's five-feet flat, somehow at that moment found the strength to own her voice as a mother and new immigrant to this country, and said to him, "Well, that's not going to happen. My daughter is not staying here. She's coming with me, and we're all taking our flight to Chicago together." The official pushed back and said, "No, no, no. You don't understand. It's a quarantine." My mother said, "You don't understand who my husband is. My husband is Dr. Raúl Hinojosa at the University of Chicago, and we're going to have to call the president of the University of Chicago, blah, blah, and blah." Somehow, I was let in.

I love that story. It teaches me one of the essences of my work and what I try to tell young people, which is to own your own voice and learn to own the power of your own voice.

I also attribute my understanding of what American democracy is, again, to my mother. It wasn't like my mom was reading all the books about what a democracy looks like, but it was Chicago on the South Side in the 1960s. I was being raised there as a Mexican immigrant. There was an organic understanding that the Civil Rights Movement existed and was involving predominantly our African-American neighbors. My mother understood profoundly that this was part of who she was as a new American.

So, when I was in third grade, my mom wrote a letter to my teacher and for all of my brothers and sisters saying, "My kids will not be in school today because we are going to see Martin Luther King speak." There were other mothers in the classroom in the school that had done the same thing, but it was somewhat controversial. When I remember that moment of being in a rally on the street in Chicago, seeing Martin Luther King, Jr., what it spoke to me about was what democracy looks like, the essence of what democracy looks like. Something that my mother and father growing up in Mexico didn't see where you never voted because there was no democratic participation. My mother understood that this was what the essence of being a citizen was. Even though, at that time, the only person who was a citizen was my father.

I moved to New York to become an actress and a dancer. But something happened when I went to my very first professional audition. I was eighteen or nineteen years old. There was not a lot of Latino theater going on. I did this audition for a movie and I did a great audition, but the director kind of looked at me and said, "Great audition. But you know, I don't know. You're not tall enough. You're not short enough. You're not white enough. You're not dark enough. You're not street enough. You're not sophisticated enough. You're not Latina enough. You're not

American enough. It's like, I just don't get you." Something in me kind of died at that moment. I gave him the power to take away the dream of me actually becoming an actress. Although Broadway is still there . . . It could happen. You never know.

I moved to New York in 1979 from Chicago, which was a relatively Mexican city. We were going to El Barrio Mexicano every weekend. I was crossing borders my whole life, whether it was from Hyde Park, the community where I was being raised to El Barrio Mexicano to leaving Chicago and going to Mexico every year by car from Chicago, all six of us in a station wagon. It's true. Because I had been crossing from the north to the south, I knew immediately that things in this country were going to change profoundly when I saw Mexicanos in the American South. It was a huge, huge moment for this country, and a big change in something that, of course, has set off many, many repercussions.

When I got to New York, there were not many Mexicanos in 1979. There were like three, and I was one of them. I had to pack up my tortillas in boxes from Chicago and freeze them for six months. I would bring my salsa and freeze it and also stock it on the shelf. Something else happened that I'm sure may sound controversial, but for me was very liberating. I grew up having a lot of issues around identity and I absolutely went through a self-hatred moment, just never fitting in, never feeling quite American enough or quite Latina enough. By the time I got to New York, I had reached a point of really loving who I was as a young Mexican immigrant growing up in Chicago. In New York, I said to myself, "there are no Mexicans here, so what am I going to do?" It was a learning moment, because what it taught me was the ability to also let go of our nationalism. While nationalism can be something profoundly empowering, it can also separate us.

In New York, I became a Pan-Latin-Americanist. I understood that I was no longer just from Mexico; I was part of a continent. I became friends with people from Puerto Rico, Colombia, Argentina, Cuba and Chile. It was an incredibly liberating experience to not be tied to just one country, but to understand that I was part of a universe. While living in a city like New York, I believe, I did become a citizen of the world.

I never really thought that I could be a journalist. Although I went to Barnard College and studied Latin-American Studies, Political Economy and Women Studies, there was no one out there like me, except for Geraldo Rivera, who was doing really good work back then. There was certainly no one like me in public television or radio.

I first got involved in radio at WKZR, the Colombia University radio station. Then, at the urging of someone from Barnard, I applied for an internship at NPR. But, I still doubted that I could do it. Anyway, I got hired for the internship at NPR. I was the first Latina at the NPR headquarters in Washington, D.C. While I loved producing for Scott Simon, I understood immediately that I wanted to be on the air. I wanted to tell my own stories. I embarked on a project to make this happen. I moved to San Diego and then moved to Tijuana, but actually worked at KPBS in San Diego; I was crossing the border every single day. I eventually made my way back to New York and got hired by NPR.

In my first couple of years as a reporter, I was spending a lot of time in the Bronx. Everywhere I've been, they've always named me the Bronx bureau chief because I care deeply about the Bronx, because it's been so maligned. I was doing stories with young people, crime and violence. I had done a story about some very bad heroin. It was called, "Good Fellows and Tango and Cash." It was very potent heroin. People were dying. People were dying in all areas around New York City, not just the Bronx. People were dying in Westchester, in the suburbs in Long Island, New Jersey, Connecticut. Reporting the story, I understood that the South Bronx had been chosen as a market point for the sale of drugs because you can get in and out easily.

Anyway, the point of this is that I did these stories about the South Bronx and I ended up at NPR in Washington visiting a few days later. An NPR personality, who shall remain nameless, came up to me and said, "Oh my God, María, those stories that you did about the South Bronx, they were so moving. But I have to ask you a question. Weren't you terrified to be in those neighborhoods?" I said, "No. I've lived in those neighborhoods in the past." The interesting situation was that she probably never would have thought to ask me if I was terrified the first day that I set foot into National Public Radio headquarters in Washington, where I was actually terrified about.

I tell this story because I always like to remember that we don't all see the world through the same perspective. It doesn't mean that one perspective is right and the other one is wrong, but that is the essence of what America is. It's a diversity of perspectives and experiences. That's why we in the media have such a huge task in making our newsrooms diverse, because we represent everyone in this country.

I use teaching moments with my children every single day that I can. That's the way to incorporate lessons into one's life. One of the teaching moments stems from the fact that I became a pan-Latin-Americanist and married a man from the Dominican Republic. I hope people respect this, but one thing I do is talk about some of our internal issues: racism, sexism, homophobia, anti-Semitism. I believe that we as Latinos must be self-critical on these issues.

When Germán was my fiancée, I took him to a wedding in Mexico. Germán is a mulatto with a ponytail and an earring. He's an artist, vegetarian, etc., etc. My family made comments like, "They don't even speak Spanish there." Even within my own family there was prejudice. Once I told my family that Germán had grown up with Juan Luis Guerra and designed Guerra's latest album cover. Then it was, "Juan Luis? We love you, Germán." It's funny that I should be telling this story, because Juan Luis is getting a Grammy award tonight. Germán, in fact, was really an old friend of Juan Luis'.

Germán and I are raising two children in Harlem. My relationship with the African-American community is one that I feel very, very strongly about. I believe it is a responsibility of all of us here to step up to the plate, because apart from the issue of immigration, which of course is huge, the issue of African-American-Latino relations, I believe, is central to what's going to happen in the future in this country.

Regarding my moments of self-hatred, I was María de Lourdes Hinojosa-Ojeda, but who I really wanted to be when I was growing up was Randy Kalish, Susie Golfer or Lisa Tim. But no, I was María de Lourdes Hinojosa-Ojeda. I hated my name. Now of course, I love it, even though I get hate mail. People write to say, "Why do you say your name like that? Can't you Americanize it?" This example is probably one of the high points of hate mail that I receive. It's part of the times that we're living in.

What do we do with our kids? Well, you take a tradition that maybe you disliked, maybe you had a problem with, maybe you wanted to be far from, and as you get older, you change your mind: "You know, I love this." My son is Raúl Ariel Jesús de Todos los Santos Pérez-Hinojosa. My daughter is María Yurema Guadalupe de los Indios Pérez-Hinojosa. You're going to be tested on that before you leave. But, with my kids, it's real life. So that, when the *paisano* knocks on the door to deliver the Chinese food, there is recognition: "*¿Qué pasó, paisano? ¿De dónde eres?* Where are you from, *paisano?* Come in." Usually the *paisano* is like, "Wow, somebody is recognizing me. Somebody is talking to me." Yeah. I do that.

When I see a woman who stands on 72nd and Columbus with beautiful earrings that I know are from Oaxaca, and I'm with my kids, I start talking to her. I say, "*Señora,* . . . Oh really? And how many languages do you speak?" "Oh, I speak Spanish, Zapotec, Mixtec. . . . " I would say to my kids, "Look at this. Here is somebody who is speaking languages that are hundreds upon hundreds of years old, existed before English existed. She's standing right here." I say to my kids, "Your responsibility to remain bilingual is because you do have a responsibility to help those who are quadrilingual in other languages, but who do not speak English. Learning Spanish is something you should feel proud of, but you also know that it's something that you can use to help those less fortunate than you."

Finally, let me talk about my feelings of where we stand in America today. When I was writing my speech, I said to myself, "I just could not spend all this time talking about myself." I believe so strongly that the moment we are living in right now in history is crucial. I have felt an urgency to tell stories in the past, but there is an urgency that I feel now that is like a fire that is moving me forward.

Something happened to me a year and a half ago, when I was in Indiana covering a story about how immigration was playing out in the mid-term elections. Now, you're thinking *immigration, big story, and mid-term elections. She must have gone to some place in the Southwest, maybe some place in the South. Indiana, hotbed of immigration. Indiana?* No, I *know it's not.* There's a 4 percent Latino population in the State of Indiana, but immigration was *the* issue that Republicans and Democrats were running on—Democrats, even more stridently than Republicans.

We had been warned that an area of Indianapolis called Little Mexico was dangerous. However, we discovered in our investigation that the crime rate was non-existent. We did an interview with a woman there, a *madrina* who kind of helped new immigrants, who came undocumented 35 years ago to Chicago. She and her sister both became citizens. Her sister is Republican and she's a Democrat. Fascinating. As we were leaving, she ran out to show me something she had forgotten to tell me about: it was a piece of paper that all the storeowners in Little Mexico had found plastered to their windows. It was a leaflet written by hand with magic marker that said, "Wanted: Armed American Citizens to hunt down illegal aliens that the government won't catch." In Indianapolis. That's horrific. The fact that we report about news of racial violence, which is horrific, but we don't seem to take these threats seriously is a problem. I do believe that what is operating right now is a culture of fear. It is the fear of the Other.

In fact, if Samuel Huntington of Harvard had his way, I am the most feared person here because I maintained contact with my Mexican roots, because I'm Mexican first. Samuel Huntington is an attack against Mexicanos. I'm Mexican. I stayed in contact with my roots. I'm bilingual. I travel back and forth. I remain culturally aware of my own experience. All of these, according to Samuel Huntington, are going to destroy America. Destroy it.

I was at CNN and interviewed Samuel Huntington. I asked, "Professor Huntington, do you have a lot of Latino immigrant friends? Do you hang out with a lot of them? Do you speak with them?" He had just written a whole book about Latino immigrants, so I wanted to know how he got his information. He said, "Well, not really. I don't hang out with a lot of Latinos." So, I said, "In all of my years covering immigration, not once has an immigrant said to me, 'Learn English? Who wants to learn English? I hate English. I want everybody to speak Spanish.'" I have heard people say, "I want to learn English but . . . " Okay, if you've seen how hard it is to learn a new language when you're working six days a week, twelve hours a day, and then Sunday is the only day that you have to recuperate, it's hard. I said to him, "You know, I have also never heard any immigrants say, 'Oh yeah, I crossed that border to reconquer my land, you know, the *Reconquista*.'" Because I've been on the border. I've interviewed hundreds of immigrants, and not one has ever told me, "Oh yeah, I'm here for the *Reconquista*."

I do not understand how we can have a country where the Other is so feared.

When I think about what's happening now, this is not just an anti-illegal alien movement; this is an anti-immigrant movement and it is an anti-Latino movement that we must confront head on. Because, at the same time that the media makes decisions to go for the divisive, ironically it gives us other options. Do you know who the children's character with the largest audience in the history of television is? Dora the Explorer. Ten billion dollars. Probably that was yesterday, so today it's probably $11 billion on

Dora the Explorer, a bilingual Latina character. ¡Qué miedo! Right? A lot to be afraid of from *Dora the Explorer*. What is the hottest— I'm sorry, I love it—the hottest new television show out there? *Ugly Betty*. *Ugly Betty* opened the door, and they're walking through it. Fascinating.

I don't know how many of you saw the episode where they had the two Cubano actors talking. Of course, *ni un* Mexicano understood what they were saying because they were speaking Cuban Spanish, which I think is even cooler because they're really going for it. I swear. *Ugly Betty* is great with the kids. But the sex change operation—having that conversation with my daughter at nine, a little difficult. A little difficult.

I make fun, but I cannot ignore the fact that we are living in an America where people are fearful of a knock on the door without a warrant, where they can come and arrest you and deport you within twenty-four hours. You are leaving behind American-born children. This is not just anti-immigrant and anti-Latino; this is against basic civil rights and human rights, a situation that has been created at this moment. At the same time, when I was interviewing Paul Cuadros, a journalist who's living in Siler City in North Carolina, he said, "Everybody talks about the invasion." There were labor recruiters from the South going into Mexico to find cheap labor. It was not a massive surprise invasion. There was a coordination. You're exactly right, Paul. I was the first reporter to get inside the Smithfield Foods Corporation, the largest pork processing plant in the world, where many undocumented Latinos work and where they kill 30,000 hogs a day. That's one every eight seconds. They want those workers there, because they are cheap.

I cannot as a journalist sit with my hands folded and not be telling these stories. That is the urgency that I feel. I want to know what the presidential candidates, who espouse family values, have to say about separating families—separating children, American-born children from their parents. I plan on asking that. When I interviewed Hillary Clinton after she had done the

Spanish-language debate, I asked her, "As a lawyer, do you believe there is such a thing as an illegal human being? If you don't, then will you be prepared to not use that term in your campaign?" She kind of fuddled around the answer, but then of course it came up during the debate.

I'm going to leave you with two thoughts. I stopped using the term illegal immigrant or illegal alien, but not because I met some radical Latino professor. It was from somebody who looked entirely different from me and who had the most different experience from mine: Elie Wiesel, the Holocaust survivor and Nobel Peace Prize winner. He said, "There is no such thing as an illegal human being. They may have committed a crime but," he said, "once you label them illegal, that's exactly how the Holocaust started."

I'm going to leave you with this final story that I tell at almost every speech, because it is uplifting. After September 11th, which was the most difficult story for me to ever report and changed me as a mom and as a journalist, I knew immediately within hours that there were undocumented immigrants who had been victimized in the twin Towers. Within two days, I had the story about Julia Hernández, whose husband Antonio Meléndez had died there. He worked at the Windows on the World restaurant. We did a story in the Bronx two days after 9/11, and everybody was crying; it's a very rare thing for a CNN crew to have the cameraman, the soundman, myself, my producer, the whole family, all of us crying. We put this story on the air and got a response. Julia was sent letters and cards, and it was very uplifting to know that, yes, the rest of the country identified with us as New Yorkers.

A couple of months later, in December of 2001, the phone rang in my office. On the other end of the line there was a man who said, "Hello. Is this María Hi-nojowsa?" I said, "Hinojosa. Yes." "Hi, Ms. Hi-nojowsa. My name is A. J. Dinkins and I'm a hairdresser originally from South Carolina, but I live now in Augusta, Maine. I live here. I'm a hairdresser and my partner,

Rudy, is a farmer. We have just raised several thousand dollars for the Julia Hernández family in our church. I want to come and deliver this money and these gifts to Ms. Hernández, but Ms. María," he said, "I have never been to New York and I have never been to the Bronx. Would you please meet me at the airport and take me to see Julia Hernández?" I said, "A. J. Dinkins, I'll be there, but I'm coming with a camera crew because I'm going to do this story."

We did this story of A. J., gay hairdresser that he is, with his hair dyed red for Christmas, and we go off to the Bronx. A. J. had never met any Mexicans, and Julia had never met a White gay man that she didn't work for. There we were in the Bronx, my beloved Bronx, and it was a love fest. I mean, who would have thought that these people, who had nothing in common, would find this love? And they did. It was just beautiful. As A. J. was leaving, he said, "Oh my gosh, I want to invite the whole Hernández family to come to my farm in Augusta." I said, "That's a wonderful thing, and we'll see if it happens."

Six months later, the phone rang, and it was A. J. "Hi María, can you bring your husband and kids up to Augusta, Maine, because I just invited Julia Hernández, the four kids plus a cousin, to come up and spend a week at my farm in Augusta." I said, "A. J., I'm not bringing my husband and my kids, but I'll be there with a camera because I'm going to tell your story."

Now, I have never been to Maine in the summer, but I know why the Bushes like it. It's beautiful. Stunning. Back in 2002, it was still pretty homogenous White. I think that's changed in the past few years. I don't know if you can imagine, here we were, this motley crew: Julia; four Mexican kids and the cousin; A. J., who had dyed his hair blonde; Rudy, the 6'4 farmer in his overalls; me; my cameraman, who is a hippy with a ponytail; and my African-American sound technician. Everybody was looking at us in Augusta, Maine. They're like, "Who are these people and why are they so happy?" Because all we were there to do was to help these Mexican-American kids, all four of them citizens, to forget about the fact that their father had been killed a year ago. When I get into my moments of sadness—it happens often— my husband says, "You know, there are people who want to tell these stories, but you will always tell these stories of sadness." It may be true, but it moves me because I do want to find the humanity in all of them.

I have this picture of me with A. J. and Julia Hernández, and a beautiful, pristine lake in Maine behind us. What this symbolizes to me is that there are people who are prepared to get outside of their comfort zones to extend a hand to the Other, the one who is so feared. They are people who are prepared to cross borders within their own country, within their own homeland, within their own communities. Julia crossing the border, to take her family to a gay couple's house for a week. A. J. prepared to open his house up to a family of strangers, essentially, and us to tell the story.

We do have a responsibility to not be silent anymore and work on these issues, to not be afraid to push back. This is a decisive moment in history. All of us here, not just those of us who are in the media, all of us, you are all leaders and you must, I believe, all engage in this dialogue.

Dolores Huerta
Civil Rights Activist
Dolores Huerta Foundation

November 18, 2008

Born on April 10, 1930, Dolores Huerta has spent her life being a fierce advocate for Latino farm workers, immigration and women's rights. A labor leader and civil rights activist who worked with César Chávez to found the National Farmworkers Association (which later became the United Farm Workers), Huerta worked tirelessly to improve the social and economic conditions of farm workers. In 1965, she, along with César Chávez, helped organize a nationwide boycott of abusive grape growers, which resulted in the California table grape industry signing a three-year collective bargaining agreement with the United Farm Workers in 1970.

Not only has Huerta helped thousands of workers and directly influenced policy to better the conditions of Latinos in America, but she also has continued to be a mentor and an inspiration to many of our leaders today, who are guided by the phrase Huerta coined, "¡Sí se puede!"

My dad was a volunteer for the mineworkers' union in New Mexico. His name was Juan Fernández. He was such an avid union man that shortly after he was elected to the state assembly of New Mexico, he got expelled because he punched out a fellow assembly member, José Montoya from New Mexico, because José Montoya had made a derogatory remark about mineworkers. My dad took it upon himself to take him out right then and there.

My dad was a really strong union person, but unfortunately my father did not raise me. My mother left my dad; she divorced him because my dad was too macho. My mother said, "I'm not going to take that." She took us to California where I was raised in a town called Stockton.

My mother was a businesswoman. She was an entrepreneur, a small businesswoman, a very, very smart person, way, way ahead of her time. She was very much a feminist and very involved in the community.

I was fortunate to have these kinds of role models in my mother and my dad in terms of my upbringing. In Stockton, I had the opportunity to join an organization, that was then starting, called the Community Service Organization—this is the organization that both César Chávez and I came out of. And when we think of the organizations in the Latino community . . . The first Latino organizations were the *honoríficas*, the mutual aid societies, where people got together and pooled their resources. For instance, if somebody died, they paid the funeral expenses. They would also celebrate the Quince de septiembre, the independence holiday, Cinco de Mayo, etcetera. We also had the veterans' groups some of the oldest ones, of course, are with us here today and those are the League of United Latin American Citizens and the American GI Forum. These were the *veteranos*. They came back from World War II and they're still here today working on behalf of our community.

The organization that became the first mass-based organization to really get thousands of Latinos involved was the Community Service Organization. The person who led that organization, I call him the Padrino of the Latino Movement, was a man named Fred Ross, Sr. He was such a great organizer that nobody knew who he was, right? That's how great he was. Someday, more of his history will be taught to all of us. He is the one who got César Chávez and me involved in organizing, as well as Cruz Reynoso, who became a California Supreme Court Justice; Herman Gallegos; and many, many others. What an organizer does is go into a community to find the leadership there and get it involved. That man, Fred Ross, was responsible for so much of what we did.

Some of the issues we fought in the CSO are really successes that still impact us today. We got rid of citizenship requirements, because before, unless you were a U.S. citizen, you could not get any kind of public assistance. That was one of the first issues we took on and won. We were able to get driver's licenses in the Spanish language. Before, you couldn't get a driver's license unless you spoke English. We got the ballots in Spanish. These are things that we still have today, and we kind of take them for granted. We've got disability insurance for farm workers. We've got the right to register people door to door, because before that, you couldn't do that. You had to go down to the county court-house and take an oath. All of these were really groundbreaking achievements that came out of the Community Service Organization. And then, of course, César and I left that organization to form the Farm Workers Union.

But interestingly, what goes around comes around, and sometimes back to the future. One of the big issues too that we fought then was to get rid of the Bracero Program. This was a foreign worker program called Public Law 78 that brought hundreds of thousands of people from Mexico into the United States, and they were very mistreated. I remember they would tell them "Aquí no hay 4 de julio, no hay 16 de septiembre." "You came here to work, and we expect you to work, and don't expect any holidays." And people were very, very mistreated. But right after we got that program stopped, our government, the United States of America, legalized more than 500,000 ex-braceros without any legislation. There was no law passed. It just kind of happened.

César and I got involved. We were arranging the documents for all these people to be able to come in to the United States, but then the government was saying, "well, they couldn't bring in their wives and their families." So, I flew to Washington, met with the Deputy Secretary of State, and we changed that regulation. Not only could the ex-braceros come in, but they could also bring their wives and children. That was a really fantastic thing. It happened back in 1964, and of course we used that to help us organize the Farm Workers Union.

Look what's happening today. In California, while the rest of us are fighting for legalization, they now have guest workers in California. They have over 1,000 foreign workers in Salinas; they have foreign workers in Sacramento; they have foreign workers in Calexico and foreign workers in Yuma, Arizona. This comes on top of the hundreds of thousands of deportations that they have had where they have split up families, these terrible anguished conditions that so many families have gone through, taking away the parents and leaving the children behind. We're doing community organizing with my Dolores Huerta Foundation. We had a young man who committed suicide because they deported his mother. These are such atrocities that our government is committing. It's almost like the message is, "Here, we want your work, okay? We want your contributions to our own economy. But we don't want you to be here. We don't want you to live here. We don't want you to be residents. We don't want you to be citizens."

Even though we have been celebrating our great achievements in this election, we can see that, institutionally, we still have a long way to go. Yes, on May the 1st of 2006, we had millions of people marching for legalization against the Sensenbrenner Bill. We had millions that were marching, yet we know that we couldn't get a bill passed in Congress. The deportations happened right on the heels of what was going on. Even though we showed that we care, that we participate in the democracy, we still have a long way to go. That's something that we really have to reflect on.

We know that Proposition 187 in California, which tried to take away citizenship from people whose parents were not citizen—that was part of 187, and it was in the Sensenbrenner Bill—that really helped California come together. We had this little revolution in California where we were able to get Antonio Villaraigosa elected to mayor of Los Angeles. We have almost 40 Latinos in our California state legislature. The Sensenbrenner Bill did the same thing for us nationally; it brought us Latinos together. It gave us this common cause that we have to work for to get another legalization bill. But in order to do that, we're going to have to do so much work. It's not just enough to come out there and march again like we did on May 1st of 2006, which by the way, we should think about because that march was the largest number of people on the street on one issue in the history of the United States of America. That is how momentous that was.

I've been getting a lot of questions as I travel around the country. People say, "Oh, wow. Now that we got Obama elected, we're going to get legalization." Wait a minute, okay? We know that Obama is going to do great and wonderful things, but he doesn't have that magic wand. We know that the only way that we're going to get legalization is if all of us work very, very hard. We've got to start focusing especially on those Congress people that we need to educate and all those senators that we need to educate so that we can at least get the bill on his desk. I don't even think we should ask Obama to do anything on legalization until we do the work we need to do in our communities.

We saw this phenomenon in this last election, where the young people left their homes in California and they went to Pennsylvania and they went to Colorado and they went to North Carolina. Well, we've got to do something like that. We've got to do something like that. We've got to get young people and us older folk to do the same thing and go out there to some of these Congressional places because we've got to educate the public. We've got to make them understand that what we're asking for the people who are here, the undocumented people that are here, it's not anything different from what has always been in our country. Because every single person that is in this country, their people came from somewhere; their people were legalized at some point. This has always been the policy of the United States of America. We're not asking for anything different from what has always been done.

In fact, if we go back to the 1920s, there were more immigrants in the United States at that point in time than there were citizens. There were many immigrants who had the right to vote. They had the right to vote in this country even though they were not U.S. citizens. Sometimes we forget that history.

Another thing that we have to educate the American public on is where this anti-immigrant hysteria is coming from. It's coming from the same white supremacist organizations that were supporting Jim Crow and segregation, the ones that kept African Americans from voting in the South. This is who these people are. If you look at the family tree of the FAIR Immigration Reform people, you'll see this is who these people are. They have been very successful because they've gone all around the country and promoted all of these laws to stop any kind of justice for immigrants.

We have got to do the same thing. We've got to go out there and educate the American public. Let them know that these undocumented people that are here what they are doing. They are taking care of our children, taking care of our elderly, our disabled, cooking our food, picking our food. The food that we just ate right now came from some hands of undocumented workers somewhere. They're cleaning our buildings and building our buildings. They are contributing to the economy with their taxes, their social security. They're never going to see that money that they've contributed. We've got to educate the public about who these people are so that they can understand that they are not criminals, that they are workers. We need to get that sympathy. We need to let them know who the opponents are.

As we continue doing our work on immigration, we've also got to look at the other issues that are going to be affecting our community. Some of those issues are the same for the rest of the American public: health issues, national health care and education. Instead of our money going to prisons, let's put some of that money into education. In the San Joaquín Valley of California, they have only built one university since 1965, the University of California, Merced. They have built seventeen prisons. These are our tax dollars!

We also need to talk about some of the issues that affect other people, such as the women's organizations. I'm a feminist. Although I have eleven children, I am very strongly for choice. I like to tell people when we think about who's attacking the immigrants, it's the same people who are attacking the feminists. It's the same people who are attacking our gay and lesbian communities.

I'm going to say to all of you out there who are leaders: this is an issue that we have to stand up on. We have got to take the lead on this issue. We have got to go out there and say we are for human rights. That includes the human rights of people that are homosexuals. We've got to stand up. We've got to be counted on for these issues.

To help us to be able to do that, share these words with the folks that you're arguing with. This is what I tell people: the right of a woman to choose how many children she wants to have, it's her right of privacy, her constitutional right. Who you want to live with, fall in love with and, yes, have the right to marry, it's your constitutional right and your right of privacy and nobody should interfere with that right. We can quote the great Mexican President Benito Juárez, who was the first indigenous president of the Americas: "El respeto al derecho ajeno es la paz." Respecting other people's rights is peace.

In California, they're blaming the African American community and they're blaming the Latino community because a lot of people didn't vote. We know that the priests and the ministers were out there saying to vote against this Marriage Equality Act. But don't blame us too much, because the problem is the campaign could have done a lot more. I was out in California, and they could've done a lot more. This struggle is not going to end soon; it's going to continue. We have to be there as Latino leaders in the forefront of this struggle, because it is a struggle for human rights. Can we go out there and do the work that needs to be done to really show our presence as we did in the last election, to bring justice to our country? We are the leaders. We need to take the risks, and we need to do the work. ¡Sí se puede!

Mel Martínez

U.S. Senator
U.S. Secretary of Housing &
Urban Development

March 5, 2008

In nominating Mel Martínez as the nation's twelfth Secretary of Housing and Urban Development, President George W. Bush referred to him as "the embodiment of the American dream." He was unanimously confirmed by the United States Senate and served as Secretary of HUD from 2001 to 2005. Under his leadership, HUD expanded homeownership opportunities to more Americans, particularly minority and low-income families, through innovative budget initiatives and partnerships with community-based housing providers. In 2004, Martínez was elected to the U.S. Senate as a Republican representing the state of Florida; he served from January 3, 2005, until his resignation on September 9, 2009. He also served as chairman of the Republican Party from November 2006 until October 2007, the first Latino to serve as chairman of a major party.

Born October 23, 1946, in Sagua La Grande, Cuba, Martínez fled to the United States in 1962 as part of a Catholic humanitarian effort called Operation Pedro Pan that eventually brought about 14,000 children to this country. Catholic charitable groups provided Martínez, who was alone and spoke virtually no English, a temporary home at two youth facilities. He subsequently lived with two foster families, with whom he remains close. He was reunited with his family in Orlando in 1966.

Martínez graduated from Florida State University College of Law in 1973 and practiced law for some 25 years in Orlando, Florida, where he was actively involved in community activities.

Martínez's story chronicles the plight of many Cuban immigrants to this country after The Cuban Revolution. Like many immigrant families, Martínez's family had to make many sacrifices in order to secure a better future for their children in the United States.

Many of us who actually immigrated to this country have particularly interesting stories. I know that there are others here today who share my background as a Peter Pan. I'll take you back to a little city on the northern coast of Cuba where I was born in 1946—I am at the cutting edge of the baby boomers, the same age as the president and the same age as Bill Clinton. That sort of dates me, a little bit of Woodstock with a Spanish accent maybe.

I grew up in a really wonderful little city. It was a place where my comfort level was at its all-time high. There, I attended a Jesuit school, Colegio del Sagrado Corazón de Jesús, a wonderful place where my father had gone to school. That tells you a little something about the continuity in my life and the secure sort of cozy feeling that I had living in this city of about 25,000 to 30,000 people.

My dad was a veterinarian. We were not particularly well-off, but we were fine, and he loved his profession. My mother was a wonderful lady of great faith and, also, as typical of the time, was just at home taking care of us. She did work on the side a little bit. She came from a family that was not particularly well-to-do. She had gone to work early in life and had not finished schooling, which in so many of our countries that's not that unusual. It happens.

In any event, this wonderful and secure environment began to erode as Cuba's political situation continued to unravel. One dictatorship was then followed by a great hope. But then that hope was dashed before too long by yet another and even more tyrannical dictatorship, which imposed on Cuba the suffocating lack of movement that communism brings about. One of the first things that happened in my life that really shook my foundation was that the school that my father had attended, and that I had attended, was summarily closed. Most of the priests were ushered out of the country. We, all of a sudden, began to see life change in so many and such dramatic ways as to really begin to wonder if we were in the same place. It's one of those things that you read and think would never happen here. Well, it was happening here in our lives. Religious freedoms were curtailed. The ability to dissent was frowned upon and particularly persecuted.

Because of revolutionary zeal, there were firing squads and people were shot. Summary trials and show trials—all of these things were happening with lightning speed while at the same time, the government was evermore present, especially through the committees for the defense of the revolution. They were the same things that have happened in communist countries when the freedom was snuffed and the rule of law disappeared. As a result, those of us who were people of faith and had been raised in an environment of Catholic education didn't feel comfortable in this world. My parents began to worry for me, worry for my safety. They had seen young people—I was only I guess fourteen at that time—not much older than I who were beginning to get in trouble. There was also the fear of conscription into the military service that would begin at age sixteen.

In the midst of all of this, the aborted Bay of Pigs Invasion occurred. My father and mother sat me down one day and closed the door to their bedroom, so as to not allow anyone to hear. They discussed with me the prospects of leaving in this effort that was very much underground and very secretive. That effort would later become known as Peter Pan. It was essentially parents sending their children alone in the care of the Catholic Church, and in cahoots with the U.S. State Department, that was providing the visas for this exodus. Peter Pan began as a little movement of helping people who were somehow implicated in efforts to try to undermine the regime, which was a lot of people at the time. It grew immediately from a couple of dozen families to what ended up being more than 14,000 of us unaccompanied minors who came to the United States between December 1960 and the Cuban Missile Crisis of October 1962. A wonderful man by the name of Monsignor Bryan Walsh in Miami undertook this ad hoc effort. He did a wonderful job, if not a perfect job, of attempting to provide for all of us.

After preparations, about six to eight months went by, and all of a sudden I was able to flee Cuba. I flew to Miami. I was picked up at the airport with another eleven children who were coming unaccompanied. I was taken to a camp in Miami where children ages fourteen to eighteen were being kept. This program went up to age eighteen. The younger ones were taken to another holding place. From this camp, it was the idea that you would be then sent out into foster homes and other similar camps, maybe of a more permanent nature all outside Miami and around the country. Then the bishop decided that we had to be placed in foster homes. That began a process of some 70 of us kids, who were now in Jacksonville, being placed in foster homes. The church was wonderful, but even more wonderful were the people of the Lord, the people who were motivated by their faith to open their homes and their hearts to children like us. Ever since, I've been in awe of these families. Imagine being asked from the pulpit to take in these teenage boys. We were all boys being placed, teenage boys who didn't speak their language.

I ended up in the home of Walter and Eileen Young in Orlando, Florida in the summer of 1962. An incredible journey ensued. It was my Americanization. It was the time that I began to figure out what this country was about. I began to learn the language the hard way. Not too many English-as-a-second-language programs were available at the time. The family spoke no Spanish, but one of their children had been taking Spanish in high school. He was about my age. With his dictionary and sign language and whatever, we began to be a family. We had a little bit of a bonding experience. They picked me up at the Greyhound Station and brought me home like at 3:00 in the afternoon. To break the ice, Mrs. Young said, "Well, would you like something to eat?" I finally figured out: "Sure." She was scratching her head thinking, *Well, what can I give this young kid that would be universal?* She thought, *Well, what teenager doesn't like a peanut butter and jelly sandwich?* She made me a peanut butter and jelly sandwich. Now, since in Cuba there was no peanut butter, peanut butter doesn't look edible to the untrained eye. Fortunately, there wasn't a family dog, so I didn't have to wonder.

Anyway, through those kinds of little things, as I said, we became a family. These people were absolutely wonderful. They weren't particularly well off, but they were particularly filled with love. They helped me a great deal. I went on to Bishop Moore Catholic High School in Orlando and began to learn the difficult ways of fitting in as a teenager. I did hear for the first time a certain epithet that I'm more accustomed to hearing today related to the immigration debate, you might say. People were asking me where I was from every time I opened my mouth, which led me on a quest to try to get rid of the accent because it was an impediment. Not only did I not know the language, but when I did learn to speak English, it didn't matter what I had to say. People were more focused on the accent than what I was saying. I had to understand the ways of American teenagers and the system. I obviously was hopelessly lost in classes because I didn't speak the language, and that continued for a while. Finally, I began to catch on and do a little better.

The great equalizer for me, the most wonderful thing that happened and that allowed me to begin my path of becoming an American, happened when they let us know about tryouts for baseball. I got to play the game that I love and was pretty good at. Baseball opened all kinds of doors for me; I had been shunned and ignored until then. Participating in sports was the great equalizer. People really didn't care if you spoke with an accent, if you could hit a line drive. The truth is that all of a sudden my teammates became my friends—some are still my friends to this day—AND allowed me to break out of just being comfortable with Cuban kids, speaking Spanish. I began to interact with the greater society of my school. For me, more important than learning the language was the process of learning the culture and understanding what America was about.

That's why when we talk about this immigration debate today, it is so important to understand that a lot of the objections are not based on the war sentiments of the American people, but are really rooted on the idea that in the American psyche, when people come to this country, they want to see them assimilate. That is what happened in my life. I began to assimilate, to learn the language and to understand the importance of not just clustering with the other Spanish kids, because that made others feel uncomfortable.

If we're in this country, we need to participate and be a part of the greater whole while also remaining true to who we are, understanding our heritage, being proud of it. I still speak fluent Spanish, and I'm very proud of it. My children also learned Spanish because it's important to them. I also understood that for me to succeed in this country, I had to learn the language of this country, and English is the language of this country.

That was all part of the process that took place at my high school. A couple of years later, I graduated and there was a gut check. I'll share a quick story with you about one thing that happened as I was approaching graduation. My guidance counselor, Mrs. McCann—I remember her well—had a bun at the back of her head and talked math. She looked at my grades and, you know, I was not doing really well because I still was trying to learn the language. She said, "You know, you're really not college material. You ought to consider being an auto mechanic." I would love to meet Mrs. McCann again today. I don't know where she is. But the truth is that we've learned a lot about how to handle people since then. I think guidance counselors today will be a little embarrassed about that one. I'm sure she meant no harm; she was just trying to accommodate a future that she thought was appropriate for a Hispanic young man. Many Hispanics are really interested in cars. That might be a really good thing for some of them to try to do.

In any event, I went on to a community college, which is all I could afford to do, and began the process of working my way through college. I was thankfully reunited with my parents in Orlando in 1966. By the time they came, I was nineteen and living with my second foster parents, really wonderful people. When I had turned eighteen, I received a letter from my dear friend, Monsignor Walsh, that I was now on my own. However, my foster parents said, "No, you stay right here with us." I continued to go to junior college and work my way through.

In advance of my parents coming to this country, I was determined to see about finding my dad a job in Orlando. I was able to line up work for him when he arrived at a big dairy farm. He went through some interviews. I became an interpreter at that point. From then on, I was kind of my family's interpreter and resettlement officer, which is a pretty common experience to us who were Peter Pans.

As my parents settled in I really felt responsible for them and helped them from grocery shopping to teaching them how to really live in America and open a bank account. My dad would not open a bank account. He kept making me carry the money. By the way, I had saved $250-some and we spent $200 of that on a car. It was a 1959 Chevrolet with wonderful fins in the back. I would get in that car and go from the phone company to the utility company and whatever, paying the bills: $10 here, $8 there, whatever it was. Finally, I convinced him that in America you get a checking account and you mail the bills in. After a few months, I was able to persuade them, and it was like that that they also became a part of living in America.

I'll never forget that a couple of years later we were able to buy our first home in this country. Later, when I was the secretary of Housing and Urban Development, I remembered that as being such an important time in our family's life. My dad would say, "*Tenemos casa propia en Estados Unidos.*" To him, that was a big deal, to have a house of our own and to feel like we were really cementing our roots and being a part of this American experience. This is why I believe that homeownership is so important. What I'm doing now is working awfully hard to help people stay in their homes, given the current crisis that we're seeing.

I went on to Florida State University. I met my lifelong friend and partner, Kitty. We've been married for 37 years. We've raised three children and now have two grandchildren with a third on the way. Kitty was wise enough to learn Spanish because my mother, for all the bilingualism I've been telling you about, hasn't got the message yet. She is still working on it. If my mother had been seated at dinner here and you had been speaking English to her, you never would have known, because she has a great smile and a great ability to sort of nod in a way that lets you think that she's understanding you while, in fact, she really isn't.

We moved back to Orlando when I finished law school, and I practiced law for 25 years. I was a trial lawyer, a courtroom lawyer, which I couldn't have done if I hadn't mastered the language. Of course, I still consider myself speaking English as a second language. The fact is that from time to time, it shows. I really managed to have a wonderful legal career, one that I was proud of and enjoyed. At some point, I felt a desire to give back and to do for others what had been done for me in some way, in addition to volunteering for a lot of things. As I'm sure many of you know, there's always a board looking for a Hispanic. There are openings in many community boards, so I served on a lot of different boards, participating in community activities.

Ultimately, I was convinced that I should run for county mayor, county supervisor or county judge. So, I did. In 1998, I was elected to that job by a vote of 60 percent of the people in Central Florida. Only 6 percent to 8 percent of the people in that community were Hispanic. I was able to utilize the skills that I first learned that day when I hit a line drive and a kid, otherwise uninterested in me, came up to me and said, "Hey, what is your name?" We began that process of Americanizing. I never could have won that election had I not become a part of the mainstream of this country. I was very proud of that.

It was the same day that Jeb Bush was elected governor of Florida. He and I had known each other and became good collaborators, he as governor and me as a mayor of one of the largest urban centers in Florida. As a result of that friendship, I ended up meeting his brother, who was then governor of Texas and candidate for president. Ultimately, he was good enough to ask me to be HUD secretary, and I came up here to be in his cabinet, the first Cuban-American to be in the presidential cabinet and one of only a handful of Hispanics over the years who has had that privilege. I was very honored to do that. I met so many of you as a result of that work at HUD and did the very best that I could.

Then when the opening came for the U.S. Senate seat in Florida, I went back to run for the senate. It was a tough and spirited race. I was pleased that in my first try at statewide office in Florida—something, frankly, that very few political figures have been able to do—that I was able to win enough support to proudly represent the great State of Florida in the United States Senate. That kind of brings us to where we are today.

Because of these life experiences, I've carried certain things with me that I think are important. I always carry with great pride my work and who I am. I consider that to be a tremendously important thing to live up to because I don't ever want to do anything that would discourage a youngster in junior high who maybe looks at Florida history books, sees my pictures in them and thinks anything other than *here's someone that I can look up to. Here's someone that I could be like.* When I speak to kids in schools, it's always important for me to say, "You can do it too." I speak to bilingual classes for children who are just like I was, just as confused, just as ignorant of what a peanut butter sandwich; I was also awfully confused about the language they're trying to learn or how they're to behave because our cultures are different. I let them have that understanding and that feeling that, yes, they too can do it. If you work hard and you play by the rules and you have an abiding faith in God, all things are possible in America. That's what got me to where I am today.

When the immigration issue came up, I felt it was my responsibility as the only immigrant in the senate to throw myself into the debate and try to make a difference for those that otherwise might not have a voice in the discussion. We have not been successful. I don't want to digress too long into that because that's really a whole other speech for another day. But the fact is that we still have that in the long list of unfinished business that is too tough to handle and too politically expedient to utilize for political gain. The fact of the matter is, we still have that one to get handled. I hope at some point in the not too distant future we will.

Finally, let me say that this is an interesting election year. It's going to be a lot of fun to watch it all evolve and develop. I also believe that you as Hispanic leaders have a unique opportunity to keep communities informed, to participate in the process, to help others to participate by encouraging people to sign up and to vote. Obviously, the mother's milk of politics is money, so also writing checks is important because that is the only way in which we will politically assimilate into the American political system. It's important for the people that all of us, in one way or another, represent. But it's also important for the country because one of the things that I have always believed is that we, as immigrants, have a unique responsibility to make our contribution and make our mark. Others before us have.

Think about Alexander Hamilton who, at the same age as I at age fifteen, also from the Caribbean, came to this country. He then became the right-hand man to George Washington as Washington led the revolutionary army to win this country's freedom. He then was the architect of the executive branch of our government. He became secretary of the treasury. He became much more than that. He was a creator of how the Washington administration was formed, which was the first one. Through history, our country has benefited greatly by the contributions of other immigrants. I think now us, as Hispanic immigrants, as a predominant immigrant group in this country, we have an obligation and a responsibility to fulfill that role yet again for another generation and make our contribution.

That's why it's so important that whatever else you do, you encourage Hispanic young people to stay in school and get an education; that you participate in efforts to make sure that that takes place and that, in whatever other way, we continue to make a contribution to our communities, whether it be through our businesses, through our not-for-profit efforts or through our volunteering. We can, in fact, make a difference. It is up to us to be responsible to that next generation of Americans to ensure that we can also answer the call and make sure that we live up to what is expected.

Robert "Bob" Menéndez

U.S. Senator

March 8, 2006

Senator Bob Menéndez's story is the quintessential American story. He grew up the son of Cuban immigrants in a tenement building in Union City and rose to become a United States Senator. He served as Chairman of the Senate Foreign Relations Committee in the 113th Congress. The Committee is one of the oldest and most revered committees in the Senate, at a time when world affairs have a dramatic impact on our economy at home.

A product of New Jersey's public schools and a graduate of the state's universities, Bob learned early on the importance of standing up for what's right, no matter how powerful the opposition. He first entered public service as a nineteen-year-old college student, when his high school would not provide books to students who could not afford them. Bob launched a successful petition drive to reform the local school board and a year later won a seat on that very board. He stood up to corruption in Union City and went on to become its mayor, then a state legislator and finally a congressman, in 1992. He quickly rose to leadership positions and has given New Jerseyans a seat at the table during critical negotiations on every issue since then: war and peace, jobs and the economy, education, health care, veterans issues, world affairs, transportation and housing.

The son of immigrants, Bob understands the importance of New Jersey's Liberty State Park, in the shadow of Ellis Island and the Statue of Liberty, at the gateway for millions of immigrants who came to this nation seeking a better life for themselves and their children. That's why he was one of eight senators who wrote and fought for comprehensive immigration reform legislation that passed the Senate in 2013 with an overwhelming bipartisan show of support.

There have been many discussions on the subject of immigration. I believe it is unacceptable here in the nation's capital and throughout our country to depend on the work of so many Latinos for the economy and then turn around and attack our communities and our families for partisan political gains. I personally have never found what is in the vision of those who seek to build walls instead of building bridges of opportunity. I don't think that we need a wall between Mexico and the United States.

We need greater engagement not only with Mexico but with the rest of the hemisphere, something that this administration—I've criticized the previous administration, so I don't look at it as a partisan remark—simply has not been engaging in. To believe that any fence or any wall will stop the human desire of people to seek opportunity simply flies in the face of human history and is actually the worst foreign policy I have ever seen us promote. If we're going to build a wall on the United States-Mexico border, well, we'll have to build a wall where the people responsible for September 11 came in, and that is the United States-Canada border. I'm not for either one of them, but let's be honest about this reality.

We need a smart policy. A policy that, as every country has the right and the obligation to do, regularizes its borders and makes sure that its borders are secure. By the same token, we need an opportunity to make sure that those who are here in pursuit of the American dream can be brought out of the darkness and into the light. Let's make sure we know who is here to pursue the American dream versus who might be here to destroy it. Overwhelmingly, I believe that people are here in pursuit of that dream. That means we need not take it to deportation but to a pathway to earn legalization in our country. Hopefully the voices of reason will rise up and explain this great reality for our country and move us in a different direction than making immigration the wedge issue of 2006.

For all of us who are citizens, particularly citizens from the Latino community, this is not just a Latino issue. It is interesting that all along Capitol Hill there are hundreds of people who say, "Legalize the Irish." In my hometown of Hoboken, New Jersey, the Irish have a long history, and there is a new wave of immigrants from Ireland. This country has a proud history of immigration, and it is that history that so enriched this country. Some of us came here involuntarily, and others came here in search of opportunity. Some flew here, while others took boats and risked their lives to get here. We are all in the same boat together today, and our community needs to raise its voices, especially those of us who have achieved the opportunity to fulfill that American dream. Sometimes it's a little upsetting to me that we sit in the luxury of our own circumstances, but if our parents and grandparents and forefathers had had that view, we would not be where we are today. So, I hope we will raise our voices along the line.

I want to share a little bit of my personal history, part of who I am today, what I stand for, what I believe this nation is, why it is the greatest nation in the world. Ellis Island, which is located in the Congressional District that I had the honor of representing for over thirteen years in the House and is within sight of where I live, has been a gateway to opportunity for millions of Americans. For me, Ellis Island is a shining example of the power of the American dream, a place that launched millions down the road to success, in a state that embodies the ideal that children from humble beginnings can grow up to achieve the same dreams as those whose families come from wealth and fame.

My parents came to this country in search of freedom. They came to the greatest country in the world and what they found was a country where people were not afraid to pursue those dreams and had the tools to help realize them. In America, freedom and opportunity are the keys that unlock success, not just for the rich or connected, but for anyone who is willing to work hard.

My mother and father did not have an easy life. When they came to this country, my mother was a seamstress in the factories of New Jersey. My father, when he was alive, was an itinerant carpenter. We grew up poor in a tenement building in Union City.

What got me involved in public life was actually an experience I had when I was in my senior year of high school. I was in a public high school and was told that because of my grades, I qualified to be in the Senior Honors Program. But in fact, I had to cough up $200 for the books. As I said, my parents were poor; we lived in a tenement and I did not have $200. I couldn't understand for the life of me why I would be barred from entering the Honors Program if I had the capacity but didn't have the money. So, I created such a raucous that they gave me the books, told me to shut up and put me in the Honors Program.

To be honest with you, I didn't feel right about it because it was okay for me but wasn't okay for everybody else who may not have spoken up and exercised what should have been his or her rights. The following year when I graduated from the local public school and was going to a Jesuit college in New Jersey called St. Peter's College, I started a petition drive to change the school board from one that was appointed by a very corrupt administration, which had wanted our $200, to one that was elected by the public. I spent a long, hot summer at the age of nineteen with a group of my friends who felt similarly that they had been cheated of the education they should have received. We got thousands of signatures on a petition drive to create a public referendum that we succeeded in passing. Then the following year, at the age of twenty, I ran for election to the first elected school board in my hometown, the one we had created. I ran against a priest, who in those days were allowed to run for public office. I won—for which I am paying in church today.

Thirty-two years ago was the beginning of my having a sense of standing up for what is right, even though it was difficult and not popular. One of the things I was told, particularly by members of our community was, "Siempre se queda igual; no hay cambio." We, in fact, not only changed the school board and succeeded in running—at that time I was the youngest person ever elected to a school board in the state—but more importantly, we began to transform the school district and reform its curriculum, in its pedagogical approach and in its diversification of where we got our educators from. We began to make progress in the school district that today is more than 85 percent Hispanic. That school district is much better off today because we created change so many years ago.

From that lesson, I came to understand that change doesn't necessarily come easy, it doesn't come to those who are not willing to commit themselves to an ideal and willing to sacrifice to make that ideal become a reality. I decided to change the city administration, and I stood up to a very corrupt city administration. During this period of time, my life was threatened; I wore a bulletproof vest for a few months. On the day before the election, the mayor I was running against was sentenced to seven years in federal prison. I lost the election the next day by 200 votes—the only election I ever lost in 32 years, the only election I intend to ever lose again, by the way. I said to myself, "Well, what did the public think about me that they wanted to vote for someone who had been sentenced to seven years in federal prison?"

At that time, I decided to practice law and use the law as a vehicle to create social change. I went to Rutgers Law School and graduated. What happened was that people who followed me in this reform movement—schoolteachers, custodians and sanitation workers, everyday common people who wanted to see a change in their hometown—began to get fired by this administration. Those same people ended up on my doorsteps saying, "We believed in you, we followed you and we are now hurt. What are you going to do?" That dragged me back in to a process in which we, along with a group of my friends that had also became lawyers by that time, litigated their cases in state and federal court for wrongful dismissal, violation of civil rights and a whole host of other efforts. We regained their employment. Then four years later, I became the first Hispanic mayor in the state's history, ousting the rest of what was left of that corrupt administration.

I learned from those early days of reforming the school district to stand up for what I believed was right, even though it was not easy or popular. It has ultimately been my compass point in terms of what I have done in the thirteen years in the House of Representatives and what I intend to do in the United States Senate.

I believe we can head our country in a much better and positive direction. I understand the power of education. I am the first and only member of my family to go to college and then to go to law school. I understand that it is the key to social mobility and economic opportunity in this country. The reality is that I would not be before you today as a United States senator if I hadn't had that educational opportunity. I also realize that the only way that I could afford St. Peters College was because of something called a Pell Grant and something else called a Perkins Grant. It became very clear to me then that I would not have had those opportunities. The reality is that but for the government creating an opportunity, we cannot guarantee equal outcomes, but we should guarantee equal opportunity. Today, we are faced with a budget that for the fifth consecutive year freezes Pell Grants. To the extent students get assistance, they get it through Pell Grants. What in essence one time was paid up to 80 percent of the value of a college education by Pell, today is only 40 percent paid by Pell.

If I did not have the combination of Pell, Perkins and worked through all four years of college, it would probably have been impossible for me to go to college. In New Jersey alone, that's 15,000 students, most of them coming from our minority communities. Their future is determined largely, in terms of the opportunity to fulfill their God-given potential, by virtue of getting this college education. And yet the President's budget eliminates Perkins totally, in addition to freezing Pell. That budget has the most significant cuts in the history of the Department of Education since it was created. A third of all of the federal budget cuts come from the Department of Education.

In a world that has been transformed by technology, in which the boundaries of mankind have been largely erased in the pursuit of human intellect, for a nation to be able to continue to be competitive and be the global leader, it needs to be at the apex of that curve of intellect. That means we need a robust and effective education system, one that creates opportunity for each and every one of our citizens. That's what I intend to fight for in the budget committee as we mark up the budget later this week, to try to make sure that we change the direction of what our priorities and values are.

It's that same type of attitude, from my experiences, that led me to cast a vote that I think was very important even though it was highly criticized at the time that I cast it. You know, votes on war and peace are also votes about life and death. I have a standard. I am not willing to send my son and daughter if the conflict is not right. I am willing to send my son and daughter if the conflict is right. If I am not willing to send my son and daughter to a conflict, then I am not willing to send anyone else's sons and daughters. In that respect, I was willing to send Alicia and Bob, if it was necessary, to Afghanistan. That's where Osama bin Laden was, that's where the Al-Qaeda was, that's where the Taliban gave him sanctuary, that's where the perpetrators of September 11th were; those were the people who killed 700 New Jersians and 3,000 Americans. That was the right cause and that was the right use of American force.

Then when we had the most sophisticated army in the world, the most technologically advanced army in the world and we had Osama bin Laden cornered in the hills of Tora Bora—difficult terrain but nonetheless we knew that he was there—we handed over to the war lords stacks of money expecting they would hand him over to us. Instead he escaped, they took the money and we are now still in search of the mastermind of those who killed 3,000 people of the United States. And what did we do? We deviated our attention to another part of the world.

I sat in the Intelligence Room and read documents that were available to members of Congress. I didn't see any clear and present danger to the United States; I didn't see any imminent threat to the United States. I have to be honest with you: desires of weapons of mass destruction? What? Evidence of weapons of mass destruction? No. I made a decision that it was wrong to vote for the war in Iraq. I voted "no," even in a district that lost 150 people of those 700 New Jersians, because I felt in my heart it was the right thing to do. At that time, I was criticized; today, as we are in the cusp of civil war in Iraq, the very same people who came to criticize me, to their credit, have come to tell me, "You were right."

The question is, will you stand up for what you believe in? Will you stand up for what you know in your heart is right, even though it may not be popular, even though it may not be easy?

The course of human history has been changed by men and women who are willing to stand up for what is right, even though it is not easy. That is what I ultimately think is the essence of leadership. I hope that in your lives each and every day you will choose to find within yourselves, whatever walk of life or whatever work you do, a moment to stand up for what is right. The question is, will you choose that moment, seize it and make life better for everyone else? I choose to do that. That is why I am going to fight for my seat in the United States Senate.

Omar Minaya
General Manager
NY Mets

September 19, 2007

Omar Minaya is the current Sr. Vice President of Baseball Operations for the San Diego Padres. He previously served as General Manager for the Montreal Expos and the New York Mets, making him Major League Baseball's first Hispanic General Manager.

Born in the Dominican Republic, Minaya moved to Queens, New York at the age of eight. Minaya starred as a baseball player at Newtown High School and was drafted by the Oakland Athletics in 1978. He had a short-lived career in the minor leagues, as well as stints in leagues in both the Dominican Republic and Italy. After injuries ended his playing career, Minaya joined the Texas Rangers' scouting team in 1985, where he helped in the signing of players, such as Sammy Sosa and Juan González.

In the mid-1990s, Minaya left Texas and returned home to join the staff of the New York Mets, working his way to assistant general manager behind Steve Phillips and being partly responsible for that team's late-1990s success. Minaya became the first Hispanic to hold a general manager position in Major League Baseball when he left the Mets in early 2002 to accept the general manager position with the Montreal Expos. He returned to the Mets as general manager following the 2004 season. But Minaya's dream of becoming a general manager for the New York Mets did not come easy. He applied for the job and was rejected nineteen times before finally getting the position. He is the embodiment of the phrase, "perseverance is failing nineteen times and succeeding the twentieth."

I love baseball. I was born in the Dominican Republic, a country that loves baseball. After my parents immigrated to New York City, I grew up in a neighborhood that idolized baseball. My father was a factory worker. My mother was a factory worker. I was fortunate enough to have two parents who were loving and always supported me. I was fortunate enough to go to the public-school system in New York. But at the end of the day, when you grew up in the streets of New York in the early '60s, there were a lot of choices that you could make. I chose baseball.

I remember playing stickball in the streets of New York, pretending I was right there in center field; I was Willie Mays or Mickey Mantle. I visualized my dream to be a major league baseball player. Although it did not happen *exactly* as I had visualized it, I did end up playing professional baseball with the Oakland Athletics and the Seattle Mariners; then, I went on to play in Europe. What a wonderful experience that was to play in Europe, to be able to understand another continent, to be able to understand diversity.

I loved growing up in New York because when you grow up in New York, you become open to many diverse cultures. That diversity God prepared for me is why I am where I am today. God has a way of working things out for us, and sometimes we look back in our lifetime and realize that God put us in certain situations for us to be able to use them later on, not only for the betterment of society but for the betterment of whatever God wishes for us.

When you look at baseball today and you examine the role that Latino players have, you realize that Latinos are in a position of leadership and have the power to impact our society and create hope and opportunity for all of us. As a general manager of a team, I have the responsibility to bring people together for the best of the organization, to bring people together whether as players, as managers, as coaches or as other business people. As a general manager, I have the opportunity to bring everybody together for the common good. As a general manager, I look at Manny Acta who's the manager of the Washington Nationals. Manny needed to be given an opportunity, and he was given an opportunity with the Montreal Expos; today he is the manager of the Washington Nationals. For those of you who are National fans, you've got yourself a good manager.

What's truly more important is dreaming. I can talk about dreams. That's one thing that I can talk about because, you know what, growing up, it was a dream for me to be a centerfielder. It was a dream for me to be out there and be like Willie Mays. But the reality is that that was not going to happen, because I did not have the physical ability. Not having the physical ability, I basically had to tell myself, "Omar, what are you going to do? What is it that God has in store for you?" I thought about that and I started telling myself, "You know what, I know one thing. I may not be a good enough baseball player because I don't have the physical ability, but I will be a success, if I put all my passion and remember all I was taught about being a good baseball player, in whatever field God leads for me. I know that."

And you will also be a success. Whatever you put your passion in and whatever you believe in, there'll be obstacles along the way. There'll be obstacles along the way and some people will tell you, "Well, nobody has ever done that." You know what, that's the challenge. Because nobody has ever done that is why you should go after it. Somebody once said to me, "Omar, no Latino has ever been a general manager." Even today, I had to go for about eight to ten interviews. I was the bridesmaid of most of these interviews. The bridesmaid: I was always the one they'd say, "You know what, we didn't hire you, but you were number two." I know we've all heard that along the way. The challenge was there. For me, it's about meeting people, being open minded.

I told myself, "You know what, there has not been a Latino general manager. I want to be . . . no, really, I'm going to be a general manager or the first Latino general manager." But how do I get there? You're not going to get there through bitterness. Along the way, you're going to come to situations where you're going to get frustrated, people are going to tell you, "We've heard this all along, they're racist." Somewhere along the line, you're going to feel, "You know what? Nah, I'm just a failure." After eight to ten times of being the bridesmaid, it's pretty easy to give up. But you know what, our parents, being immigrants, our heritage, too many people struggled too much to get to where we are today. We are blessed to be able to live in this beautiful country, although right now as immigrants we have issues that we have to talk about. But you know what, we've been given the mantle. We've been given the baton to move forward. It is our responsibility to do that. And when you've been given that responsibility, we have to continue the faith and the networking. We've got to continue to believe in ourselves and help others believe in themselves.

There was a movie about growing up in New York called A Bronx Tale. I'm a big fan of A Bronx Tale because I was a street kid like the protagonist by the name of "C." That movie deals with diversity and deals with those issues. It talks about talent. There's nothing worse than wasted talent. When it's all said and done, I told myself, "You know, Omar, as a baseball player, I did my best." I was not a good hitter. I was a great hitter in high school, those aluminum bats were great—you know what I'm saying? But reality kicked in. First, it was fastball and there was 2 and 0, or it was 1 and 0 and they threw that change up, and then they threw that pitch inside, I grounded to second, and it was the same, over and over, over and over again. I tried my best, but didn't make it.

I told myself as a general manager. Now, we get into who controls the budget. Because you can be a great player—you know, Jackie Robinson said he wanted to see a black man as a third-base coach. That's what he said. But we're in areas right now where we don't want to see a third-base coach. We want to see a manager. We want to see a *general* manager. We want to see a team president. We want to see a team owner. All of us have to encourage our group. I grew up, as I said, in a very diverse place and that's a blessing. I believe that for us to move forward, we must be able to interact with everybody.

I know we are having issues right now with immigration. The fact is that we can change that. We have the ability to change that. And we will change that. I guarantee you that. We'll change that because this is what America is about. I feel very fortunate and blessed that God has put me in a position to be able to share my experiences with young people as much as with older people. I do believe that in our society we have a lot of wisdom available to us, but it's up to us to use it.

When I became a general manager, I went to John Schuerholz. If you know, the Atlanta Braves have won a lot of championship divisions, and I thought he's the best general manager. I've always believed in going to the best, to ask advice from the best. Don't be afraid to ask questions. Be honest when you talk to people and just tell them how you feel. Hey, I was fortunate enough to work with the President of the United States, and I tell you what, he's a friend since we worked together in Texas; to this day, if I have to ask him a question, I will not be afraid to go ask our president a question. But one thing that I learned along the way was that whether it's the President of the United States or we are working Shea Stadium and the people that clean the spikes of the players, when you talk to them, they're all the same. Believe me when I tell you to not be afraid to go and ask questions, no matter who it is. You'll be surprised whom you'll be able to get your best advice from.

I asked John Schuerholz, "John, what does it take to be a good general manager? What does it take?" He gave me a very simple answer: "Omar, let me tell you something about yourself, okay? I know a little bit about you. Tell me a little bit about your parents. Just tell me a little bit about your parents." I told him about them, and he said, "Listen. To be a great general manager, just listen to what your parents say. Just keep that in the back of your mind. And if you do that, you will be a success."

I want to share that with everybody, especially young people. I just want to share that for me it's an honor to be a general manager of the New York Mets, to be the first Hispanic general manager. Trust yourself, and don't ever stop dreaming. We are blessed to be in this country. Don't stop dreaming, because if you stop dreaming, you are shortchanging those that came before you and those that are in front of you.

Gloria Molina
County Supervisor
Los Angeles County

June 4, 2008

Trailblazer Gloria Molina is the first Latina in history to be elected to the California State Legislature, the Los Angeles City Council and the Los Angeles County Board of Supervisors. As a Los Angeles County Supervisor, Gloria Molina developed a reputation as a fiscal guardian committed to achieving good government reforms and addressing quality of life issues—particularly for the one million residents living in unincorporated areas. But her main focus has been on strengthening Los Angeles County's public health care system, first by securing $1 billion in federal funds from President Bill Clinton in 1995 to rescue the county's struggling health care network; then by helping develop the county's public-private partnership system of health care into the largest in the United States.

While at the California State Legislature, Molina lent her political muscle to many issues, but it was her lengthy but successful fight against building a state prison in the Boyle Heights neighborhood that made her a local legend.

Molina grew up as one of ten children in the Los Angeles suburb of Pico Rivera to a Mexican-American father and Mexican mother. She attended public schools in her hometown and attended Rio Hondo College, East Los Angeles College and California State University, Los Angeles.

My father used to say, "*Con un sueño, trabajo y ganas, todo se puede lograr.*" With a dream, hard work and determination, anything can be accomplished. Now, one would think with such positive inspiration that it had all been planned, that I would have known as a child that one day I would be here. But nothing could be further from the truth.

My parents are from Casas Grandes, Chihuahua. I'm first generation. Although my father was born in the United States, he was raised from the age of three in Mexico. Of course, he always longed to come back to the United States. I'm the oldest of ten children. I was raised in Los Angeles. We all lived together in a small two-bedroom house. And, of course, I was always reminded that it was my responsibility to set the example for my brothers and sisters. This is a tradition in Mexico, and I was very proud to follow through on that tradition. My parents had dreams for each and every one of us. But those dreams were really rather limited. My father aspired for me to graduate from high school and go on to be a legal secretary. That would make him so very proud. He wanted all of his children to learn English and not have an accent. That was very important to him because he didn't want us to be discriminated. Of course, he wanted for every single one of us to graduate from high school. He'd been a construction worker all of his life and, as he said, worked with his back and his hands and did not want us to follow in that tradition.

Tradition was part and parcel of my growing up. Certainly, my brother was expected to become a lawyer or a professional. The girls were expected to become teachers, secretaries and moms. But my dreams were much larger than that. They weren't political at all. It was my intention to become a fashion designer, believe it or not. After two art classes, I clearly decided—and I think it was decided for me that I had no talent in that area whatsoever—to start college with an interest in social work. It's interesting that my mother was very bothered by my wanting to attend college. After all, she'd only attended the third grade. She felt that for my future, graduating from high school was more than enough. After all, I was to become a wife and a mother. She was also bothered by the fact that my father had had an industrial accident. He had been in a cave-in, and we were living on his disability check. Another fine Mexican tradition is that the oldest has to be responsible for the wellbeing of the family, so an additional paycheck was necessary. Consequently, I had to go out and work. I attended college while working full time as a legal secretary.

I was involved in all kinds of issues in the community, and one of the things I decided to do was to volunteer at a local community center on the east side. I started working with young women, tenth graders who unfortunately couldn't read at a tenth-grade level. It bothered me tremendously. I went to go visit the teachers at the high school and was confronted by a group of teachers who said, "Don't worry about these girls. After all, they're not going to graduate from high school. They'll probably get pregnant before then. We don't expect them to graduate. So, if I were you, I wouldn't worry about them." Well, that certainly got my adrenaline going, and it hasn't stopped since.

At the same time, on the eastside, the Chicano Movement was just beginning. At college, all of us were members of MASA, the Mexican American Student Association. This was when it was okay to be a hyphenated American. And, of course, MECHA followed soon thereafter.

The Chicano Movement was so exhilarating to me. Listening to Chicano activists talk about what we needed to do about the inequities, the injustices; it was wonderful. I joined up as quickly as I could. I was a wonderful follower. Unfortunately, the women of that organization were relegated to the task of mimeographing and making menudo for all of the fundraisers. Every time we wanted to raise our issues—and we had many, such as employment training, child care, higher education—we, of course, were quickly castigated and put in our place. I participated in various events, but anytime we would raise our issues, we were accused of trying to divide the movement.

Well, at the same time, I attended various consciousness-raising meetings. That's what they were called back then in the infancy of our present feminist movement. I listened to all of these white women talk about these macho men who were discriminating against them, who were relegating them to subservient roles. It was a real problem for me to listen to that because, growing up, my father was very proud to be a macho. Machismo in Mexico is a proud tradition. A macho is someone who is a responsible, respected man, someone who takes responsibility for his family, and it's a very honorable role. So, them using that word was a real problem for me. I certainly was a victim of the racism that was going on in the community, but I was also a victim of the sexism that was going on in the community.

The war in Vietnam and the fact that our Chicanos were going to the frontlines, and we were losing many, many more than we represented in this country as far as population, led me to decide very quickly that this was going to be my focus. I got involved in the Chicano Movement and I was working every day on those issues while I working full time. At the same time, I quietly—I wasn't a very engaging person at that time, a leader of any sort—participated in various discussions with other Latinas and other Chicanas in the community. We certainly felt the discrimination. We certainly felt the barriers to our moving forward. We started talking about putting together an organization, a network where we could become advocates.

I came across the opening of the Chicana Service Action Center by a group of very, very assertive women, including Francisca Flores, who was an activist in the labor Movement in the 1940s and '50s, Lilia Aceves and various other women who had decided to open up an employment training and counseling facility. I was very glad to finally find this network of women. They convinced me, and we joined up with them. They said that we should form a chapter of an organization known as Comisión Femenil Mexicana Nacional, a national Chicana advocacy group. We thought, *absolutely*. We developed a chapter as quickly as we could in Los Angeles, later to only find out that the organization only existed on paper. There was no such organization. But our very first meeting attracted more than 200 Chicanas. We clearly understood the importance that the dialogue we were having with ourselves was going on everywhere, and that Chicanas needed to have a network, an organization and someone to advocate on their behalf.

We took action as quickly as possible. We started building our leadership skills by speaking in front of people, many times certainly not prepared, but we were learning our way through. We were writing proposals to develop various programs for women. We were writing articles about many of the issues in our community. We were moving forward with a very strong action plan. We developed more employment training programs. We developed supportive services for Latinas and Chicanas and their families. Because a woman can't go to work if she doesn't have good childcare services, we developed the very first bilingual, bicultural childcare center. We also went as far as suing L.A. County—for which I now serve on that Board of Supervisors—to stop the forced sterilization of Mexican women at the county general hospital.

We had a very, very active plan, and we were very excited about the work that we were doing. Of course, that led to getting involved in the political process. Certainly, it wasn't what we were planning on doing, but by nature of getting involved in many of those issues, you become part of the political process.

I became very adept and developed an army of what I call "the lickers and the stickers." We were a very valuable commodity to most of the grassroots campaign for the Chicanos that were running for office. Every time one of them decided to run, they'd call on me and I'd put together a whole group of people. We became a very, very valuable commodity, as I said, to any of those campaigns. I was a regular.

Eventually, I got an opportunity to work for the newly elected assemblyman, Art Torres. He, at that time, was called an administrative assistant. I really welcomed the opportunity to work with him in the community on many of the issues. It was just exhilarating to be a part of not only his campaign but eventually his staff.

I wanted to learn much more about political organizing, so I asked for an opportunity to work on the Carter-Mondale campaign that was coming through the eastside of L.A. Instead I became the "Chicana" in the California campaign—you know, you only have one at a time, you can't have too many. I was sent up and down the state to organize for Carter-Mondale. Unfortunately, most of the Chicanos didn't know who Jimmy Carter was and, in many instances, didn't have the interest. But luckily, while we didn't win the state of California, we did win the White House. At that time, I was called by a very dear friend of mine, Rick Hernández. He had been the western region desk and later became a muckety muck at the Small Business Administration. He called me and said, "Why don't you apply for this job at the White House?" I thought, *Wow, what an exciting opportunity to go to the White House and be with all of these White House politicos that know what's going on and how to do it. I could learn so very much.* I certainly was excited. It was so very impressive, and I was so fortunate.

Well, my very first day on the job, I received an envelope on my desk. It had two little flags on it: the American flag and the flag of Iran. We were invited to join Jimmy Carter on the White House lawn to welcome the Shah of Iran. I was very excited, my first time on the White House lawn. Now, I had been involved in the Chicano Moratorium in East L.A., and in the school walkouts on the eastside, I had been part of anti-war protests throughout L.A., and I had been involved in feminist protests, but I never expected to be gassed on the lawn of the White House, which is exactly what happened that day. It seems that many of the people who were against the Shah were creating quite a stir right outside of the White House. That's what happened to me on my first day.

That evening, as I walked out, the White House police said, "We need to walk all Persians to their car." I said, "Persian? I'm not a Persian. I'm a Mexican." They said, "Oh, from Mexico?" I said, "No, from East L.A." Of course, it was very clear that we were non-existent to many of the people here in D.C.

Well, at that time, we were fortunate to have a few members of Congress, such as Congressman Ed Roybal and our very own Congressman Robert García. Very few people who were there were not able to really fight all of the inequities that so many of us knew existed in our community and that I knew that at that time. I needed to go back home and find a way that we could get more Latinos elected to the U.S. Congress. It was interesting because I was working in the Office of Presidential Personnel and my responsibility was to, again, "get Hispanics appointed to commissions." Not the top commissions, by the way, those little smaller commissions. "Make sure you only put one on, okay?" That was my role at that time. I enjoyed the work, it was wonderful work, but clearly, I needed to go home. We needed to go home and be part of organizing in our own community to make sure that we had a stronger and better presence in the beltway, and that was very important.

When I returned to Los Angeles, I started working full time for then Speaker Willie Brown. And then, again, I also volunteered—I was a volunteer for everything—for a group called Californios, a reapportionment committee that was operating in Los Angeles. We knew that because of the growth of the Chicano population throughout California, we were entitled to two additional congressional seats. We're very excited. Many of my feminist friends thought, *why not?* One should go to a Chicano and one should go to a Chicana, if we're going to be fair about this whole process. We approached many of those Chicano-elected officials that we had supported all of this time, walked in and made our request that we thought we should have one of the seats in Congress. Well, we were laughed right out of the room. What was interesting about it is that we had approached various

Chicana lawyers because we thought that they would be the most qualified to run. They laughed at us as well. They said it was tough enough to get a Chicano elected, let alone a Chicana.

We went away, licked our wounds and, luckily for us, there was an opportunity that turned up in my own backyard. Assemblyman Torres decided to challenge one of his senate colleagues, and that vacated that assembly seat. Again, we went to the various Chicana lawyers, but they said, "Uh-uh, we don't have a chance of winning. We're not going to run for that seat." At the end of the day, it was very clearly decided that I had to be the candidate. I knew the district. I had worked the district. I knew enough about politics. I decided to do it. We had to move forward and take the risk. We weren't sure we were going to win but we were going to do all that we could.

I was very fortunate. We were able to raise money. We got into an action plan. We had a campaign going. It was very fortunate for me to be the oldest of ten because when you're walking the district, having nine brothers and sisters with you is a help. We walked that district one and a half times. In 1982, I was the first Chicana ever elected to the California State Legislature. I'm very proud of that. I'm very proud to say that what my mother said to me many, many years before, about setting the example for others served me well. Since then, I have been followed into the California legislature by some of the most talented and wonderful women that you will ever meet. I'm very proud to have been the very first one. But many others followed, such as our wonderful Congresswoman Hilda Solís.

In 1987, I decided to run for the city council. I should mention, by the way, when I first decided to run for that assembly seat, the politicos said, "No." They already had a candidate in mind. We had to run against them, despite they're believing that we could not win. Would you believe that after winning the state legislative seat and deciding to run for the city council, I went back to those politicos and said, "Look, I want to run for the city council," and they said, "Oh, no. We've got our own candidate."

They didn't support me back then either, and I had to beat them again.

In 1987, I became the first Chicana on the Los Angeles City Council, which was very important to us. The next battle was for the Los Angeles Board of Supervisors. Five white men represented the County of Los Angles, a very powerful board from the standpoint of what it does and what it's responsible for. Five people represent ten million people (Its budget this year is over $22 billion.) It has a tremendous amount of responsibility. But the way the district lines were drawn was very clever and certainly didn't allow for any minority to serve, even though we had a large Latino population and a very, very large African American population.

As a result of a case MALDEF brought to the Supreme Court to challenge reapportionment, a seat in the first district was carved out to be a Latino district. I ran with ten other candidates, including unfortunately my former boss, Art Torres. I was elected as the first Chicana to the County Board of Supervisors, a position that I serve in today. I'm very proud to carry out that work.

When Congressman Roybal was ready to retire, he came to me and said, "I'd like you to run for my seat." Frankly, I was very happy doing the work that I was doing. By that time, I was married and had a child. We were very fortunate to have Lucille Roybal-Allard, who had followed me into the California legislature, ready to go. She was able to follow through, serve and follow in the footsteps of her father. Lucille is a wonderful congresswoman. I love her dearly. She's one of our great leaders. I'm so proud that she has been one of the Latinas that has been motivated to get involved in the political process. We had wanted, from day one, to get a Chicana in the U.S. Congress. By the time that Lucille got there, there were others, but unfortunately still not enough. We have to do much more work, elect many more Latinas to the U.S. Congress.

Nevertheless, I'm elated at the number of women that I see in positions of power, in advocacy organizations and in corporate positions or on major foundation boards. I'm very proud to see so many Chicanas in position of power. It's wonderful. I am glad that I am but one of many who continue to struggle and take on risk to carry on these kinds of roles.

By the way, I want you to know that while my mother had a real problem in my attending college, she saved money most of her life so that her youngest, the ninth and tenth—they're twins—would be able to go to college without ever having to work. She was so proud that day when they graduated with their degrees. I'm so glad that my mother realized how important it was for all of us to go to college. I was very proud of her that day as well.

The reality is we have so much more to do. We need to realize that it requires both men and women to be at the table when it comes to public policy. It can't be one or the other. We need to continue to have that kind of unity when it comes to the issues of public policy. I'm looking forward, like everyone else, to a new administration. I wore a pantsuit in honor of my candidate. I look forward to being a part of the Democratic campaign to win the White House back. I do know that whoever goes into the White House will have to go through the Latino community to get there. Hopefully, they will recognize and understand the unbelievable talent we have in our community and will appoint Chicanas and Latinas to positions, such as Secretary of State, Supreme Court justices, even vice presidents, making our community better and stronger every single day. It is wonderful to be a first, but it would mean nothing if you did not have the following of so many people like you.

Richard Montañez
Author & Executive
PepsiCo

March 11, 2014

Richard Montañez vividly recalls the day when the CEO of Frito Lay sent a video message to the employees. "He told us to act like an owner. I looked around and didn't see a lot of reaction from my co-workers, but for me it was the opportunity to do something different." Montañez had started working at Frito-Lay as a janitor in its Rancho Cucamonga plant in 1976. He took this task to heart and did not let the fact that he'd grown up picking grapes with his family or that he had not finished high school discourage him from calling the CEO on the telephone and telling him his idea for a new product. The rest is history. The new product he created was Flamin' Hot Cheetos, an idea that became a billion-dollar-a-year product. "I've created several other products but I can never tell that story because people stop at Flamin' Hot Cheetos," says Montañez.

Montañez leads Multicultural Sales & Community Promotions across PepsiCo's North American divisions, leveraging best practices internally and externally to develop community partnerships. He is recognized as the creator of the "Flaming Hot" line of products, including "Flamin' Hot Cheetos," which influenced future ethnic products and the first Frito-Lay Hispanic marketing team. In 1990, he helped write and launch the Continuous Improvement Initiative, the first operation cost *improvement team. In addition, he helped influence Hispanic products and marketing promotions for KFC and Taco Bell.*

When I started with Frito-Lay in 1976, I didn't have a whole lot going for me. I had no education and was told I would never be anything. But I had one thing: vision. This is what vision did for me. When others saw what I was, vision saw what I would become. The very thing that disqualified me, vision qualified me.

I've been with my wife since we were kids. We've been married 35 years and been together 40. But when we got together, we didn't have any dreams. That's why I tell young people, "You know what, dream. Let it be wild. It's okay, throw it out there."

My dad and my grandpa were good men, but they didn't know how to dream. All they were doing was working. I started working full-time when I was in the third grade. My grandfather picked grapes, my dad picked grapes and I picked grapes. We didn't have time to dream, but we had hope and our hope was that someday we would have a better future. Hope that maybe someday we didn't have to worry about how we were going to feed our kids that day. Maybe someday we'd have a bank account. Maybe someday, Judy, you and I will be able to write a check. Maybe someday, we'll live in that neighborhood that we used to go trick or treating in and they'd throw us out because they said we don't live in there.

I remember not wanting to go trick or treating in the barrio—there was no candy in there. Judy and I used to go across town where you get the big Hershey bars. But after a while, after a few knocks, they would realize, "You know what, this is not your neighborhood, is it? Go back." We were never hurt, because we didn't know what discrimination was. We didn't know what it was; we just knew we didn't belong there. We had to go back to the other side of the tracks.

Young people, I want to tell you today; listen to me, young people. You don't need anybody's permission to become great. If you feel you need somebody's permission, I'm here to give it to you today. You have my permission to be great.

For me it all began in the 1960s. You see during the civil rights movement of the 60s, I wasn't old enough to make it, to have an impact on the movement, but I was old enough for the movement to have had an impact on me. Let's go back to 1963, third grade in a one-room building. My mom would get me ready for school because we were being bused from an all-Spanish-language school to an English school. I was crying, and Mom asked, "*Chillón, ¿por qué lloras?*" "Cry baby, why are you crying?" I answered, "*Porque ya no quiero ir a esa escuela.*" "Because I don't want to go to that school anymore." "Why not?" "*Porque todos hablan inglés.*" "Because everybody speaks English."

My uncle took me to the corner bus stop. And guess what bus showed up? It was green. I asked my *tío*, "Why can't I get on the yellow bus? Why do I have to get on the green bus?" He said, "I don't know, *m'ijo*. This is the bus they sent." It wasn't until years later that I realized that it was society telling me, "You're not good enough to get on the yellow bus. You have to get on the green bus because we're going to parade you across town so that everybody can see these kids are not good enough for the yellow bus."

We got to school. I didn't understand a word the teacher was saying. But there was one sound that's international. Every young kid knows this sound and it's the sound of the recess bell. So, there we were and we heard it—what a relief! There were about eight or nine of us, I really don't remember, but we grabbed our lunches and sat down. We were all getting ready to eat our lunch, and I pulled mine out. I was getting ready to take a bite and, just like that, everybody was staring at me. So I put my lunch back in the bag. Why do you think I put my lunch back in the bag? It was because it was a burrito. You've got to remember this was 1963, and the world hadn't seen a burrito yet. Contrary to popular belief, Taco Bell didn't introduce the burrito to the world; me and my mom did. But I put that burrito right back. Why? Because I was embarrassed, because I thought, *why do I*

*have to ride the green bus? Why do I have to eat burritos? I don't want
everybody staring at me. Why can't I fit in? I want to be like those other
little boys.*

I went home and I told my mom straight up, "*Mamá, hazme
un baloney sandwich con un cupcake como lo que comen otros.*" "Mom,
make me a baloney sandwich and a cupcake, like the other kids
eat. Because I don't want to be different." But my mom, being the
marketing genius that she is, said, "No, *m'ijo*, this is who you are."
She made me two burritos and said, "Here's one for you and here's
one to share with a friend." Wednesday, I had my burrito nightmare. Thursday, I shared a burrito with a friend. Friday, I was selling burritos for 25 cents apiece.

That's when I started to find out that, "Well wait a minute,
maybe there is something special about being different. Maybe
it's okay to speak a different language. Maybe it's okay to eat different food." I finally realized that none of us were created to fit
in. We were created to stand out. Young people, live your life,
stand out, regardless of what anybody thinks. Remember, creating history is just a matter of seeing and pursuing what others
can't and won't. Look, everything created has a step-by-step pro-
tocol, and sometimes you just need to break out in order to break
through.

Young executives, listen, stay away from people who discourage you. Hang out, instead, with people who encourage you. You
know what it is to discourage someone? It means to go into their
hearts and pull out their courage, and they're never the same. You
know what it means to encourage someone? It means to grab
courage and put it in their inner being, where they'll never be the
same. That's who you need to be spending time with: people who
encourage you.

I quit school at such a young age that I had such jobs as
killing chickens for a living and working at a car wash. That's
probably the one regret I have: I don't have a formal education.
Yet, I speak and teach leadership classes at universities across the
country.

I had no formal education, but I know for a fact that I'm probably the most uneducated brilliant person you'll ever meet. I was teaching an MBA class to about twenty students. It was a six-week course, and I scheduled my time to make sure that I was in on that Thursday. A young MBA student asked me, "Well, Mr. Montañez, all my professors have a degree. Where did you get your degree?" I was writing something on the board, I turned and looked right at him and said, "The University of Cucamonga." He said, "Where's that?" "Never mind. Private school. You couldn't get in."

He tried to start it again, "Well, Mr. Montañez, one more question." I'm like, "Yes?" "All my professors have PhDs. What about you?" I looked him straight in the eye and said, "Oh, I got a PhD. I've been poor, hungry and determined."

Young people, you need to know that nothing outside of you is bigger than what is inside of you. Go ahead, release the limits that have been placed on you and set free the unlimited life that you and I are intended to live. We're all brilliant human beings, and we all hold the gift of genius.

Let me tell you where I got my courage. Back in the third grade every Tuesday, they had after school reading. One trailer would pull up outside for the Latinos and the other trailer would pull up for the white kids. And every Tuesday at three o'clock, we'd get in line. But one day, I had a revelation that led to a revolution that became an evolution in my life. Young people, remember that. Get a revelation because it will lead to a revolution that will create evolutions.

One day, on a Tuesday, I decided to break ranks and got out of the line that I was told to get into. That was the Latino line. I got out of that line and got in the white line. I had a fear that I'd never had as a child. My own Latino classmates, intentionally or unintentionally, were calling me back, "*Ricardo, estás loco.*" "You're in the white line. This is the line you're supposed to get in."

But this is what I said, with fear, but I had something inside of me that was greater than the fear. I looked at them and I said, "They got cookies inside. I'm going to get us some cookies."

I remember walking in, but I was scared. I saw two white ladies and wondered what they were going to do when they saw the little dark kid? But I had something inside that was greater. I was hungry. My pain of hunger was greater than my fear of being different. What if I could just get a cookie for my friends and me? So, I got closer and closer. You know what those two ladies did? They filled my pockets with cookies.

You're all wondering what the moral of that story is. First, if you're hungry, young people, if you're hungry for that position, for that career, fear will leave. If you're hungry to live in that neighborhood, fear will leave. If you're hungry to run for that political office, fear will leave.

One day, my neighbor said, "They're hiring at Frito-Lay." I got an application. I couldn't read or write, but I had my beautiful wife fill out the application. I went back and it was like 11:30 at night. In those days, they didn't do background checks, and I thank God they didn't do background checks.

I got hired at Frito-Lay. I remember telling my dad and my grandfather. My grandfather said, "¿Qué hacen allí?" "What do they do there?" I didn't really know how to explain potato chips. I just said, "Papas fritas." "Okay, bueno, m'ijo. You're doing so good."

I was a janitor but you would think in the Montañez family that I just graduated from Harvard because something was happening. There was a revolution that was taking place in the Montañez family. Somebody was breaking away from the grape fields and going into a factory job as a janitor. And somebody said, "You're just a janitor." There's no such thing as just a janitor. There's no such thing as just a waiter. Every waiter in this room, I want to tell you that someday you can manage this hotel.

I began to mop those floors. My dad and my grandfather said, "You make sure that they shine. You make sure that those floors look like a Montañez mopped them." I began to take everybody's trash out. I didn't care whose it was, I took it out. I cleaned, and people would walk in and say, "Wow, this floor smells good." I had influence. I was a janitor, but I had influence.

Then one day the CEO sent out a video that said, "I'd like everybody to act like an owner." Here was the opportunity for a janitor to act like an owner. Is he serious? I didn't know what our company was all about. I began to research it, found out that we were a sales and marketing company. Then one day, destiny—because I'm a firm believer in destiny—I saw it. I just got a revelation of what I could do.

I did what a typical Latino janitor would do and I called up the CEO. This was many, many years ago. Remember when corporate America was in command and control? Corporate America had not seen empowerment yet. I believe that I changed corporate America. I believe that I introduced the word empowerment to corporate America. Some people said, "You're so full of yourself, Richard." And I said, "I am and you should be, too." Fall in love with yourself because when you fall in love with yourself, there's a freedom to be yourself.

In those days, there were no emails; we had phone books. You could find anybody who was anybody. So, the first one was the CEO. What did I do? I went to one of the secretaries and said, "Say, can I use the phone?" "Oh, you can't use this phone," she said. "This is just for . . . " "Oh, it is? I'm going to call the CEO." And she's like, "Oh yeah, you can use my phone. I've never seen anybody get fired on the spot."

I called him up. In those days, we were in every country that the government would allow us, worldwide. All the other CEOs would call up our CEO. His executive assistant, who is a visionary and still is my friend today, said, "What country are you calling from?"

"United States," I said.

She said, "You're the president of the . . . ?"

"No, I work in California." And she was like, "You're the general manager in California?"

"No, I work in the Rancho Cuca . . . "

She was, "You're the director of operations."

I said, "No."

"What are you?"

"I'm the janitor."

A visionary. Young people, many times greatness will come in a ridiculous form. You've got to be willing to look ridiculous. And leaders, many times a great idea will come in a ridiculous form. Can you see it? She did. I tell her my idea, and she says, "I'll be there in two weeks."

I hung up, the happiest man you've ever seen. Wow, I didn't know what I had just done. Then, there came the plant manager—there's always someone in the room ready to steal your destiny. "Who do you think you are?" he confronted me.

Because, see, the phone call had just come down. "Hey, who's this guy that just called the CEO?"

This was many, many years ago.

"Who do you think you are? Are you going to do the presentation? Everybody's coming. Now, I got to fix everything. Now, I got to paint the place."

I remember I went home and discussed it with my wife, something I've done my whole career. "I don't know what I did. But now they're coming, and you know . . . " She says, "We're going to go and get a book on how to create a marketing strategy. Don't worry, Richard, your destiny is to stand before great men. Don't worry."

We went to the library and checked out a book on how to create a marketing strategy. You know what we did? We copied it word for word. So, the day finally came. We didn't have technology, right? Remember the transparencies? I had made a bunch of them. I went to a store and bought my first tie for $3.50. I had my neighbor fix it so in the morning I just had to slip it on.

And finally, there they were. The CEO himself came with every high-level executive in the PepsiCo organization. I didn't realize what I had done. I started the presentation, word for word, and I was feeling it. Then all of a sudden, a question came up. There's always somebody in the room to steal your destiny. It was one of the highest marketing executives in the company and he raised his hand and said, "Well, Richard . . . "

And it was going so well. It was going too well.

He asked, "Well, Richard, just how much market share are we talking about?"

I froze. "The market share?"

We hadn't read that chapter yet. I almost fainted. I was that little boy again. When will I fit in? I'm making a fool . . . who do I think I am presenting to some of the most educated men and women in my organization? But then I remembered going into the stores where the racks were—we call them gondolas. With the most ridiculous smile you would ever see, I held my hands out and said, "This much market share." How ridiculous is that? How much market share? This much market share!

Do you know what the CEO did? I didn't realize what I had done. But the CEO stood up and said, "Ladies and gentlemen, do you realize that we have the opportunity to go up to that much market share?"

Then there was a young vice president who later became the CEO, Al Kerry. He's the CEO of Pepsi today. He stood up and told his sales team, "Do you think we can get that market share?"

I've come to realize that I'd become a legend by being ridiculous, but I've accepted who I am. So be it. So, what if I'll never look like a regular vice president? I don't even tell people what I do because nobody believes me, anyway.

"Oh, come on, Richard, quit lying. What do you really do?" they say.

"I oversee the . . . "

"No, no, what do you really do? What do they pay you to do?"

Well, I just give it up. "I don't do anything. I'm still mopping floors."

I want you to understand, there's always somebody who's going to try to steal your destiny, and you need to be prepared.

You need to be looking for it. I also want to tell you that corporate America is looking for you. Your job is to break the doors down. That's what Dr. Andrade did years ago; he broke the door down for us. And then leaders like Mickey Ibarra came in. It's kind of embarrassing: my bio says I've been invited to the White House several times. But Mickey had a key to the White House. Men broke the doors down. Other men got the keys, and you know what they did with them? They made copies and began to pass the keys out. That's what we're doing here. We're giving you the keys to success. We're making room for you. We're telling you that we have your back. That's the new generation.

The rest is history. The new product I created—Flamin' Hot Cheetos—became a bestselling product. I've created twelve other products, but I can never tell that story because people stop at Flaming Hot Cheetos.

I always try to explain, "But I got several other products."

"No, no, just tell us the Cheetos story."

I finally accepted who I was and what my calling was. I knew that I didn't have a career; I had a calling. Out of that, my wife and I were able to create our own foundation. Last year, my family—three boys, two daughters-in-law and five grandkids—fed more than 20,000 people. Last year, my wife and I bought 5,000 pairs of brand new shoes and gave them away to kids who needed them. Last Christmas, we gave away 2,000 wrapped presents to kids who needed them. And people say, "Why do you do it?" This is what I love to say: "Because I can."

The first time I got a call to fly on the corporate jet, the CEO called me up and said, "Richard, I want you to fly from L.A. to New York, to get on our jet to come to D.C. because I want to introduce you to . . . " He began to develop me. He began to mentor me. I'm so happy. Corporate jet! I had never even flown, let alone on a corporate jet. My wife and I did what any Latino would do in those days. We didn't have any luggage. We went to Sears and bought that piece of luggage. I was going up for one day and Judy packed it as if I'd be gone for a month. I mean, I'm like going for one day! I pulled up to the hangar and there were two pilots there staring at me and they're like, "Uh-hun."

So, I say, "Watch it with that."

"It's not going to fit," one of them says, looking down at my suitcase.

Then I go, "Well, you've got to put it in."

I was the first one there and I sat in the first seat I saw. I could see the hangars, I could see the limos pulling up. It was the CEO and the board of directors, and they were all boarding the plane. They all walk by and say, "Hi, Richard. Hi, Richard." Then the CEO, "Hi Richard." For some reason, I almost feel like the bad guy.

The flight only took thirty minutes. Later that evening, I'm sitting there over dinner with the senior vice president of HR, and she's just giggling.

"I just love your spirit, and you don't care, do you? "

"What?"

"I don't know if I should tell you."

I'm like, "Tell me, please."

She says, "Well on the way over here, you sat in the CEO's seat."

The first thing I thought was, "Man, typical Latino, even on the corporate jet I call shotgun." Some things never change.

I remember that after we flew back to New York on the corporate jet, we took a commercial flight out of Kennedy. I sat in a window seat, put my head on the window and started crying. I remember saying to myself, "Again, it's that little boy with the burrito. When am I going to act like the other executives? When am I going to start looking like them? Where will I fit in?"

Now, that little voice that talks to me and talks to you said this: "Don't you realize just what happened? Intentionally or unintentionally everyone on that plane had so much respect for you that none of them was going to tell you that you were in the wrong seat."

The CEO himself said, intentionally or unintentionally, "It doesn't matter to me." He just sent out a statement that if anybody could sit in his seat, it was me.

That little voice said, "Richard, it doesn't matter where you sit. What matters is where your heart is." And I took hold of that. Since then, I've been sitting wherever I want to sit.

Dr. Miles Munroe says, "No one is born successful, but we are all born to succeed." Vision is a source of life and hope. The greatest gift ever given to mankind is not the gift of sight but the gift of vision. Sight is the function of the eyes. Vision is a function of the heart. No invention, development or great accomplishment was ever done without the vision first. Vision is the key to unlocking the gates to what was, what is and what will be. Vision sets you free from the limitations of what the eye can see and allows you to enter into what the heart can feel. It is vision that makes the unseen visible and the unknown possible.

Janet Murguía

President & CEO
National Council of La Raza

May 15, 2013

Janet Murguía grew up in Kansas City, Kansas in a family of nine: seven children and their parents in a small house with one bathroom. Her parents came to this country with very little, in terms of education and resources, but their belief in this country and the opportunity it would have for their family guided them.

Murguía's parents have always been a source of inspiration for her. "This is an extraordinary nation when you think about it. Two people with very few means from a very small town in Mexico worked very hard, sacrificed much and dedicated themselves to the education of their family and service to their community. I am a witness to and, in many ways, evidence of their American Dream." Although Murguía's mother only had a fifth-grade education, she instilled in her children the value of a good education. Janet Murguía attended the University of Kansas, where she received bachelor's degrees in Journalism and Spanish, and later a JD from the School of Law.

She began her career as a legislative counsel to former Kansas Congressman Jim Slattery. She then worked at the White House from 1994 to 2000, where she ultimately served as deputy assistant to President Clinton, providing him with strategic and legislative advice. She also served as deputy director of legislative affairs, managing the legislative staff and acting as a senior White House liaison to Congress. Subsequent-

ly, she served as deputy campaign manager and director of constituency outreach for the 2000 Gore/Lieberman presidential campaign. In 2001, Murguía joined the University of Kansas as executive vice chancellor for University Relations, overseeing KU's internal and external relations with the public, including governmental and public affairs.

Since January 1, 2005 Murguía has served as the president and chief executive officer of the National Council of La Raza (NCLR), the largest, national Hispanic civil rights and advocacy organization in the United States.

I draw on my parents' story, on my heritage and on my roots when I come to work every day. It is what sustains me. The source of that strength for me has been my family—they are my inspiration—and my roots growing up in a Mexican-American neighborhood in, of all places, Kansas City, Kansas.

My father came to the Unites States in the late 1940s. He was born in Oklahoma but returned to his parent's small rural community of Tangancícuaro, Michoacán, Mexico, as a young boy, not even ten years old. With very limited English, he actually came back to report for military service towards the end of World War II. Like most immigrants, he was also looking for a better way of life. He worked at various jobs, a little bit at an ice plant, a little bit at the stockyards and then finally worked as a steel worker. Once he settled in, he sent for my mom and my oldest sister, and they moved to Kansas City, Kansas.

Both my parents could be described as simple, humble, modest people. When my mother and father were reunited in the United States in the 1950s, the contrast between their lives in Mexico and this country was quite dramatic. Growing up in rural Tangancícuaro in the 1920s and 1930s was like growing up in the rural United States in the late 1800s. My father talked about riding a horse to deliver goods for the shopkeeper he worked for, my mother washed clothes and dishes in a nearby stream and ironed clothing with the kind of metal irons that needed to be placed on hot plates. Neither one of my parents were able to pursue an education in Mexico due to very difficult personal and family circumstances. My dad's father died when my dad was sixteen years old, and he had a family of twelve. My mom's mother died when she was fourteen, and she had a family of six. They've been moms and dads for a long time. But you know what? They were awfully good at it. They lived like pioneers during those times, even after coming to the United States.

With seven kids—my six brothers and sisters—my mom didn't work outside the home. But the nine of us lived in a very small house that had only one bathroom. I think we all knew that we had to do a lot with very little. We had basically one room where the kids slept dormitory style. I remember Mary and I would put our shoes and clothes in a box, in a closet, and that was where everybody had their things. When we went to school back then, it was rough, but we were together and my parents really provided for us. I remember Mary and I going to school and we'd have our Monday-Tuesday dress and our Wednesday-Thursday dress and then our Friday dress. We didn't get a phone in our home until I was in the eighth grade. I'm the youngest. My mom washed clothes in a ringer washer with no dryer until I was in college. We knew about going to the *lavandería* and having to dry our clothes and fold them and do all of that. My parents worked hard, and sometimes it was tough going.

Society presented its own set of challenges as well. There were times when my dad was laid off from work and we had to rely on some government assistance. You know what? It was really tough to see my dad go through that period of time, because he was a very proud man. He would take work wherever he could, but somehow, we got through it. In Kansas City, in the 1950s when my parents went to the movie theater, they had to sit in a separate section of the theater. My father and other persons of color had to use separate bathrooms early on at the steel plant. So, I know about the challenges that our community has faced over the years. My dad worked very hard, taking overtime whenever he could. My mom pitched in by babysitting and getting some money there, but then she never made a lot of money.

By the early 1980s, though, five of their kids were in college, all at the same time, thanks to scholarships, work-study and financial opportunities and a lot of hard work. After all was said and done, six of the seven kids received postsecondary education degrees. My oldest sister, Martha, the one who didn't get to receive a postsecondary education degree, is mentally challenged. But you know what? Even though she didn't have her degree, I think that she has taught us the most of all in our family. She taught us a lot about the human spirit and character because Martha worked for more than 30 years at a downtown restaurant in Kansas City, and she took three buses to get to her work. So even Martha, who didn't have her degree, made sure she was contributing in her own way.

Interestingly enough, four of us went to law school. My brother Ramón was the first in our family and in our community to attend Harvard Law School. It was a great moment of pride for my parents. Today, Ramón is a lawyer in private practice in Kansas City and a civic leader. He's one of the founders of the Greater Kansas City Hispanic Scholarship Fund, which now has more than a million-dollar endowment. He's one of the first Latinos to serve on the board of trustees for the Kellogg Foundation, one of the largest philanthropic foundations in the country.

My brother Carlos was the first Latino to be a state court judge in Kansas. He served in that position for ten years. In 1999, he was confirmed by the U.S. Senate to be a federal judge in Kansas after being nominated by President Bill Clinton. Carlos is the first Latino to serve as a federal judge in the district of Kansas.

Then there's my twin sister, Mary. Yes, she looks a lot like me so be careful, because you can't tell us apart. I'm just a little better looking, but you have to look very closely. We'll just keep that between us. It's our little secret. Mary is a judge on the United States Ninth Circuit Court of Appeals after having served for more than a decade as a federal judge in the district of Arizona.

She was the first Latina to serve as a federal judge in Arizona. She and my brother Carlos are the first brother and sister in the U.S. history to serve on the federal bench together. I know that we're capable of contributing and making history.

As for me, I decided to go into government service instead of practicing law, and I ended up working in the west wing of the White House. Looking back, it is obvious that education was very important to my parents and to each of my siblings. Despite my parents' own lack of formal education, they recognized that education really wasn't just a goal. It was a value. I share my parents' story because I believe my parents are primarily responsible for what my brothers and sisters and I have been able to do. It is because of some very basic principles and values that they believed in and that they instilled in us: faith in God, a strong work ethic, love of family, knowing the importance of a strong community, lots of sacrifice and a clear appreciation for what we have and what is offered in the United States. I saw these values played out in so many ways. El ejemplo y los principios que nos dieron were lived out in front of us.

My mom, who only had a fifth-grade education, would be in the kitchen usually by the stove or with dishes in the sink, and here would come in my madrina Virginia, my madrina de bautizo. She was older and didn't know how to read or write at all. She'd carry her letter from her daughter from Mexico, and back then we didn't have all the access to telephones and everything else, and so that letter was her lifeline to her daughter. My mom would clear the table. My mom in her limited reading capacity would read this letter to my madrina and then would sit and write out a letter, even if it was phonetically, back to her daughter.

I think I learned compassion from my mother and about service in the simplest of ways. She'd always be the one thinking about Doña Carmen down the street, who was the elderly lady, and maybe she needed some caldo because she wasn't feeling good that day. She'd send us off to deliver the caldo for Doña Carmen, even though Doña Carmen would always kind of regañar us for not wearing dresses, for playing football with my brothers and everything else. But there we were because my mom had said we needed to go there.

My dad was one of the toughest and most resilient people I knew. He worked for 37 years at the steel plant, where during the hot Kansas summer it was ten times hotter than it was outside that plant. He would cut steel wearing heavy full gear, heavy steel toe boots, the big hat and the big jacket. In those deep freezes that only Midwesterners know, he would also work just as hard and never faltered even if he was sick and should have stayed home.

This is an extraordinary nation when you think about it. Two people with very few means from a very small town in Mexico worked very hard, sacrificed much and dedicated themselves to the education of their family and service to their community. I am a witness to and, in many ways, evidence of their American Dream. I have seen it come true for my family, and for me. It is a credit to them and a credit to this country. They wanted us to know that despite the challenges, in this country no matter who you are or what color you are, there is opportunity if you are determined to find it. My dad had his own way of expressing this. He would say to us, "Remember, you're no better than anyone else, but you're no less than anyone else either." He would remind us, "*El sol sale para todos.*" "The sun shines for everyone." My mom would say, "*Con Dios por adelante todo es posible.*" "With God's help all things are possible."

My parents' words and my parents' values are what led me eventually to Capitol Hill, to the White House, and now to NCLR. I wanted to help families like mine who needed a helping hand, a leg up or just an open door. I had mentors and supporters who opened many doors for me—because no one gets where they are alone. One of those doors led to a job in the White House. I needed those doors opened, because I didn't have the type of connections a lot of my colleagues did. At my first White House meeting—I'll never forget—was at the Office of Legislative Affairs. On my left was a gentleman by the name of Goody Marshall, and on my right was Paul Carey. I found out that Goody Marshall was the son of Supreme Court Justice Thurgood Marshall, Jr. Paul Carey was the son of three-time New York Governor Hugh Carey. I thought to myself, *how did I get here?* The doors kept opening for me during that time.

I was privileged to be able to ride on Air Force One several times across the country and across the world. One moment I'll never forget was when I was privileged to be able to fly in Marine One with President Clinton, playing cards with Bruce Lindsey. I was sitting next to Melanne Verveer; we were flying right over the New York skyline at sunset, at eye level with the Statue of Liberty. That's the privilege that I had been given because I had a chance, and someone opened the door for me. President Clinton believed in me enough to give me this chance to work in the White House.

I know with those privileges come great responsibilities. I know that for my parents, it was always really hard for them to understand exactly what I did. I kept explaining, "I work on Capitol Hill." But they never quite got it, right? You all know. "*Eso ¿qué es? Okay, qué bien.*" "Okay," my mom would say, "*pero ya, vente.*" She'd say, "*Ya, pon todas esas cosas en una caja y ya vente.*" But I would answer, "Well, I'm in the White House now." My mom would just kind of go, "Okay, *está bien, pero, ¿cuándo vas a venir?*" But when I was able to go home and show her a picture of the president, Pope John Paul II and me, she looked at that picture and said, "*Está bien, tienes un buen trabajo.*" Now, that impressed her. But moms have an amazing way of both being your biggest fan and the one who brings you back down to earth. I remember one time, because I would call her regularly at certain times . . . I remember that time and days slipped by, and that was not good. I thought she was going to understand that I was doing work for the First Lady. I explained, "*Mamá, no te pude hablar porque estaba con la Primera Dama y no podía llamarte.*" "Mom, I couldn't call you.

I was with the First Lady, I couldn't call you." And she listened. Then she said, "*Yo soy más primera que la Primera Dama.*"

I'll be honest with you. My parents always had a way of keeping me grounded. In fact, I'll never forget when my mom and my *madrina* Sally, another *madrina*, were talking in the kitchen. Mary and I were outside. My *madrina* Sally says, "*Comadre, debes de estar muy orgullosa de tus hijas. Una es juez y la otra trabaja en la Casa Blanca.*" She would say, "Comadre, you should be very proud of your daughters. One of them works in the White House, and the other is a judge, a federal judge." My mom just sat there and said, "You know what? I'd be really proud if they knew how to make flour tortillas." "*Estuviera muy contenta si supieran hacer tortillas de harina.*" So, we're still working up to achieve my mom's full view of success.

But look, I had the privilege of working in the White House when I know not everybody else got that chance. I did realize that I could compete, not in spite of, but because of my story and what I brought to the table. That was hammered into me when I had my most proud moment in the White House. That was when I was able to take my parents to see the president in the Oval Office. I know some of you have heard this story, but I want to share it with you again because to me it was a defining moment. Here my parents were, their journey had led them to come visit me here in Washington D.C. and to see the president. I remember my mom being so self-conscious about her shoes because she had to do a lot of walking in the city that day, and she said she didn't have her good shoes on. They were so nervous. But I'll never forget, when she walked through the doors of the Oval Office, tears were coming down her face. She said, "*¿Cómo llegamos hasta aquí?*" And the president welcomed them in. My dad stuck out his arm and said, "Mr. President, thank you for giving my daughter this opportunity." President Clinton put his hand on my dad's shoulder and said, "You know what, Mr. Murguía? I hired Janet. She walked you into this office, but you're the ones who got her here."

That is the story of our community. That is the story of our contributions, and each and every one of you knows and understands that story. I am proud to now be at the helm of the National Council of La Raza to work in partnership with so many other champions and with each and every one of you, because, you know what, our journey continues. There's much more work to be done. I know that we can count on all of us working together to get that immigration reform bill done and get it over to the finish line, to get Tom Pérez on the cabinet as Department of Labor secretary, and to continue to do so many other things.

Soledad O'Brien
Journalist, Producer & Anchor
CNN

September 22, 2009

Journalist, producer and entrepreneur María de la Soledad Teresa Marquetti O'Brien knew that with a name like that, she would be dealing with identity issues all of her life. The daughter of a white Australian father and a black Cuban mother, O'Brien developed the skills to stand up for herself very early on. She has used her mother's wise words as a beacon to help her make some of the toughest career decisions: "My mother used to say to us, 'People do not define you. God defines you.'" She learned early on that when obstacles are put in your path, move around them, walk around them, climb over them and get around them. That is why from the time she got her first job as a journalist, she refused to change her name when asked by her television network. After a long career as a broadcast journalist for major networks, she recently founded Starfish Media Group, a multiplatform content production and distribution company to tell her own stories.

When you come into the world with the name María de la Soledad Teresa Marquetti O'Brien, you're going to be dealing with identity issues your whole life. I am a first generation American. My dad is Australian, and he's white. My mother is Cuban, and she's black. Of course, who you are and where you're from matters a lot when you're one of six children raised in an American suburb, where no one can seem to manage to pronounce your name and you don't look like anybody else. But because of my parents, I know who I am and what I am. I'm a mixed-race Latina and first-generation American, acutely aware of how nuanced the conversations about identity have to be.

My parents met in 1958 in Baltimore, Maryland. My mother would tell us the story of how she used to walk to daily mass. She was studying at Johns Hopkins University, and my dad was working on his PhD. She would walk to daily mass and my dad would drive because he had a car. As he drove by, because they sort of recognized each other, he would wind down his window and say, "Would you like a ride?" My mother would say, "No, thank you," because you don't take a ride from a man you don't know well. I was like, "Gosh, even on the way to daily mass?" I mean, if there's a safe guy, it's the guy going to daily mass. But I digress.

So, day after day, my father would drive by, "Do you want a ride?" "No, thank you. No, thank you." Until one day, she said yes, and they decided to go on a date that night. Every single place they went, because it was Baltimore in 1958, and my dad is white and my mother's black, they wouldn't seat them together. Every place said to my father, "You can come in but she can't come in, and you certainly can't come together." My mother told us the story about how she took my father back to her apartment after they were turned down at restaurant after restaurant—she's an amazing cook of incredible Cuban food—and she made him dinner. The entire point of her story was, "See. If you can cook, girls, you can get a man." I kid you not, truly. We took from the story much more than that. I'd like to say I don't make it, but I make it happen. That's the kind of cook I am.

My parents decided at the end of 1958 to get married in Baltimore, Maryland. In the state of Maryland, interracial marriage was illegal; and so they got in their cars, drove to Washington, D.C. and they got hitched. Then, they drove back to Maryland and lived as a married couple. Their friends would tell them, "Whatever you do, do not have children because interracial children will never fit, in this world." I'm number five of six. My mother was a terrible listener every step of the way, which she used to tell us. They also used to say, "When obstacles are put in your path, move around them, walk around them, climb over them and get around them." My mother would tell us, "People do not define you. It's not up to people to define you. God defines you." Then she'd go into a long reason why I'm not going to church enough, "but people do not define you." Because of that, it matters so much that we are here because we get to be the role models for those who maybe didn't have a mother and father like mine. It pushed us every step of the way to be what we wanted to define.

When I was growing up, there was Gloria Rojas. Gloria Rojas was a reporter on, I think, the NBC channel. We're a real NBC family. We'd watch Gloria Rojas. She would do the most Anglo delivery of the news: "At City Hall today, blah, blah, blah, blah, blah, . . . then later today, we're expecting to hear from the governor, blah, blah, blah," until she got to her closing. Then she'd say, "Reporting live, this is Gloria Rojas." I remember thinking, "Wow. If Gloria Rojas can be on TV, María de la Soledad Teresa Marquetti O'Brien could be on TV too." I was being interviewed in Wisconsin, a young woman who is half-white, half-Japanese said to me right before the commercial break before we did our interview, "You know, at my station"—she must have been twenty—"they call me a young Soledad O'Brien." I said, "Girl, I'm the young Soledad O'Brien." Remind me never to hire her at CNN. But I think when I'm feeling charitable, I think what she was saying was people like us don't necessarily fit into that box. Our time has arrived. They don't get to define us. We get to define us.

My sister, Estela, was a couple of years ahead of me at Harvard College. She was a physics major. She would tell me all the time how her professors and the administrators would tell her, "Minorities do not succeed in physics, and women do not succeed. You should drop this major. You will not make it." I was writing an article once for *Time Magazine* about it, so I called her and said, "So you've got a lot of subtle pressures." She said, "No, no. It wasn't subtle. People would call me and tell me minorities don't succeed and women don't succeed. You should drop your major." She went on to get her degree in physics from Harvard, then got her master's in astrophysics, and then went on to get her M.D. and her PhD. She's an eye surgeon now in Harlem. I guess minorities do succeed sometimes in physics. But she was told every step of the way, "You cannot do it. You will not do it." I asked her, "Why did you think you did it, if everyone around you was saying you couldn't?" She said, "Because mom made it clear that others don't get to define us."

My mother had come to this country for an opportunity, and there wasn't a human being who was going to stop her. I remember when I started looking for reporting jobs in 1993. I had an interview in Springfield, Massachusetts. We did the whole tour of the station. Usually, they show the backroom where the equipment is. That means that you're in, you're going to get the job. They don't show you the backroom if you're not going to get the job. The news director sat down, he was like, "I've got to tell you, we only have a spot for one black reporter, and you're not dark-skinned enough. You won't look black on TV." I remember thinking literally, "*Wow, should I be more offended?*" Forget the Latinos. There was no Latino job at all. But the black job: there was only one or I wasn't going to get the one job that existed?

At Hartford, a couple of days later, I had an interview with the news director. It went very well until he said to me, "Soledad, that's such a hard name to pronounce." I said, "Really? I grew up in an all-white neighborhood in Long Island and no one had trouble there." He said, "Yeah. Would you think about changing your name?" I said, "Well, loosely translated, I'm named after the Virgin Mary. Since I don't want to get struck dead by lightning on the way home today because I changed my name, no." But each time, I would call my mother and tell her, "I don't know where I fit in. I can't fit into this box that has been created for what people are supposed to be like." She would say, "Bide your time. People do not get to define you. You define yourself. There will be a place that wants you, and you'll get to do the work you want to do."

She was right. I spent my career in local news, and then went to the network. Lately I've been working on documentaries. I've had a chance now to do stories on people who are undercovered and people who are covered most often one-dimensionally, demonized at times, painted with a very broad brush, or whatever you want to call it. It's really been a joy. It's truly been a privilege to tell stories about people from whom we have so much to learn, who have amazing stories, who have a million stories, for whom four hours is going to be a drop in the bucket for 50 million people who have really interesting stories. And you know what? They're not the ten stories everybody does. They're the other 49 million stories that no one does. What a great opportunity. I need ten hours at least.

I have four small children. It's in part because of them that I am so happy that I get to devote my time doing stories about the community, our community. It's allowed me an opportunity as well to explore identity—our identity as community, my identity personally—and how much that identity matters in a nuanced and meaningful way. Our documentary, *Latino in America*, and the book that goes along with it, is my chance to tell the story of how people of different races and different backgrounds from 21 different countries can all be grouped into this thing called Latino. How does that work? What do we have in common? What does it mean to be Latino today? I got to discover a lot about my mom and myself in the process. My mother who told me, "I will never be interviewed for your book," finally sat. Yeah, toughest, most hostile interview ever: she finally sat down and talked to me about her trip from Cuba to the United States.

Latino, of course, is not simply this grouping of people who speak Spanish. It's not the same as being Hispanic with just hints at origins. It's not about being Latin from Latin America. It's an experience. It's what happens once we get here. And, as you said, we've arrived. We have arrived. The Garcías are one of the pieces we'll do in our documentary on the first night. The name García is number eight, out of the top ten most popular American names in the United States. That kind of says it all right there.

In 2007, the number of new U.S.-born Latinos outpaced those immigrating to the United States. This boom of Latinos is an American phenomenon. Twenty-five percent of kids in this country are Latinos. And we're living everywhere, not just on Calle Ocho in Miami or in East L.A., but in Shenandoah, Pennsylvania, St. Louis, Missouri, and Orlando, Florida. To say that Latinos are the future of this country—you'll hear that a lot—is not enough. We are the present of this country. We're here.

In Orlando, Florida, I interviewed a guy named Carlos Robles who is American-born. He is American bred. He was taking accent reduction classes because he's struggling to get a job. He can't get a job because no one can understand his English. He was raised in Puerto Rico and trying to make a go of it in Florida. It's with his story that we explored the complexity of our country's relationship with Latinos. He is a U.S. citizen trying to get rid of the accent that he acquired on U.S. soil. At the same time, our country has room for a wonderful woman, Marlene Ferro, a Latina living in a Miami suburb. Living in Miami means she's going to throw her daughter a *quinceañera* that is expensive. She is going to find 30 kids to put in her backyard, all of them second or third generation Americans who can speak fluent Spanish and who have been dancing salsa all their lives. If you ask these young people, "Are you Cuban or are you American?" they look at you confused. They say, "I'm both. What do you mean by that question? I'm both."

In Miami, that's okay. It's less clear if that's okay in places like North Carolina, where I interviewed Bill and Betty García. They are trying really hard to teach their kids that there's meaning in the fact that their dad's a Nuyorican and their mother a Dominican. What does that mean? Well, the children push back. Like any fifteen year old, they don't want to be dragged to the art show.

They don't want to study their history. Because they're brown-skinned kids in North Carolina, they think they're black. Their parents say, "Let's talk about your identity. Who are you?" It's a struggle that lots of families have that search for identity. They don't speak Spanish. They can't communicate with their cousins when they come back to New York. Who are they? Where do they fit? The parents struggle and the kids struggle too.

I interviewed one of the sons and said to him, "You mother is offended that you don't embrace her culture. She tries to cook for you. She tries to dance with you. You push her back." He said, "You misunderstand. I'm embarrassed that I can't. It's not me being embarrassed of her. I'm embarrassed of me." That changed everything. Then, of course, there's a story we know, the story of Luis Ramírez who was living in Shenandoah, Pennsylvania when he was reduced to that stereotypically illegal immigrant crossing the border. He was beaten to death by a group of teenagers who were convicted in the end of simple assault, not murder, not homicide. They were convicted of simple assault. His story is clearly the story of how vulnerable so many people are.

You saw Eva Longoria. She's a ninth-generation American. Her people were here before the Mayflower. They beat them out. And yet, at the same moment she's existing, Luis Ramírez is existing too. She, of course, is the star of *Desperate Housewives*. When I asked her what it meant to be a Latina, she literally was perplexed in that same way. She said, "I'm an American. I'm an American with a Mexican heart." She celebrates her heritage and does not allow herself to be reduced to a stereotype about her heritage. That's really, I think, what we all want, anybody wants. It's a very complex and challenging thing, this Latino identity. It's as much about how we see ourselves as how others see us. It's as much about opportunities we embrace as opportunities we push away. Complexity, of course, is most apparent in places where there are high concentrations of Latinos.

I've been to Miami so many times. I gained ten pounds in Miami this year. The food at the airports in Miami. I mean, that's ridiculous. You cannot help but marvel at the Miami that Latinos have built. It's amazing. It is amazing when you think of this sleepy Jim Crow town that it was compared to, to what it has become today. It boggles the mind. Bilingualism and entrepreneurship have made Miami this hub for "bajillions" of dollars of commerce with Latin America.

We interviewed Senator Mel Martínez in our documentary. He came to Miami, as you all know, as a child refugee from Cuba. He arrived at Boys Town, was given a visa and a place to live. He got an excellent education, support and love every step of the way. He will be the first to tell you, it allowed him to rise to one of the most powerful jobs that you can have today in this nation. At the same time I was interviewing him, I was interviewing a young woman, who I'll call Martha since we can't tell you her name, who'd also come to Miami. She'd been captured by the Border Patrol, and she was living at a detention center (which is what Boys Town is now for: unaccompanied minors who come across the border); it's still Boys Town, but a few years later. She was waiting adjudication on immigration charges and had been recently released into foster care. What happened to her and what would happen to her if she didn't get support and a visa? Would she become a Senator Martínez down the road? We don't know.

My travels have also taken me to Los Angeles several times—also excellent food. As you know, L.A. experienced the highest numerical growth of Latinos last year. L.A., of course, is a place where I think, as Latinos, you feel like you've arrived. Everybody is speaking Spanish. Latinos are absolutely in every position of power. And there's not as much question, I think, about what are you doing here. Certainly, when you compare it to a place like Charlotte, North Carolina, we dominate the political scene and the cultural scene. And it's there that I met a young woman named Cindy García. She attends Fremont High School in East L.A. The L.A. school systems did not build schools for 39 years while, at the same time, the population was exploding. Of the 680,000 students in L.A. schools, 200,000 attend class in portable classrooms. After a certain number of decades, honestly, they should not be called portable classrooms anymore. They're just the classrooms.

It is a mirror of what Latinos face across the country. Latinos are the nation's most needy students. They are the poorest, the most likely to attend the most overcrowded classrooms. A study done by the National Council of La Raza determined that Latinos are missing from Head Start programs and preschools. This young woman who we follow, Cindy García, desperately wants to graduate. She fully understands that she will be missing out on the American economy if she does not graduate and move on to the next thing. Half of all the nation's school children by 2050 are going to be Latinos. Cindy García is a metaphor for a whole bunch of Latinos.

If Cindy and all these other students fail to be educated, there are tragic consequences not just for them but for the rest of us as a nation. We lose, not just them—everyone loses. The problems that Cindy faces are very much Latino problems and at the same time are problems made in the good old USA. They speak volumes about why identity matters. She is devoted to her family. She misses school to help her mother care for her siblings. She misses school to translate for her mother the demands of social workers, officials, anybody that her mother needs to deal with. Cindy needs school, but she doesn't go.

She has literally not enough hours in a day to study, and her school is called the dropout factory. Seventy-one percent of the students in Cindy García's school dropout. I mean, think of that staggering number. Seventy-one percent of these students drop out. Being Latina for Cindy García is a blessing and a curse. She works so hard that it is breathtaking to watch her work. And in any other circumstance, this girl would be a star. But she needs support. She wants to succeed so badly, and there are so many obstacles in her way.

Her story is probably the one that stays with me the most. I tell it to you today because there really is no certainty that Cindy graduates. Every week that goes by, we think, *will Cindy make it? Oh, she's going to make it.* No, she's not. Oh, she's going to make it. Oh, she's not going to make it. There is no certainty. And if she does not graduate, we have to understand that it's our loss as a community. We define who we are. We get to change a community and change it for the better, enrich society, embrace education and build compassionate consciousness of our community.

I want Cindy García to have what I had, which was what my parents gave to me when they came, exactly what they came to this country for, a place to get good opportunity, education, support, self-esteem, a fundamental belief that whatever it is that you want to do, you can do it. When my mother would say that to me, I didn't roll my eyes. I truly believed her. I was like, "Okay, I can do it." We have to recognize that Cindy's story belongs to all of us and that we have to pledge to make the Cindy Garcías of this nation a success. As our demographics change, there are a lot of potential Cindy Garcías. Cindy García's problems have to be our problems, and we have to embrace them. We have to make our successes their successes too.

That is what being Latino in America is. It's succeeding, fulfilling the dream and the promise that we came here for, and then turning around and grabbing everybody else and making it happen for them too.

Federico Peña

Mayor
City of Denver

August 26, 2008

Federico Peña is a senior advisor in the Denver office of Vestar Capital Partners, a private equity firm that he joined in 1998. He was formerly the U.S. Secretary of Energy and the U.S. Secretary of Transportation in the Clinton Administration. Prior to serving in the cabinet, Peña defeated a fourteen-year incumbent, William H. McNichols Jr., to become the first Hispanic mayor of Denver from 1983 to 1991. Born in Laredo, Texas, Peña earned a B.A. (1969) and a J.D. (1972) from the University of Texas at Austin and The University of Texas School of Law, respectively. He currently serves on corporate boards and is a Trustee of the University of Denver.

Peña traces his mother's roots back 240 years, where the founder of Laredo, Texas, Colonel Tomás Sánchez was his fifth great-grandfather. Peña credits his parents' emphasis on education and being proud of their heritage as the reasons why he has been successful. He believes that what he has been able to accomplish in his life comes from, "that self-centeredness, that confidence, that feeling that you're standing on a rock because you've been here for a long, long time."

I think my story is very similar to the stories of everyone else in this room. We, in our own ways, have faced obstacles from wherever we have come from and in whatever we have done. In some way, we have persevered and overcome those obstacles. Sometimes we've been knocked down, but we've always picked ourselves up. That's why so many of you are here today. There are millions of Latinos and Latinas all across our country who have done what you have done and what I have done, in the sense that they have gone far beyond what their parents had accomplished and what they ever thought was achievable. Because of that, our nation is great.

Our nation will be greater in the future because, as we know, this nation has always been a nation of immigrants. With the new wave of immigrants whose sons and daughters are winning gold medals at the Olympics, whose sons and daughters are the valedictorians of their high school classes but whose families are then threatened with deportation, we are nevertheless one America. We are America. On Thursday, I will once again be with the immigrants who are going to be marching in the north side of the city as I did three years ago, when 80,000 came here to Denver and marched to the state capitol.

I was born in South Texas. My mother and father had six children. I was the third oldest in the family. My brother, Oscar, was two years older than I was. Then his older brother, Gustavo, was two years older than he was. My mother had triplets in 1948, fifteen months after I was born. As the story goes, nobody had a clue, particularly not the doctor. Please don't quote me, as I might get letters from doctors in Brownsville. As the story goes, my dad was in the waiting room and the doctor came out and said, "Mr. Peña, congratulations." Then he came back five minutes later and said, "Mr. Peña, congratulations again." And you know the last line, right, "Mr. Peña, congratulations again." So, my father and mother had six children in the course of seven and a half years.

The point that I want to make is, like so many mothers and fathers, their main commitment was to us, their children. They sacrificed everything for us. From day one, it was always understood and expected that we were going to excel in school and that we were all going to go to college—which we all have done.

Unfortunately, three of us became lawyers. It was because of our parents who understood their roots, which went back 240 years in Laredo where the founder of Laredo, Texas—Colonel *Tomás Sánchez*, was my fifth great-grandfather. He had ancestors who fought, on my mother's lineage, during the Civil War, one of whom, Santos Benavides, used to ride his horse from Laredo to Austin, Texas, as a member of the first territorial legislature. Because Santos could only speak Spanish, he needed a translator, which offended some people in the legislature back then. In some ways, some things have not changed.

That's the story of how I was raised. I was raised with the understanding that I should always be proud of my heritage, my family and my roots. Whatever I have been able to accomplish in my life, it has come from that self-centeredness, that confidence, that feeling that you're standing on a rock because you've been here for a long, long time. Many of you have been here for a long, long time, particularly those of you from New Mexico who have helped guide me in my life.

After high school graduation, I moved to Austin, Texas, which I thought was a foreign country located 300 miles from Brownsville, Texas, and I entered the University of Texas. It had 35,000 students—a student population larger than my hometown population. When I set foot on that campus, I realized that less than one percent of the entire student body was minority, including African-Americans, Latinos, Native Americans and Asian Americans. Less than one percent of the campus was minority. I can recall walking through the campus from one end to the other and not being able to say hello to one person because I didn't know anyone. But I was there for four years and somehow, I persevered.

When I applied to the University of Texas School of Law, I took the law school standard admissions test. For those of you who are lawyers, you take the LSAT. I am a terrible test taker and I did poorly, very poorly. I won't tell you how poorly. I don't want to discourage any of the young people here. But I wanted to go to the University of Texas School of Law, so I applied. I remember the assistant dean—God bless his heart, he is no longer with us—said, "Federico, you can't be admitted. Your scores are too low. Based on statistical analysis, we predict that you cannot succeed in the University of Texas School of Law. If for some good fortune, with some luck you are able to graduate, you won't pass the bar exam. And so, you're taking a seat in the school that ought to go to somebody else, whom we know, based on their test scores, will absolutely succeed and go on to become a great and brilliant lawyer."

I didn't accept "No." It wasn't the first time that I had not accepted no. I kept bothering him. Every two or three weeks I'd go back and see him, "Come on, Dean. You've got to let me in." There has never been a lawyer in my entire extended family, and I want to be the first. He said, "No. Your scores are too low." I continued to press my case and, finally, a few weeks before school started, when they had I think five slots left for other people, he said, "Well, you've been so persistent and you apparently want to be a lawyer . . . We'll, finally, let you enter the law school."

Fast forward. Irony of ironies, years later I was invited back to give the commencement address at the University of Texas School of Law. I was made an honorary member of the Order of the Coif, and now I'm a distinguished alumnus of the entire University of Texas System. I have a feeling that a lot of you in this room can relate to that story.

I moved to Denver after I graduated from law school. I had earlier passed the bar exam in Texas as I did later in Denver. My brother, Alfredo, was going to law school in Denver. I don't think I knew anybody else. I was on my way to California to continue my civil rights work in affiliation with California Rural Legal Aid. It would have been interesting had that happened, but I stayed in Denver and went to work for MALDEF.

I made the decision not to become a corporate lawyer, but to become a civil rights lawyer because I believed that was the right thing to do. It was in my heart. I was involved in the first tri-ethnic, school desegregation lawsuit in the United States: *Keyes v. the Denver Public School System.* That case went all the way to the Supreme Court and back, and back up again, and back. My responsibility was to represent the Latino students and teachers who were not originally represented in that case, and we were able to do that.

It was an interesting time because that's when somebody named Corky Gonzales was in this city, and he was marching everywhere. He created a lot of excitement in this city and a lot of challenges. When you're a civil rights lawyer doing the kind of work I was doing back then in that tumultuous time—my work was quite challenging. But somehow, I persevered. And we thank Corky for his contributions.

When I decided to run for the state legislature, someone told me I couldn't do that because I was not from Denver. When I moved into my district, there was a gentleman there who had been a community activist for 25 years who was running. I was the outside shot. I walked for five-and-a-half months door-to-door, and I was elected to my first term. At the end of my second year in the legislature, I was elected the minority leader, which is very unusual for a thirty-two-year-old freshman legislature. The election was so tumultuous that the person I beat for that position, who was a great Democrat for many years, left the party and became a Republican. But we did what we could in the state legislature as the minority party.

I left the legislature, and friends came to me and said, "Why don't you run for mayor of Denver?" My response: "Why should I do that? There's an incumbent who's been here for fourteen years. He's got lots of money in his war chest. He has 99 percent name recognition. I have one percent name recognition. My first name is Federico. My last name is Peña, why would . . . " People encouraged me to run, and so I ran. There were so many naysayers. People would say, "Denver's not ready for a Hispanic mayor. You're from Texas. You're too short. You're not very well known and you don't have any money." But I sensed in this city back then what I feel in this country today: this undercurrent of discontent, the sense of thousands of people in this city who wanted to contribute, who wanted to participate and felt they weren't being given an opportunity. I was one of them. I said we are going to bring a coalition together of African-Americans, Latinos, Asians, environmentalists, labor and neighborhood people and gays who had never participated in a mayoral election in this city. We brought everybody together. My theme was, "Imagine a Great City."

The night before the primary election, I got a call from a reporter, whom I will not identify. He said, "I'm required to call you because I'm calling all the candidates running for mayor. How do you think you're going to do tomorrow morning in the primary?" There were seven people running for mayor. I said, "You know, I have this strange feeling. I think we're going to come in first." There wasn't laughter, but there was this silence on the phone for about ten seconds. He said, "But we have you coming in fifth." So, the next day, as it snowed in the middle of May in Denver, we had record voter turnout in the history of Denver for any mayoral race. I came in first.

The next day, after the election, that reporter came back into my campaign office. He took out his little note pad. For those of you who are reporters, you know those little pads you have. He closed it up and he put it in the back of his pants. He folded his arms and he said, "Okay, tell me what's happened to my city." I had to explain to him what had happened to our city. And so, as they say, the rest is history.

We went through a tough time in rebuilding this city. But most of all, I want to echo the comments that others have said. When I decided to finally run for mayor of Denver, I also looked to somebody else. His name is Henry Cisneros, and he was the mayor of San Antonio before I was mayor of Denver. He came here one day to speak to a crowd and, of course, Henry's an extraordinary and gifted orator. I listened to him and I thought,

Maybe there is some way I can possibly run. All of us, in our own way, have been inspired by others.

When I went to Washington, there were some people who said that people with a last name like Peña would not be appointed to the Department of Transportation, because that's sort of a different kind of nontraditional appointment, or whatever people refer to it as. But we were very proud of the work that we did there. I was very proud of serving two departments—the Department of Transportation and later the Department of Energy—and I came back home and started a business. I'm a businessman now.

When I talk to young kids and they ask me, "What should I think about? I want to become an astronaut. I want to become a doctor. But I'm not sure I can do it." I say three things. Number one, believe in you. Believe in yourself, what's in your heart. If you truly believe you can become an astronaut and if you want it badly enough, go do it. I don't say, "It's too hard. You're too short. You're from another planet." Go do it.

The second thing I say to them is, believe in where you have come from. You have a proud history, a proud tradition. It is deep. It is rich. It will give you strength. Remember it and stick by it. And the third thing that I say to young people is, don't forget to seek some guidance from the one above, because there will be in your journey some ups and there will be some downs. There will be some highs, and there will be some lows. And you always need to have that guiding force in you to keep you focused straight ahead.

We have come a long, long way. Each of you in your own way has gone through your struggles and accomplished much to be here today. We're all thankful for the guidance we got from our families, or relatives, or someone who inspired us, who encouraged us and who had confidence in us. Our responsibility with the extraordinary political power that we now have in this country—people like Antonio Villaraigosa and others who fully realize this when they live in a city like Los Angeles—is just starting. It's just emerging.

We already know that the census has advanced the time before 2050 when our country is half minority and *we* will be almost 35 percent of the United States population. With that potential, with that opportunity comes responsibility. All of us have the responsibility to make sure that as our communities grow, as we contribute to our country, that we find a way to do what we can to eliminate the extraordinary dropout rate in our school systems. We cannot advance with 50 percent of our children dropping out of school. It will make no difference if we are the largest population, if we're dropping out of school. It will make no difference if we are the largest population, if our kids are still in our jails. It will do no difference if our kids don't have good jobs.

We are America. Our responsibility, our obligation is not simply to celebrate what we do in this city this week. It's not simply to recognize the great achievements that so many people have made for many, many decades in our country so that we could be here today. Our responsibility is to look to the future and say we have to do whatever we need to do now to make sure that all these young kids do better than we have done and move this country forward; so that they can become the next presidents, become the next CEOs, become the next chairman of boards, become the next astronauts and scientists and Nobel Prize winners. In the year 2050 all of us can say—if we're still around—that we were proud of what we did in the year 2008 because we made sure our community continued to be great in this country. That is our responsibility. That is our obligation.

Thomas E. Pérez

Chair of the Democratic National Committee & U.S. Secretary of Labor

October 25, 2013

Thomas E. Pérez was nominated by President Barack Obama and sworn in on July 23, 2013 as the nation's 26th secretary of labor. He has committed to making good on the promise of opportunity for all, giving every working family a chance to get ahead and putting a middle-class life within reach of everyone willing to work for it.

Pérez's story is the story of immigrants coming to America looking for a better life, looking to help. His parents were born in the Dominican Republic, "My maternal grandfather was the Ambassador to the United States from the Dominican Republic until he spoke out after the massacre of the Haitians in the 30s. It was a brutal massacre: roughly 20,000 people senselessly murdered." And after he spoke out, Perez' grandfather was declared persona non grata. His family moved to the United States and, after his father served in the U.S. Army, settled in Buffalo, NY.

Pérez grew up in family that loved to discuss politics around the dinner table. Throughout his career in local government, Pérez strived to expand opportunity for people. Now in his role as secretary of labor, he is making sure that the American dream is a dream that is accessible to everyone.

My late mother was a real role model for me. She told me years ago, when I was a kid, "Tom, everything happens for a reason." She was a person of deep faith who went to church every single day until her health started failing her; and she always used to say, "Everything happened for a reason."

About the year 2006, I was on the Montgomery County Council, a job that I loved because we were able to help people. We were in the frontlines. I was running for attorney general, and it was a dead heat. It was a three-person race, and we were surging in the right direction. We were just about to get on TV because there were people like Mickey Ibarra and Ken Trujillo and others who had invested in our campaign. We were ten days out of the campaign, and my phone rang. Someone was telling me that the state Court of Appeals, the highest court in Maryland, had just kicked me out of the race on a technicality. I was going 70 miles an hour, and I hit a brick wall that I had never seen or anticipated. It was not one of my better days.

My mother had died roughly ten months earlier, and I remember thinking, *Okay, she said, everything happens for a reason.* The reason wasn't jumping out at me at the moment. She also used to say, "When a door closes, windows open." But I thought I was in solitary confinement. I saw nothing but darkness at that moment and for weeks afterward, because I couldn't quite figure out what had happened. Fast-forward a few months to January 2007, when Governor O'Malley appointed me as secretary of labor. We now had an opportunity to go across the state, building partnerships with businesses and others, helping people who needed the skills to compete, making sure that work places were safe. Now, working with our local colleagues and local government, we were able to address the foreclosure crisis, which had hit so many communities, including Prince George's and elsewhere, disproportionately. We were able to do so much.

Then, a couple of years later, President Obama nominated me to serve as the Assistant Attorney General for Civil Rights, which was the dream job for anyone who's been a civil rights lawyer. In June of that year, Senator Edward Kennedy called me. He only had a couple of months left to live, and I had worked for him as special counsel on civil rights issues. When you worked for Senator Kennedy, you were part of the Kennedy family for life. He called to say, "This is a really important job, and I am so excited for you." I had the privilege of going around the country, expanding opportunity for everyone, and working together to make sure that the corrosive power of fine print didn't result in the American dream becoming the American nightmare for homeowners. We also worked with so many other people on police reform, education reform and so many other critical issues.

Earlier this year, I was literally getting ready to go on a trip to Malaysia to talk about human rights and about how Muslim, Christian and other populations can co-exist. I was sitting at Washington National Airport when the phone rang. It was the White House: "We'd like to talk to you about the Department of Labor job." After I picked myself off the floor, I said, "Well, I'm actually heading to Malaysia." I moved my trip around a little bit to come back a day early, took a 36-hour flight back and interviewed with President Obama the Friday before the inauguration. I was able to get confirmed roughly three months ago, on July the 21, 2013.

I really do feel that we are a product of the American Dream. My story is the story of immigrants coming to America looking for a better life, looking to help. My folks were born in the Dominican Republic. My maternal grandfather was the Ambassador to the United States for the Dominican Republic until he spoke out after a massacre of Haitians in the 1930s. It was a brutal massacre: roughly 20,000 people senselessly murdered. And after he spoke out, he was declared persona non grata. My father was part of the student movement there and he had to get out of Dodge. My parents got married and came to America.

My father went into the U.S. Army as a legal immigrant. Legal immigrants have been serving this nation with distinction since the Revolutionary War. The first fatality in the most recent war in Iraq was a legal immigrant from Guatemala who came here, was undocumented, had his status adjusted, enlisted in the

U.S. Army, made the ultimate sacrifice and received his citizenship posthumously. My dear Uncle Hugh was proud of showing the war wounds he sustained in World War II while fighting on behalf of the United States of America.

My family and my extended family were proud to serve this nation. They were proud of their Dominican roots and their American roots, and they were proud to be here. They were proud to serve, especially my dad. After he got out of the service, my folks settled in Buffalo, New York. They did that for one obvious reason: they wanted weather that was similar to that of the D. R., and they found it.

I sat through a lot of dinner table conversations about politics, because when you've been kicked out of a country and disrupted in the way that they had saw bad things happen the way they had, it has a profound effect on your life. That was the currency of our dinner table conversation: politics and what's happening back home. My folks never went out to dinner. They never went on vacation. "Why would you go rent a house for a week when you own a house? That would be one house too many." That was my parents' logic. We went on one vacation in the last twelve years that my dad was alive. One vacation, because it was unnecessary. My parents also taught us that adversity builds character. The year 1974 was a character-building year, not just for Richard Nixon, but also for Tom Pérez. It was a character-building year because, frankly, if on January 1st you had said to our family one of your parents is going to die, there would have been unanimity that it would've been my mother, not my father, because she had chronic health issues. She went to New York early in 1974 for major surgery, because there was no surgeon in Buffalo with the competency to do it. So, she went to Columbia Presbyterian in New York, which gave her an opportunity to get back to Mecca; which any Dominican in this room knows is Washington Heights, 152nd and Riverside Drive, The Riviera. And so, she had that surgery, came back home and things were getting back to normal.

My aunt, who was living in Colombia with her husband, had been staying with us for a few months because we needed some help. She was going to leave the Monday after Easter Sunday, and Easter Sunday was the first heart attack my dad had. Now, I was the youngest and they thought, *We need to make sure that Tom is sheltered from that.* That was a very laudable aim but a learning moment for me. Tell your kids the truth. I thought everything was hunky-dory and then, a few months later, my dad had his fatal heart attack.

Things were kind of tough, and we had the service in the D.R. My parents' dream had been to raise their kids here and return home. But it didn't quite work out for either of them. They did raise their kids here and they did a pretty good job, because my siblings are all doctors. I didn't become a doctor because I watched my brother operate one day and, after they peeled me off the ground, I decided I needed a new line of work. But that is a true story.

I remember one of the most important lessons my folks taught us was really a Biblical lesson: "To whom much is given, much is expected." And so, when I used to teach in law school, I would challenge my students as the last assignment in the semester to write their own obituary. The reason I asked them to do that was I wanted them to be able to say they loved every job they've ever had. Lawyers are the most risk-adverse group of folks I've ever met. They get into these jobs that are sometimes monetarily rewarding, but not necessarily spiritually rewarding. I wanted them to reflect on what they wanted their legacy to be. I'd tell them, "After you're gone, what are people going to write about you? Don't start thinking about that the day before you die because it's a little bit late. Think about that while you're in school."

I'm very blessed, because I feel like I was able to answer that question with the help of my family and my community. The answer to that was this: I was put on the planet to make sure we expand opportunity for people. When I was in local government, that's what we tried to do. I'm so proud of the fact that the county that I had the privilege of representing has a history of welcoming people, of inclusion, of making sure that the American dream is a dream that's accessible to everybody.

In my federal service, I had been so blessed to have the ability to go out there in communities across this country to address some of the biggest challenges that we confronted. One of the things that I recall so vividly in my first ninety days on the job was getting to go to the 50th Anniversary of the March on Washington, because that really brought together my two lives: civil rights and labor rights. I remember listening to President Obama and other people talk and thinking about the tremendous progress that we have made. Make no mistake about it: we've made so much progress.

As the President correctly pointed out, it does a disservice to those people who died in the process to suggest that we have made no progress. It really does a disservice. But at the same time, it would do an equal disservice if we didn't acknowledge, in the words of Senator Edward Kennedy, "The unfinished business of America," the unfinished business of civil rights and the unfinished business of making sure that everybody has access to economic justice and economic opportunity. That everybody has the same opportunities to build those ladders of success that my parents gave to my siblings and me by focusing on education, by making sure in our family there was no such thing as a vacation, because they were investing that money so that their kids could get to college and do what they wanted to do. That's what we learned, that's what I learned and that's what I have tried to devote my life to.

And so, I have to thank all of my colleagues for their support and President Obama for his support and confidence. I have to say thank you to those folks back in Maryland in 2006 who thought they could kick me, get me down and get me out of a race. My mother was right, everything does happen for a reason.

William "Bill" Richardson

Governor
New Mexico

February 27, 2007

For more than 30 years, Bill Richardson has been a distinguished public servant: a U.S. Congressman (1982-1996), U.S. Ambassador to the United Nations (1997-1998) and Secretary of Energy under President Bill Clinton (1998-2000). In 2008, Richardson sought the Democratic nomination for president, dropping out after the Iowa and New Hampshire primaries. As a diplomat and special envoy, Richardson has received four Nobel Peace Prize nominations and successfully won the release of hostages and American servicemen in North Korea, Cuba, Iraq and the Sudan.

Before being elected governor of New Mexico, Richardson was chairman of Freedom House, a private nonpartisan organization that promotes democracy and human rights worldwide; he also served on the boards of the National Resource Defense Council and United Way International. He has been an adjunct professor at the John F. Kennedy School of Government at Harvard and received several honorary degrees from institutions of higher learning that include Tufts University and the University of New Mexico.

As Governor of New Mexico from 2003 to 2011, Richardson's bold governing style moved New Mexico forward in several important areas, including clean energy, education, transportation, healthcare, immigration, environmental protection and one billion dollars in tax cuts to New

Mexicans. He vastly improved the state's job numbers and improved economic development by bringing the movie industry to New Mexico,
which resulted in more than 140 major film and TV productions. He
also built a light-rail system from Albuquerque to Santa Fe and part-
nered with Virgin Galactic to build a commercial spaceport.

Richardson was born in the United States, raised in Mexico for
much of his childhood and then educated in U.S. schools. He believes
that living his life as a bicultural Latino—living in two worlds—gives
him a unique advantage when running for office in the United States.
Being a bicultural Hispanic has made him sensitive to other points of
views, to other cultures, to other countries, to other ways of getting things
done. That's how you sow respect for each other.

Why am I standing here? I truly believe it's because of my
bilingual upbringing, my mother: ninety-two-year-old María
Luisa López-Collada. I talked to my mother just three days ago.
Here is my only emotional message to everybody. Spend more
time with your mom and dad, especially in the later years, because
you're going to have those remembrances. My mother used to call
me Willito, not Bill or Billy, but Willito. "¿Cómo estás, Willito?"
"Very good, Mother." "Are you still governor of New Mexico?"
"Yes, Mother, I am. In fact, Mother, I want you to know, last Janu-
ary 20, I announced for president." She said, "¿Presidente de qué?"
There, I was put in my place right away. But that was my mom.

I remember those many times at home in Mexico City. I
remember so vividly my mom only talking to me in Spanish.
We'd be at the dinner table, my sister and me . . . only in Spanish.
But my father, actually when he did talk to me—he was a very
stern father—it was always in English. That's how I went to
school, both languages simultaneously, not classes divided, but
half the class would be maybe in English and the other half in
Spanish. You moved between those two worlds. I remember also
dreaming in Spanish. Here I was, eighteen years old and dreaming in Spanish. Then as I got older, the conflict: Am I an American? I want to thank my dad because I wouldn't be a candidate for

president if it weren't for my dad. We lived in Mexico City, my mother Mexican, my father an American. Although born in Nicaragua, he was an American citizen.

So, we lived in Mexico. But my dad was so determined that I'd be an American that we drove in one of those old cars to Pasadena, California just for me to be born, because he was so proud that his son would be a full-fledged American. I was born in Huntington Hospital in Pasadena, then we left immediately. As I ran for the presidency, they tried to get money contributed and asked me, "Well, what are your roots in Pasadena?" I said about three hours. That's it, I have none. "Well," they said, "if they move up the California primary, we're going to be pushing that." There we were.

I remember growing up and loving baseball. I love it. Girls, studies really ranked last. But baseball, I just loved to play. I'd go to the games, and whenever I was in the United States, the New York Yankees and Mickey Mantle and Tom Tresh and Elston Howard— you understand that great tradition of the Bronx Bombers. In baseball today, the best players are our people: Latinos.

My life was a bicultural life, but I was conflicted in high school in the United States. They'd call me Juancho because I was Richardson but my English wasn't perfect. So, I was Juancho. When I would go on vacation or go to Mexico City and was playing baseball—I was a pretty good hitter—I remember somebody yelling from the stands, "Strike out the gringo." I wasn't either. This is a true story.

Later in politics, I always felt that being bicultural, learning two languages, living in two worlds, being Hispanic was an advantage, because we're sensitive to other points of view, to other cultures, to other countries, to other ways of getting things done. You sow respect for each other.

In Sudan, we got the American journalists out; we got the ceasefire with Fidel Castro. We spoke Spanish. I remember we got three political prisoners. The conversation didn't start out too well. I started out in Spanish and President Castro said, "I want you to go to a baseball game." I went to a baseball game with him, and then we had a second meeting. He said, "What did you think about our baseball?" I said, "Great hitting, but your pitching is awful." It was like 14 to 11. He said, "No, no, no. You're wrong. You're wrong. There you go. You're a gringo. You don't know anything. We have good pitching." I said, "Well, you might keep the score down—14 to 11!" So, a little disagreement but a connection started. Then I said, "My God, I see Reverend Jesse Jackson. You gave him a bunch of prisoners. What about me, the Hispanic?" We brought three back, and I was very, very proud of that.

I ran for Congress in New Mexico. Obviously, I'm Hispanic, but I'm not a native born New Mexican. My name isn't López, although it is. I'm Bill Richardson. There are also Native Americans, maybe 12 percent; especially in the primary, 18 percent are Native Americans. I'm navigating between a bunch of very, very attractive important candidates—now Congressman Tom Udall and Roberto Mondragón, an icon in Hispanic politics in New Mexico—and there's me, Bill Richardson. I had to get votes anywhere I could. The Hispanic vote, a big bulk, goes to Mondragón. I get my chunk. We split the Anglo vote with Udall. And then the Native Americans, God bless them, went with me, so I won by 3 percent. Every time I go to the Native Americans, I say, "Whatever you want, you can get it because you remember where you came from."

This is another thing, since we're getting personal. You've got to remember who brought you to the dance. In other words, right now, a governor running for president or whatever. You get a lot of people telling you how great you are, and that nothing is wrong. But I want you to remember those that were with you when you weren't doing so well. That's who your friends are. Those are your friends. That's why Jack Otero and Bobby Garcia got me on the Commerce Committee—your first committee can be key.

Bobby, the Steering and Policy Committee, with members—you have to get the majority of the vote. What Bobby told me was, "You've got to tell this Congressman from Texas whose name is Charlie Wilson that you're going to be sensitive to oil and gas. You've got to do it or he'll vote against you, and you won't get enough votes." Bobby maneuvered it, and I became an oil and gas advocate. What Bobby didn't know is that New Mexico depends on oil and gas, so it was very easy for me. Bobby engineered that for me. I served in Congress as chief deputy whip, the first Hispanic whip.

Now, today, the great thing about Bob Menéndez since he was elected, is he's now chairman of the caucus; he beat everybody, and now he is a U.S. senator. Many of us got in there by our numbers; we got appointed, but it was Menéndez who obtained the highest ranking in Congress. And now, Joe Baca is a whip. He is a big, big, big star in the House. But it was the Bobbys and the inside early guys, Congressman Eddie Roybal—God bless him, he passed away. It was that 1982 year when ten of us came in to Congress like a rush; Texas guy, New Mexico, Arizona guys. Ten of us came in. Most of them are still in the House, you know. We started growing. Now, we're 30, 35 in the House, and it's bipartisan.

I want to just conclude with this. Running for president, let me tell you, it's fun. The world handshaking record, I'm going to shatter it. Many, many times over, I traveled the whole country. I love this country. I just think that the experience of running, making lives better and trying to bring people together is rewarding. "Why are you running? You've got all these other stars." Mickey kind of introduced me today. He called me "the long shot." By the way, I announced four weeks ago. I started out at one percent. Today look at the polls: I'm at eight percent. I'm moving up. I'm moving up. I've got to move up a little more.

There's a second tier. I'm kind of alone in the second tier, with these formidable opponents. But I am raising funds. It's going well. Many of you helped me this morning. Thank you. There are two races for the president, for the votes and for those that fund your campaign because the country is so huge; the media markets are so expensive. You have to strike early. You can't say I'm not going to do well in Iowa, in New Hampshire, in Nevada, and I'll come back in California in June. It all happens right away.

Running for president, I was asked, "You are a Hispanic candidate. How do you use your Hispanic-ness?" I said, "Well, here's how I use it." You know how they put us in boxes all the time? The Hispanics, okay, they only care about immigration or civil rights. They don't care about other issues. The reality is our community isn't just centered on those "Hispanic" issues. We care about jobs, education and the war in Iraq. We're mainstream. We're the biggest market in this country. We're part of the mainstream. You get both political parties. How do you get the Hispanic vote? Oh, well, you trot out the mariachis and you start singing. That doesn't work anymore. They still do it, by the way. You come out and you see how the outreach is and some of the radio acts and stuff. Now it's blogging and Internet. It's so different. Technology and kids using this blogger technology on the Internet, it's changed all.

I'm an American governor. I'm proud to be Hispanic. Am I only running on Hispanic issues? No. Am I trying to get the Hispanic vote? Yeah. Am I going to be the first American president to do more for Hispanics than any other president? Yeah, I am. It's not just our issues. It's not just dropout trends. It's not just having a sensible, comprehensive immigration plan. I said to President Bush, "Mr. President, I congratulate you on North Korea. You talked to them directly. Guess what? By engaging in direct diplomacy, they actually did something. I congratulate you on this agreement. Why don't you do it with Iran and Syria?" He acknowledged that and then said, "I'm for comprehensive immigration. I'm going to push this. I'm optimistic. I'll help because we need to have this happen."

Whether we're dealing with these issues that are pictured as issues that relate to us or they're pictured as issues that relate to the American mainstream, I'm going to be in it. I want your help.

This is an office that is pretty important. I wouldn't have jumped in if I didn't think I was ready. I'm ready. In fact, I think I'm the best qualified for this job.

It's a long journey, ten months away. A lot can happen in ten months. I think the American people, if they see the track record and your passion, and they see that we're going to go in a grass-roots campaign, we're going to be respectable in the fundraising arena. They will give us a chance. I think the most exciting thing about this election is that the barriers are broken. Whether we elect an African-American or a woman or a Latino, those days are gone. The American people want leadership. They want commitment. They want somebody who's going to deal with problems.

One of the things that happens when you run, you lose control of your life. Look at all this. I mean, I have no say in anything I do. I can't eat. I can't have a cigar. I've got to wear these fancy—it's not that fancy—suits. I've got to comb my hair. I got to do things that I wasn't able to do before. But I want to just say to all of you, I thank you, I need your help. We can win this thing. If that happens, we make history.

Adam Rodríguez
Actor & Screenwriter

May 22, 2014

A native New Yorker, actor and screenwriter Adam Rodríguez is best known for his role as Eric Delko on the internationally acclaimed CBS crime drama, "CSI: Miami." Most recently, he was cast as Cookies love interest on Fox's hit series "Empire." Adam currently stars opposite Channing Tatum in the Warner Brothers feature film "Magic Mike XXL" (2015), directed by Steven Soderbergh.

Rodríguez credits his parents with instilling in him a sense of confidence that allowed him to dream big at a young age. Back then he dreamed of being a baseball player. But when an injury cut his dream short, he started taking acting classes as a way to spend time. Unfortunately, at that time, there weren't many actors that looked like him on television or in movies. After years of playing lead roles in both media, Rodríguez now appreciates his role as a mentor to young actors and hopes that his work will inspire another Latino kid to pursue his dream of becoming an actor.

My mom and dad are two very proud hard-working Latinos who always instilled in me a belief that anything could be accomplished. This was possible due to the tremendous amount of love that we received at home. We never, ever lacked for love. My parents were always working, and my sister and I were often left to our own devices. But I knew I was in charge; I took on the big brother/absentee dad role—and I say "absentee" only because he was out working for us. That kind of love lets you know that you are never alone, believed in, cared about and thought about on a constant basis. That kind of love is the kind of love that gives you the confidence to know that you can accomplish anything and allows you to dream big. My parent's love made me feel like there was nothing I couldn't accomplish because, if these people believe in me and love me this way, why shouldn't the world love me this way? Why couldn't I do something that would make the world feel as good as these two people make me feel?

Part of my life was lived, especially in the early years, bouncing back and forth between the Bronx and a town called New City, which is a suburb of Manhattan. I would shuffle back and forth between these two places while my dad was going to law school in Boston and my mom was taking care of my sister and me most weeks. My dad would drive home on the weekends. We had a lot of family that helped out.

I was shuffled back and forth between these two worlds but I didn't really fit in. New City is a town that's predominantly Irish, Italian and Jewish. Latinos, other than the Rodríguez family, pretty much did not exist in this town. There were plenty of times when you were just made to feel different, from the way you looked to your last name. This is not to say the whole place was bad, it wasn't, but it was different from the Bronx, where everybody I knew there was Latino. I found myself not fitting into in either place, which was a weird position to be in, especially for a kid. You have this confidence and love at home, but you don't know who you are yet. You're trying to figure that out, and a lot of your peers sort of influence you determining that.

I felt like an outsider for a long time. I felt like I was alone. That ended up being the greatest thing that could happen to me, because it gave me an opportunity as an outsider to look in, as opposed to being in the middle of it all.

During that time, while I'm figuring out my escape, my babysitter often was a television or a book or a movie. I would get lost in these stories and developed a real love for getting lost in the stories and the people that were telling them, whether they were writers that I love to read or actors that I love to watch, television programs that I love to watch. I would get lost in the morals, for example, that they would teach on an episode of "Different Strokes"—whatever the lesson was just resonated in me. I wanted to be a part of affecting people that way some way.

I didn't even think about being an actor at that time. When I was a kid, I dreamed of being a baseball player. That was the way I was going to reach people. That was the thing I loved to do, and that was the way that I was going to be able to connect with people and one day be able to take care of my family. That was the way I planned to build the kind of life that I envisioned myself having as a grownup. I had a really clear vision that I wanted to reach people, and that drove me. But when baseball went away from me due to an injury, and that dream disappeared, I really had never thought of doing anything else. Then my dad said, "Hey, there's this acting class you should check out." I went and I did it. It suited me; it felt good. At that time, unfortunately, I never considered being an actor because on the television shows and movies that I was watching, there really weren't that many actors that looked like me or had Spanish surnames or really had anything that I saw myself in. I could imagine being the hero, but there was no reality to that. Sure, there were a few Latinos sprinkled here and there, but certainly not enough to make you believe that that was a viable career choice.

I went to this acting class for years and, even though I enjoyed it, I still didn't consider acting for a living. Baseball went away and if I wasn't going to play baseball in college, I just felt like college at that time wasn't really the right move for me. But I enrolled in community college anyway, because it was part of the ticket for me to live in my house at that time. Otherwise, I was going to be out on my own. You know, it was college, military or a full-time job, and I figured college and a part-time job sounded like the easy way out.

One day, I was in this class and doing this scene in front of all of these people, and I just completely lost myself. Somehow in the moment of losing myself, I had this revelation like, this is it! This is what I want to be doing. It felt like something I would wake up and love doing every day. I realized that that was what was going to be the most important thing to me in my life: waking up and having a passion for what I do every day. Acting was going to be that.

From that moment on, I decided, that's what I was going to do. Although it was a long path—getting a job as a stockbroker, working as a waiter and a bunch of other things—I was always clear that the path was set. I never once doubted that I could achieve this. I was able to dream it, and there was no doubt in my mind that this could happen.

As the years went by, I continued to study and perform in plays here and there. Then a guy who went to the Army with my dad and was a New York City police detective ended up being a technical advisor on NYPD Blue. My dad hadn't seen him in years. I was walking into the house one day, and my father was having a fit wondering how this guy that he was in the Army with ended up on television with the guys from NYPD Blue. Through a series of events, my dad got in touch with him and they re-connected. We ended up seeing this man, who became a godfather to me and gave me an opportunity to audition for a show. That was my big break. It was for a show called Brooklyn South. And I got the gig. I went and auditioned against a bunch of other people and managed to get that job. I had just moved out to L.A. It was all brand new to me. I was very, very fortunate.

I knew with that opportunity that that was just going to be the beginning. It was an opportunity to start walking this walk I had always dreamed of, to be this man that I had always envisioned. It was the first moment that I knew that some eyes were really on me, and I made a very conscious choice to carry myself a certain way and to know that in carrying myself that way, I was carrying all the people that I represented with me. I knew that I was that guy now that some kid was going to be watching on TV. Hopefully, he would be inspired to not doubt that being an actor was a possibility for him, if that was what he really wanted to do.

I'm standing here today, almost twenty years into this career, and I realize that by making that choice to carry myself that way, by being consistent in that choice, by never forgetting the things that inspired me to want to do this in the first place, people do take notice, people are moved by this. You inspire people.

And that really has always been my dream, to be a leader. Whether it was playing sports or being the one voice of reason in a group of friends, I have always wanted to lead people to something better, to more. I am humbled and I am honored that you think enough of me today to have me up here as one of those people. I assure you that I will continue to work hard, and if the opportunities are there, wonderful. If they're not, then I'm going to make them. But to continue to be a beacon of hope and inspiration for our community and even for people outside of our community, that this is the example, this is what we can achieve, and this is still in a time when opportunities aren't as prevalent as I would hope they would be by the time I got here.

We've got to keep going. We keep pushing and we keep doing the kind of work that we're all doing here, which is why we show up today. I just thank you all for your support and for the love and the inspiration that you provide me with, because I really don't do this just for myself. I do this with our entire community in mind.

Ken Salazar
U.S. Secretary of the Interior

July 29, 2015

A former U.S. Secretary of the Interior, U.S. Senator and Colorado State Attorney General, the Honorable Ken Salazar has had an illustrious career in law and government. Currently a partner in one of the nation's top law firms, Wilmer Cutler Pickering Hale and Dorr, Salazar draws on his deep experience in energy, environmental and natural resources to lead his firm's efforts on tribal issues.

A Colorado native, Salazar served as U.S. Secretary of the Interior from 2009 to 2013 and represented Colorado in the U.S. Senate from 2004 to 2008. Before his election to the Senate, he served as Colorado Attorney General from 1999 to 2004, and as executive director of Colorado's Department of Natural Resources from 1987 to 1994. In addition, Secretary Salazar practiced law for eleven years at two Denver firms.

Salazar earned his undergraduate degree from Colorado College in 1977 and his law degree from the University of Michigan in 1981. He also received honorary doctorates of law from Colorado College in 1993 and the University of Denver in 1999.

As Secretary of the Interior, Salazar established ten new national parks and ten new wildlife refuges. Salazar is proud that in the creation of those national parks, he was able to help create a César Chávez National Monument in Keene, California because he was "working with a president who understood and honored my recommendation to

him that we honor the history of the migrant workers and the farm
workers." In 2012 President Obama accompanied Salazar to Keene and
*signed the proclamation that created the 400*th *unit of the national park*
system, the César Chávez National Monument.

I want to tell you the story of my grandmother, Antonia, and
my grandfather, Juan. They were both born in 1884. About 1890,
they were trying to homestead a 160-acre property right on the
border of New Mexico and the state of Colorado. While they
were out there, my Uncle Wilito became sick. My grandmother
bundled up Uncle Wilito in a blanket, my grandfather hitched
up the horses to the wagon and they went to the nearest doctor
in the town of La Jara, about twenty miles away.

As they were going to the doctor's office, my Uncle Wilito
would look up with his big green eyes at my grandmother say,
"Ay, *mamá, ay papá, ay Dios. Ay, mamá, ay papá, ay Dios.*" Well, about
a mile before they got to the doctor's office, my Uncle Wilito
looked up at her eyes and said one more time, "Ay, *mamá, ay papá,*
ay Dios," and died in her arms. I always thought about my grandmother, about how strong and how tough she was. No education
but strong and tough. How could she lose a child like that and
keep going? It wasn't just my Uncle Wilito who she lost before
he turned five. In those days without good healthcare, especially
in rural America, she lost four other children before they
reached the age of five through the diseases of those days. I
would always wonder what it was that kept my grandmother and
my grandfather going.

Well, she had faith. She had faith in a future that would be
better for her surviving children, because she had three children
that did survive—my father, Enrique, and his two sisters. And
she knew she had to give it all up to make sure that they had the
best in life. She passed away long before I got into public life, but
she certainly could not have imagined that one of the children of
her only surviving son would someday become a United States
senator or Secretary of Interior and have a brother, John Salazar,

who became a member of the U.S. House of Representatives. She couldn't have imagined that all eight of her grandchildren, the children of her surviving son, would all become first-generation graduates in this country. But she had a faith that you all have and that I have that somehow, we keep up the struggle; that somehow, we keep up the hard work; that somehow, we keep up the organization; that somehow we keep creating this wonderful network of our community; and that the corners around us in the future are going to be better than today.

When I started thinking about running for Colorado attorney general in 1997, I went to the office of the governor of the State of Colorado, Roy Romero, a great friend, a great supporter of mine, and said, "Governor, I'm thinking about running for attorney general." "Ken," he said, "I don't know whether you can win because you have some rocks in your knapsack that I didn't have in mine." He said, "There's never been a Latino elected to any position ever in the history of Colorado statewide, and I'm not sure that you can run a statewide race, but I'll do everything within my power to help you win." Well, when all was said and done in 1998, out of all the constitutional offices, including the two United States senators for the state of Colorado, they were all Republican, except for mine. I became the attorney general of Colorado, defying all the odds that people had against me.

There are so many great Latino leaders around the country, and Mickey Ibarra is one of those people. When I was serving as attorney general for the great State of Colorado, I remember going to Washington, D.C. and seeing the monument as I was coming across the Potomac River and going up to the White House. An elected attorney general, I was fighting to help preserve a part of Colorado that is in the very southern part of the state, a place called the San Luis Valley. President Bill Clinton, the Secretary of Interior and the congressional delegation and I were thinking about moving forward with the creation of the Great Sand Dunes National Park at the foot of the Sangre de Cristo Mountains in the San Luis Valley. I didn't know how exactly to get it done. But I knew that I could somehow just thread the needle and figure out a way of getting into the White House, that there was a guy there by the name of Mickey Ibarra. And because he knew my history and my past, he would make it happen.

Somebody said, "To create a national park like this will take at least ten years. That's what happened in the Black Canyon of the Gunnison. That's what happened in other national parks we've created." Well, because of Mickey's help, President Clinton signed the bill into law creating Great Sand Dunes Park within one year. I'm delighted that one of the proud mementos that I still keep in my office is a picture of President Clinton, a copy of the bill, and one of the pens that he used to sign that into law.

Latinos are present in every state, from sea to shining sea, from Barrow, Alaska, the northernmost point of the United States of America and the Arctic, all the way down to the Keys of Florida. We are everywhere and we need to be involved, we need to be engaged and we need to support each other. We live in a time of tremendous angst, and it is still a great challenge to try to find the right level of inclusion and representation of what I believe is our destiny—to become an inclusive America. We have come a long way, but we still have a long way to go.

I have had the great honor of working with presidents of the United States and leaders of different countries. When I was attorney general, I remember getting a call from a wonderful friend of mine who I had met in law school, a young man who grew up in Toledo, Ohio and whose roots are traced to a little town that only has one commercial establishment on Main Street, Romeo, Colorado. His name was José Padilla, the general counsel of DePaul University. José was telling me about a case that was pending in front of the United States Supreme Court where the affirmative action program of the University of Michigan had been challenged. He asked me whether I would be willing to lead an effort on behalf of the states to make sure that our voice was heard in the United States Supreme Court.

As a result of that call, I started thinking, *Well, here I am, a Latino, an attorney general from the state of Colorado. How can we get some other voices to help us in the Supreme Court? Well, I thought, maybe the person who had written this wonderful article in the* New York Times *called* An Inclusive America *could help.* President Gerald Ford wrote the article. So I said, "Maybe this president will take a call from an AG." I called President Ford and somehow got through. I ended up having this wonderful half-hour conversation with him. "This is why I wrote the article," he said. "Because I remember going to the University of Michigan and, if you weren't white, you were not welcome to be a part of that football team." Gerald Ford was a great star in the history of the University of Michigan football, but he knew that there were people who were just as good but weren't allowed to participate just because of the color of their skin. And so, he says, what the University of Michigan is doing is absolutely right. Then I said to him, "Mr. President, will you help me? Will you co-author a letter with me that goes out to the 50 attorneys general of the country asking them to join in the amicus before the United States Supreme Court?" And Gerald Ford said, "Yes. I'd be happy to help."

When we won that case in the U.S. Supreme Court a year later, there was an opinion that was authored by Sandra Day O'Connor in which she cited our brief among other briefs that had been filed. I will always remember that first part of Justice O'Connor's opinion, where she said that affirmative action and diversity in an inclusive society was something that was an imperative for our country. She said for the national security of the United States of America, it was important to understand, celebrate and support what our armed services were doing to increase diversity within the services; and for that proposition, she cited the brief that had been filed by the former members of the Joint Chiefs of Staff. And then she went on to speak about the global economy, how understanding the world and supporting and celebrating diversity was so important for the United States in these times. For that proposition, she cited a brief that had been written by many of the companies in the Fortune 100 list.

Then she went on to speak about education and how in education it was important to create diversity and understanding among people, and that's why the affirmative action program was important. I've had conversations with Justice O'Connor over the years, and that decision is still one of the most moving decisions in the history of law that I have ever read.

I always think about how we have made progress as a society and yet how much more progress we still have to make. I think about what's happening at our border with Mexico, which is only 1,500 miles and yet has probably a thousand times more security than we have across the northern border with Canada. We have those who would want to build a wall between the United States and Mexico, including a recent presidential candidate who has said so. Yet, I remember Ronald Reagan and others who went to the Berlin Wall and the famous speech that Jim Baker helped write, where he pointed at the Berlin Wall and he said, "Mr. Gorbachev, bring down that wall." And still, you have proponents with their anti-immigrant sentiment essentially creating a wall across Mexico and the United States. That's not where we need to go.

As we think about that particular angst of our country, it's important for us to make sure that we are telling the story of our people. It's important that people know the history of the migrant trail. It's important that people know the contributions that were made in all the wars of this country from the Revolutionary War to World War II. Those of us who lost family members, who were not allowed to be buried in the national cemeteries of our country in World War II, which led to the founding of the American G.I. Forum and its fight for equality in the late 40s and 50s. We need to remind the people of the United States of America about those struggles.

It was a tough decision to be become United States Secretary of Interior because I loved being a United States senator. I loved being an advocate for the great laws that I sponsored and authored as a U.S. senator. I loved working very closely with Ted Kennedy, John McCain and President Bush on the successful passage in the Senate of a Comprehensive Immigration Reform Act. I loved working on those issues because they had a moral purpose and really were defining the future of our country.

After many conversations with the president, the then president-elect and with my friends in the Senate, such as Senator Dan Inouye, I did accept the position of secretary. In part because I was not only the custodian of America's natural resources from sea to shining sea, but I also had the honor of being the custodian of America's heritage. That meant that the passion I brought to the job every day was really a continuing journey that all of you have. It means that, yes, in the creation of those ten national parks, I didn't have to wait ten or twenty years to create a César Chávez National Monument because I had a president who understood and honored my recommendation to him that we honor the history of the migrant workers and the farm workers. President Barack Obama went with me to Keene, which is also the Nuestra Señora Reina de La Paz National Historic Site, in September 2012 and signed the proclamation that created the 400th unit of the national park system, the César Chávez National Monument.

It was because I also knew that President Obama had my back on the border issues that I went to my counterparts in Mexico. I worked closely with President Enrique Calderón and others to create the only border crossing that has been authorized since 9/11, in a place called Boquillas, Mexico, where we united Big Bend National Park in the United States with the border in Northern Mexico and three million acres of ecosystem in Northern Mexico. It was because I cared a lot about that border and about the relationship between Mexico and the United States that I helped move forward what became a historic compact in the sharing of water and water storage facilities, flows of water in the Colorado River into the Mexican Delta in Mexico. It is an accord that was witnessed by President Calderón as Secretary of

State Hillary Clinton and Patricia Espinosa for Mexico signed that accord.

I tell you those stories only because one of the great angsts of our time really is this whole relationship between the United states and our Latin America. After the presidential election in November 2016, we will see what happens with this border and those relationships we have, north and south, in this hemisphere.

There was only two, three, four days perhaps after the November 2004 election when I walked into the White House for a 7 a.m. meeting. There were nine new senators-elect at that time, seven of them were Republican; two of them were Democrat. The nine newly elected senators had this conversation with President George W. Bush, then Vice President Cheney and two of the senior aides for that breakfast that morning. Because President Bush had campaigned very hard for the seven Republicans, he hadn't campaigned for Barack Obama or for me. When he came in from the residence around 7 a.m., he went around congratulating the senators who were there. He went up to David Vitter from Louisiana, and said, "Hey, Vit. You did it." Senator Vitter replied, "I did exactly what you said, Mr. President. I organized out in the rural areas and came back at the very end to New Orleans and I won." The president went down the line and addressed Barack Obama: "Well, Senator, congratulations. I look forward working with you."

Then he got to me, the last one in the line of nine and said, "Oh, congratulations, senator. You're the one that shouldn't have been here and you got away." So, I gave him a big hug and he said, "Los hermanos Salazar ganaron." I actually developed a very positive constructive relationship with him, but I still remember that breakfast because he did know the seven Republican senators very well; he did not know Barack Obama or me. So most of the conversation was between George W., myself and Barack Obama. I said to President Bush at that time, "You are a former governor. You understand the relationship between the United States and Mexico. You understand the importance of commerce and culture and educational exchange. Since the time of John Kennedy, the United States foreign policy has really been one that has been East-West. We focused a lot on Russia and Europe and China, but the Alliance for Progress, which John Kennedy launched in the 1960s, was a new era for Latin America." I reminded the president that when I spent some time in Central America, that at some of the poorest villages of Costa Rica, they would go into these little huts and there'd still be a picture of John Kennedy hanging there because the United States was paying attention to the relationship with the South. I said to the president, "You have four more years, Mr. President. And I'm here as the U.S. senator. I will work on those issues." That is part of that reason why I enjoyed very much working with him on the issue of immigration reform and the issues of our North-South relationship.

But we obviously have to do a lot more. There's a lot more as we deal with this particular angst of our time. There are a lot of other angsts that we have to deal with, including the fact that our education system needs to create more opportunities like those that many of us have had here in this room—which I've had.

As I think about my own life's journey and the leadership and the positions where I've worked with multiple presidents in this country, served the people of Colorado as their U.S. senator, served the people of the nation as Secretary of Interior; I think back to where I started. I think back to El Valle de San Luis. I think about a mother and a father who taught us the way, who didn't have a college degree themselves but somehow understood that education was a keystone for their children's success. My mother, at the age of nineteen—I don't know how many of us at the age of nineteen would do this—found her way to a train to go across the country to work in Washington, D.C. during World War II. During that war for five years, she worked at what was then the War Department and helped move it into the Pentagon.

I think about my father, how he went to Washington, D.C. as well, but then after the bombing of Pearl Harbor, enlisted in the United States Army. And even when he was in his last years of life was so proud of his service to his country that he told all of us, his children, that the only thing he wanted was to be buried in his uniform of World War II, an honor, a wish that he had that we kept.

I think about my uncle Leandro, who never came back from the war because he was killed in Northern Italy. I think about how my mother got the news when she was in Washington, that her brother, two years older and the closest of her siblings, had died in the war. I think about the stories of the American G.I. Forum and it's founding in South Texas because of the fact that we had a right to be treated equally, we were giving it all for our country as we always have, and what all that means to us today. So, your stories are important; our stories are important; my stories are important.

I remember often, as I've talked to people in every one of the 50 states, hundreds of different times, about how inspired I am about who I am and where I come from. I never get tired of telling the story. When I step out of the front door of my mom and dad's house, where my family has lived on that same ranch now for about 150 years, that if I look out to the east, there are beautiful 14,000-foot mountains and they are named Sangre de Cristo. They are the Sangre de Cristo Mountains because, according to legend, a Spanish priest was dying, was seeing the sunrise over the mountains in the early dawn and the crimson red of the mountains, and he exclaimed, "*Sangre de Cristo! Sangre de Cristo!*" That name still rings true there today.

If I look out to the west, the western part of the valley, and the name of those mountains is the San Juan Mountains. My grandfather was named Juan Bautista after those mountains. If you look at the ranch that we have there in the San Luis Valley, the river that runs through it is called El Río San Antonio. When you look at the nearest big town, 30 miles away, a huge town, two stoplights, ten thousand people, its name is Alamosa. And so, you see how the landscape has forever etched our history just in that one particular place.

But it's true, whether you're from Ludington, Michigan or you happen to end up in Chicago after World War I when so many of our people came to Chicago to find a new opportunity, or you ended up in places like Maine or even in Barrow, Alaska. You look out from the point of Barrow and you're looking out at the Chukchi Sea and the Beaufort Sea; they're at the end of the world. It's dark there. Three months out of the year, you never see the sun. The indigenous people who live there live a hard life. But there are people in that little town of Barrow, 800 people, who are actually Latinos. It was always an honor for me to go up there and meet them. We are everywhere. Let us tell our story.

I talked about the values which really have brought us all here, the value of hard work, which if you didn't have it you wouldn't be here today; the value of education as a keystone to opportunity; the value of high ethics to make sure, as my father would often tell us, to keep your nose clean. It's important to keep the name, having high integrity. And most importantly, don't ever forget where you come from and don't ever forget that none of us ever got to where we are by ourselves. I got where I am today because I had leaders like Dr. Andrade who cared. I had leaders like César Chávez and Dolores Huerta who inspired me. I had wonderful experiences, such as visiting Washington, D.C. and standing in awe in 1994, thinking that in one big building there was a guy by the name of Henry Cisneros who was running housing and urban development. I looked on the other side of the street and there was a Department of Transportation, and the person who was running it was a guy by the name of Federico Peña. We've come a long way. Today, whenever I go to the United States Supreme Court, I am so honored that we have Sonia Sotomayor as a member of the U.S. Supreme Court. We've come a long way. And it's those values that continue to drive us to succeed.

María Elena Salinas

News Anchor
Univision

September 10, 2015

One of the most recognized and influential journalists in the United States, María Elena Salinas describes herself as an advocate journalist whose mission it is to empower Latinos. But despite all their gains, many Latinos remain disenfranchised from mainstream America. Salinas began her journalistic career as a reporter, anchor and public affairs host for KMEX-34 in 1981. Her insightful reporting on the impact of daily news to the increasingly growing Hispanic community in Southern California quickly earned her the credibility that would lead her to the anchor chair of the national Spanish language news program, "Noticiero Univision" in 1987.

Her reputation as a serious, objective and highly trustworthy journalist has garnered her universal respect and allowed her to secure high-profile interviews with prominent global figures, ranging from Latin American heads of state to every U.S. president since Jimmy Carter. In 2004, Salinas was a moderator of the first-ever bilingual national Democratic presidential candidate debate on Hispanic issues. Three years later, she co-hosted the first-ever Democratic and Republican presidential candidate forums in Spanish on the Univision Network

Salinas has been a spokesperson for "Ya Es Hora" for many years, motivating Latinos to come become citizens, register to vote and come out to vote. Salinas has dedicated her whole career to informing and empow-

ering our community and now is even more determined than ever to
advocate for the Latino community.

There are two different sets of challenges that I have faced: one as a woman in the news business and the other as a Latina journalist.

As a woman, the biggest challenge is dealing with machismo, sexism and the double standard, however you want to call it, but it does exist in our industry as it does in our culture, unfortunately. If it's true that women have to work twice as hard to get half of the recognition that men do, women who work in Spanish-language media have to work three times as hard to get one-third of the recognition that men do. But the good news is that we can because we have that God-given ability as women to multitask and do many things at the same time—we learned it at home. I know, at least I did.

My father was a brilliant man. He was a wonderful, loving, caring man, but he was kind of old school. He believed that the woman's place was in the home. We have to understand that he was born in 1909; so it was the sign of his times. He believed that it was important to educate his daughters so that they could become good wives someday. Yes, he taught us morals and he taught us values, things that were very, very important to him. On the other hand, there was my mother, my mother who worked and worked and worked and worked. She was a hard-working woman, a seamstress. She worked long hours behind the sewing machine and cutting table, and was the best mom that anyone could ever want to have. We were very poor at that time but somehow, we never felt that there was anything missing in our lives. We led a happy life.

When I bring my daughters to Los Angeles and take them to the place where I used to live—it's right across the street from Sports Arena on Figueroa—it just makes me feel like I'm at home. I don't care if I get stuck on the 405. I don't care if there's smog or traffic. I just feel good. It just feels like I'm home. When

I see Figueroa, I say to myself, "My God, that's where I grew up." That house we used to call "La Casa de las Cucarachas" was our apartment. When I'd wake up in the middle of the night in my closet—because my bedroom was a walk-in closet—I'd go to the kitchen, boom and *cucarachas por todos lados*. So, now, the "La Casa de las Cucarachas" is a parking lot. But still, when I drive by there, I have those memories. I really thank my mother for never allowing us to realize that we were poor, that we were missing anything, that there was anything lacking in our lives. We were just very happy and we had a very good example in them.

You know, growing up in a home with an intellectual dad and a hardworking mother kind of prepared me for what I do, for a career in journalism. I inherited from her a strong work ethic and from my dad a social conscience.

I've always said that women can do everything men can do, and we do it better because we do it in high heels. Really. I mean, can you imagine Jorge Ramos being pushed out of Trumps' news conference wearing stilettos? I don't know if he would handle that very gracefully. Jorge has the fight with Trump, and I'm the one that gets the hate mail. They tell me, "Go back to your country. Go back to Mexico." Here I am in L.A., the city where I was born, in the community where I was raised, in a country that I love and that I owe loyalty to. It's incredible that I still have to prove that I'm an American. I'm an American. I'm a Mexican American. Hyphenated or not, I'm an American. I'm as American as apple pie, even if I eat the apple pie after a nice plate of *chilaquiles*, which is my favorite breakfast.

Anyway, so that leads me to the challenge that I have faced as a Latina journalist.

Thirty-four years ago, I started working at Channel 34. Thirty-four, the magic number. It's a good number. Things were very different then than they are now. Some are some are not. KMEX was a small station, considered by many a low-budget, low-quality station that no one watched except for recently arrived immigrants. As a rookie reporter I covered politics, and there are some people in this room who remember that and whom I interviewed during that time. When I covered politics, I remember going out and trying to get interviews. The kind of response that I would get, especially from candidates for national office, was, "You're from Channel thirty what?" They didn't know we existed. The picture became clear to me when I realized that they didn't know *we* existed because we were not participating in the political process.

As many of you know, in the early 80s in Los Angeles, although we were 25 percent of the population, we had no political representation. Not in city hall, not on the board of supervisors, not on the board of education. So when a seat on the city council opened up all of a sudden, there was the possibility of a Latino being elected, and there was a Latino running. So I went out and I did interviews on the street. It was in the Boyle Heights area, I remember. I interviewed sixteen people and out of those sixteen people, fifteen people were not voting. They didn't know there was an election. They weren't participating for whatever reason. They weren't registered. They weren't legal. For whatever reason, but they were not voting. In fact, and I told my news director, Pete Moraga, *que en paz descanse*, that I couldn't do the story because no one was participating in the election. How could I do a story about whom they were going to vote for if they weren't going to vote? He explained that my story was right there in front of me. We don't have political representation because we're not participating, because Latinos are still disenfranchised from mainstream America. Not only did it give me a good journalistic lesson, but it marked my career. It set the tone for what I knew would be my mission: the political empowerment of Latinos in the advancement of my community. I knew from that moment on that my reporting had to go above and beyond the daily news. My reporting had to include informing Latinos of their rights, but also of their responsibilities in what was to many their newly adopted country.

There were about fourteen million Latinos in the United States at that time. Fast forward three decades, and we are now 55 million Latinos. Los Angeles is about half Latino, about 50 percent Latino. We have plenty of political representation at all levels. KMEX is now the number one station in the country, regardless of language. I'm no longer the rookie reporter trying to explain to politicians why Spanish-language media are relevant. Yes, we've come a long way. We in Spanish-language media have grown hand-in-hand with the Latino community. No more low-quality, low-budget stations that nobody watches. We compete with mainstream media in quality and in quantity of viewership. Our audiences have become more sophisticated and more demanding. We don't want to keep it all to ourselves. We want to share it with those who are not lucky enough to speak Spanish or understand Spanish.

You know, there are so many people who have worked so hard for so long to defend the rights of Latinos; elevate our image; highlight our many contributions to be recognized as an integral part of society. And it's worked. Look at how many of you are here representing big corporations; how many of you are here as elected officials or appointed officials; how many of you are running a business or leading a foundation. Now, high school dropout rates among Latino students have dramatically dropped, and more and more Latinos are going to college, thanks to the work of many of you.

In politics, our influence has also been felt. I now see and I've seen in the past couple of decades how just about every major campaign includes staffers to work with the Latino community for Latino outreach or deal—"deal," that's an interesting word—with Spanish-language media. I'm not saying that they love us now or that we have a love affair with the campaigns and with the politicians, but they are paying attention to us because they know that they can't win an election without Latinos. They know that the best way to get to Latinos is by having respect for them and by having respect for their language.

You know, there is so much to celebrate and so much to be proud of. Unfortunately, it's not all good news. We've been reporting these days how disproportionate the number of Latinos are arrested and end up being victims of police brutality. Tens of thousands of families have been separated by deportation. Thousands of Central American kids have been separated from their families and have been jailed, detained at the border. Sadly, there's one thing that through all of our hard work we have not been able to overcome or to change: that is racism.

You know, we don't really have to worry about that guy who comes out and says immigrants are criminals, drug dealers and rapists. He's eventually going to disappear. I'm convinced. I'll bet on it. I'll put my money on it. But we do have to worry about the millions who buy it, who support him and who agree with him and who keep him at his current levels in the polls. He's not there because of fake numbers. He's there because there are actual people who believe what he's saying and who have those pent-up feelings and think that now it's okay to verbalize them and to show them. Those are the people we need to worry about.

The political climate for Latinos has definitely suffered a setback. This is a new challenge for you as community leaders and also for me as a journalist and for many of my colleagues in Spanish-language media. You, of course, need to continue leading by example, and I as a journalist need to continue to denounce injustice and oppression when I see it, calling prejudice and discrimination by its name, to question authority, and to condemn abuse. I can't be a bystander, and I won't. I need to tell success stories of people like you in this room, and I also need to tell the stories of those who are victims and are rejected by society.

This has been a good year for me journalistically. I've been very lucky to win three awards: a Gracie Award, a Walter Cronkite Award and a Peabody Award. And now I'm nominated for an Emmy Award. Thank you. And it's all for a program that I did last year, the children's border crisis, *Entre el Abandono y el Rechazo, Between Abandonment and Rejection*. By the way, that's a name that one of my bosses didn't like. He said, "No, it's too long. No, it's too convoluted. No, people won't understand." Well, when I came back from my journey to Central America, I knew that that was the only possible title, because when you talk about these kids, you understand that they are *entre el abandono y el rechazo*. Abandoned by society, by their government, sometimes by their families, and rejected in a country that is not willing to take them in and open the door to the land of opportunity. But I'm not telling this story to brag about my accomplishment, but because of the important meaning of these awards. You know, the Peabody's are given to stories that matter. There are seventeen judges, and they all have to agree; it has to be unanimous. They all agreed that mine, along with the other awardees' stories, mattered.

As far as the Walter Cronkite Award is concerned, this is what was said about my story: "It was balanced and revealing reporting from the point of view, not of politicians, but of families in their countries of origin which brought viewers face to face with women and children directly affected. This is a kind of story often left out of the immigration debate." This is what the Walter Cronkite Committee said about my story.

While mainstream media was focusing on the political battle at the border with this issue, where politicians were accusing each other of causing the crisis and the children were being put into detention centers or deported, my crew and I went to Guatemala and Honduras and El Salvador and showed the conditions of violence, poverty, drug wars and gang-infested neighborhoods that drove these kids out of their countries. This was a humanitarian crisis that needed a human face; it wasn't just a political debate.

Now, there's been a lot of talk lately about advocacy journalism. I know that we are accused of being advocates. We're not journalists, they say, we're advocates, as if it was an insult. You know, like when they say, "You're liberal. You are a liberal," and you say, "Eh? So, what? Are you trying to insult me?" Okay. So, when they say, "You are practicing advocacy journalism," I don't feel insulted by that. I don't feel insulted because, wasn't that what they said about Rubén Salazar when he reported on the injustice toward the Mexican-American community, first in El Paso and then in Los Angeles many years ago? What an honor to be in the same category as Rubén Salazar.

I believe that reporting the trials and tribulations of immigrants is not advocating. It's contributing to a healthy debate on the issues that otherwise would sound like a monologue with everyone accusing Latinos for all the ills of this country. Now, I've been reading a lot about Rubén Salazar in order to gain some perspective, especially on what's going on right now. I found an interview that was done by Bob Navarro with Rubén Salazar. When he left his job at the Los Angeles Times—he left his job as a reporter and went to work for KMEX Channel 34—they couldn't understand why he would do that, why he would leave such a reputable job to go work for a station, as I said before, that nobody watched, low-quality, low-budget.

This is what he asked, this is the exchange. What Bob Navarro was telling him during that interview was that Salazar was becoming an advocate because that's what Spanish-language TV did: advocacy. Three months before Rubén Salazar was killed, Bob Navarro asked, "But is advocacy the name of the game? Can you work as a functional day-to-day reporter in the position of advocacy?" And this was Rubén's response: "I'm only advocating the Mexican-American community just like the general media is advocating really our economy, our country, our way of life. So, I'm just advocating a community, which, by the way, the general community has totally ignored. And so, someone must advocate that because it's easy for the establishment to say, 'Aren't we all the same? Aren't we all Americans?' Well, obviously, we're not. Otherwise, we wouldn't be in the revolutionary process that we are now."

Can you believe that was 45 years ago? Forty-five years ago and here we are having the same conversation in this country. Well, some things have changed and some things have not. We're not the same Latin community that we were in the 60s and 70s or even the 80s when I started my career as a reporter. *Hoy, sí, tenemos voz y voto, y por eso ahora, sí, haremos la diferencia.*

You know, there's a silver lining to all this and to this climate of immigrant bashing. It has united the community in a way that I have not seen in many, many, many years. Latinos are finally realizing that they have to take control of their destiny. More than ever I see Latinos motivated to go out and vote. I have been a spokesperson for "Ya Es Hora" for many, many years, motivating Latinos to come out and become citizens, and if they qualify to register to vote, to come out and vote. Like I said, it's been my mission. I dedicated my whole career to informing and empowering our community, and I feel privileged to have had that opportunity. But my mission is not over. Now we have to start again. But it's okay. I'm not afraid to start over again. I'm not afraid of work. My momma taught me how to work. She gave me a good work ethic. I'm ready to continue taking on the challenge.

Ricardo Sánchez

Lieutenant General
U.S. Army

September 22, 2010

*Retired U.S. Army Lt. General Ricardo Sánchez was the command-
er of coalition forces, responsible for all military activity in Iraq from
2003 to 2004, the period immediately following major combat during
Operation Iraqi Freedom. When Sánchez relinquished command of the
troops in Iraq to General George Casey in 2004, investigations into tor-
ture at Abu Ghraib prison were being conducted. That scandal and the
capture of Saddam Hussein played out on Sánchez's watch.*

*Sánchez grew up in Starr County, deep in South Texas and one of the
poorest counties in the nation. At the age of fifteen, when the Army Junior Reserve Officer Training Corps came to his high school, he immediately signed up. From his humble beginnings and throughout his life,
Sánchez understood the value of perseverance and never accepting defeat.
Sánchez chronicled his experiences in his book,* Wiser In Battle: A Soldier's Story, *in which he relates key events in his life and military
career with a special emphasis on lessons learned that prepared him for
his leadership role as coalition commander in Iraq.*

I have done absolutely nothing extraordinary in my life.
What I have done has been driven by the oath of office that made
me a soldier. That oath demands loyalty to our Constitution and
has as its foundation in a very fundamental commitment to do

our duty. As Robert E. Lee said, "Duty is the sublimest word in our language. You should do your duty in all things. You can never do more. You should never wish to do less." I pray that I have lived up to my professional oath.

I am an old soldier who is blessed with commanding warriors from 40 different countries over the course of my time leading international forces in battle. I am a husband who has been tolerated for almost 37 years by a beautiful wife from South Texas. I am a father who has tried to instill values, character and patriotism in his children and blessed with two daughters—I have four children—with my two daughters, the oldest of the family, having volunteered to go to Iraq as members of the Army and Air Force Exchange Service because it was their duty to serve their country, not because they had to go.

And now finally, María Elena and I have entered the next amazing phase of our lives. We are grandparents. Don't ask me to show you a picture of my granddaughter because I've got about 320 of them in my iPhone, okay? It'll take you about 30 minutes to go through them all, the latest one from yesterday.

Given my beginnings, the odds must surely have been against me. But I didn't know what the odds were as I grew up in Starr County deep in South Texas, the poorest county in the nation, back then when I was growing up and pretty much still so today. By any standard, in spite of all of my challenges, the Lord has blessed me with success, happiness and friendships that go well beyond anything I had a right to dream of when I was young. I grew up in a very simple world where the simplest things in life were often times very hard to come by: a hot bath in winter, a new pair of shoes during the school year, a second-hand sports coat and warmth in our home. I learned to appreciate the simplest things in life at a very early age. Joy came from winning at marbles, the rare restaurant meal and a new family car, which I would find out later was over ten years old when my father bought it.

Economic opportunity for me was getting a job as a custodian or a gardener so that I wouldn't have to pick cotton. In fact, I was such a lousy cotton picker that I made more money sweeping stores and gardening than I ever made in the cotton fields. My pay was $1.50 a week working two jobs as a custodian and errand boy. The most I ever earned in a week picking cotton was $0.75. I was blessed with a mother who valued education even though she struggled until middle age to get her high school GED. I remember all of us walking to the high school campus and playing in the schoolyard while she attended night classes. This was a first example of perseverance that I remember.

My first personal challenge with perseverance came when my fifth-grade math teacher told me, in front of all my peers, that I was a dummy and would never do well in math. Maybe this was a motivation technique back then, but I'll tell you very honestly, I was peeved. Okay, but it worked. After that incident, I told myself that never again would I be embarrassed by anyone in that manner and especially not in math. I took away the lesson that I had to work extra hard to prove myself worthy; and probably the most impactful lesson that I learned was that I had to prove wrong those that had very low expectations of me. This would prove critical because that was the stereotypical environment that I would face immediately upon entering the Army. Nobody expected Hispanics to succeed in the officer corps.

The value of perseverance and never accepting defeat was reinforced later when I went to see the high school counselor to get help in completing an application to the military academies. Instead of helping me—and I can hear it as clear today as the day she said it—she said, "What you need to do is you need to go be a welder just like your father." She didn't help me. With the help of my junior ROTC instructors, Sergeant Grigsby and Major Marshall, I was awarded both Army and Air Force four-year ROTC scholarships, and also nominations to West Point and the Naval Academy.

Many took credit for helping. Teachers and counselors have a special responsibility to encourage young people, instill confidence, set high expectations and praise them in order for them to succeed, but it is ultimately the parents that must accept the responsibility for their failures, their attitudes, their successes and their motivations. Our society must recapture the focus on education that has been slipping away from American society if we are to retain our greatness as a nation. I hope that I have taught my children, and I hope to teach my grandchildren and all those that I have been blessed to influence that they must dare to dream of greatness, that they must never allow anyone to keep them from realizing their dreams. Many will try but all must fail. You can control your destiny, but it requires unrelenting perseverance and a never-accept-defeat approach to life.

Now, also during my early days in Rio Grande City, I learned that character, family and love of country were important. My parents knew that doing the right thing all of the time was important. When I made a commitment, I was expected to follow through regardless of how difficult it was. Facing the consequences of my actions was not negotiable. Integrity was absolute. We were expected to tell the truth. Somehow my parents always knew when I had gotten into trouble before they asked us about it. Lying was futile and made the consequences more severe. The lesson for me was clear: Always do the right things, even when no one is watching because someone will be—those damn neighbors.

This is a definition of discipline that is embraced by many but adhered to by few. All of us are fallible and will sometimes fail in this quest, but this should not deter us from constant pursuit of this nearly impossible goal. I have never forgotten that a man of character is valued. Only you can compromise your integrity. If you choose to compromise your integrity, then it's gone forever.

When I was in the throes of dealing with Abu Ghraib, I sought counsel from some of the most senior general officers that are alive today, those that I had worked with. I was told by a very senior general, whose name all of you would immediately recognize, that I was too honest for my own good. Unfortunately, I knew of no other way to live my life. The life lessons and values that I learned in South Texas were indelibly seared in my soul as I transitioned after college into a world that was foreign, complex and unforgiving. I had never seen a black person until I was a senior in high school. English was a second language. Discrimination was not a part of my life because all of us were Hispanics. Ninety-nine percent of us were Hispanics in Rio Grande City, and the five or six Anglos that were in my senior class spoke Spanish perfectly for survival.

Service to our country was this idealistic notion that was the most likely avenue to escape poverty. Very quickly, María Elena and I learned that American society was still struggling with immigration and non-discrimination. What I didn't know was that I was entering a profession, which has set the standard for equal opportunity and non-discrimination for over two decades at that time. I would live a sheltered life.

In my initial assignment, I very quickly understood what it was to be a minority, a Hispanic and a non-West Point graduate, when I was told by my commander that my first efficiency report was going to be about 10 percent lower than the average because of where I had come from. He expected that it would take me about six to eight years, half of a career, in order for me to catch up with the rest of the junior officers in the unit. I didn't know any better. I didn't know to complain. What I did know was that I had to work relentlessly and a hell of a lot harder if I was to have a chance of success in that unit.

After being in the unit for about eight months, I was rewarded with the lousiest job in the unit, dining facility officer, because I had volunteered in my quest to improve myself to serve on an inspection team that found gross problems with the unit's dining facilities. Back then, we called them mess halls, and they were truly a mess. But the commander told me, "Well, Lieutenant Sánchez, you found the problems, now you get a chance to fix them." I did. After almost two years, I had to serve as a staff officer, upon assignment to the operations staff, I was given a desk in the corner with duties that consumed about one to two hours a week. I was reviewing training schedules, that was my sole duty, and that was if I took my time.

I volunteered for everything in sight. After four months, I was nominated and selected to be an aide to one of the general officers in the 82nd Airborne Division. On my exit call, my boss, a captain at that time, told me that he had fought very hard to keep me from being assigned to his section because all of his experience with Hispanics up to that point had been bad. The commander had forced him to give me the job. It all became clear, the stereotypes, the prejudices, the low expectations of Hispanics were deeply embedded within the officer ranks, and it would take a couple of generations for us all to completely overcome those biases. There was no question that if I was to succeed, I would have to demonstrate exceptional commitment, and my duty performance would have to go way beyond what was expected of an average officer.

I was doubly disadvantaged: I was a Hispanic and from an ROTC source of commission. This barely changed during the course of my career. And by the way, that boss and I are good friends to this day. I admired him in retrospect because he had the courage to sit in front of me and tell me that he had fought real hard to keep me from joining his team, but then after four-and-a-half months, he had been the one who personally recommended me to be the aide-de-camp to the number two general officer in the division.

These experiences were never far from my mind as I maneuvered my way through the challenges of being a professional warrior. Without the ability to share experiences, problems and successes with a fellow Hispanic officer created significant problems for me, and I never had a Hispanic role model. In my initial assignment, I served with a Puerto Rican officer but did not have a Hispanic officer in the same unit again until about fifteen years later. I did not serve with a Hispanic of higher rank until I was a colonel in 1993, twenty years after I had joined the Army.

Along the way, the need for adaptation, flexibility and introspection was ever present. Immersion into the culture and value systems of the military was indispensable to my success. What I struggled with was the different perspectives and approaches that my heritage and my cultural values drove me to and what was necessary for success. At times, they were competing demands.

One cannot deny that there is a need for mentors and role models who are willing to assist our minority subordinates in understanding and helping them work through the challenges of our profession. Without Hispanic mentors, I had to rely on those superior officers who had embraced, truly embraced the value system of the Army and who had discarded their biases that still existed in the general population of American society. Fortunately, I met some along the way who understood that I needed professional guidance. They also understood that my perspectives might be slightly different. They underwrote my mistakes.

Having served with great warriors, such as Robinson, Boyle, Eddins, Hausch, Meigs, McCaffrey, Wallace and others, I learned that the most desirable trait in a warrior was courage. Now, you might ask, "Okay. So, what's new for a warrior?" I'm not talking about physical courage. Because I learned during my time in uniform that in battle, a soldier does his duty and his reaction to adversity is instinctive, sometimes resulting in amazing feats of physical courage and sometimes resulting in cowardice. However, the greatest challenge for us is displaying moral courage, and this is applying it across every profession.

Moral courage is that indispensable characteristic of a warrior that demands selflessness when faced with a need to consciously decide whether you will stand up for what is right, knowing all along that all of the possible personal consequences are unfavorable. Will you be willing and able to weather the storm that will inevitably follow? Now, moral courage is an uncommon trait, virtue, during the toughest of times and it is the greatest challenge for most of us.

Many encouraged me to speak out during the Fall of 2007 against the strategy that had gone awry, but no one was willing to stand up and be counted in the maelstrom to follow. Now, Robert E. Lee stated that true patriotism sometimes requires a man to act exactly contrary at one period to that which he does in another, and the motive which impels in them the desire to do right is precisely the same.

Now, very early on, I learned that a warrior must always control the high ground. This is a life lesson for all since it applies to all that we do. As we face challenges, we must never leave the moral high ground. You must have the commitment and faith to stay on that moral high ground knowing that you will prevail. There will be many anxious moments and some very tough seas to navigate, but in the end, your conscience will be clear. As Dr. Martin Luther King stated, "However frustrating the hour, it will not be long, because truth crushed to earth will rise again, and no lie can live forever."

Now, if you stay on that moral high ground, all controversy surrounds you, there will be many with opinions and many will express them freely, especially the media, but few will be informed and even less will know the truth; you must have the patience, the courage and the willingness to stay out of the fray because you cannot win.

As a young captain, one of my bosses told me, "Never wrestle with a pig because you'll both get dirty and the pig will love it." I never forgot that. That was Colonel Watha James Eddins. When you are engaged in controversy, "You are like a wounded zebra on the Serengeti. The herd is mildly interested in your survival. Their first priority is the protection of the herd. But if you survive, they will bring you back into the herd." This was a description given to me by one of those generals I sought counsel from while dealing with Abu Ghraib. This is a very accurate metaphorical comparison, but it must not deter you if you find yourself in those situations.

Now, without question, the greatest challenge for a military leader in high command lies in the politics of war. This isn't surprising, and all Americans should understand it since war is an extension of politics. The American way of war is fractured because modern war demands the integration and the synchronization of all elements of national power, and we as a nation have not quite figured out how to do that effectively. The challenges of interagency operations oftentimes overwhelm and undermine our war effort in total, and as a nation to this day we continue to struggle. It's primarily because we have no mechanism to ensure unity of effort. The partisanship that has fractured our political processes is also a contributor to these challenges.

I have come away from my professional experiences with an undaunted spirit of faith that is unshakeable and a love of country that is still unsurpassed. I have been asked by some of my foreign military friends, "How can you be so loyal today given what your country did to you?" My answer is simple. I was blessed with seeing firsthand that American democracy has evolved into something that is not understood around the world. Americans do not appreciate our democracy unless they have seen other countries struggle with these issues. We have made great strides in advancing to the ideal human condition that our forefathers envisioned when they enshrined the Bill of Rights as the first ten amendments to our constitution. We are truly without a question the greatest democracy on earth. We do not understand when other people tell us that they do not want what we have in America because it is tough to accept.

While serving as a commander of U.S. forces in Kosovo from 1999 to 2000, I encountered a highly respected Kosovar leader who repeatedly asked me at a social function, "What are you? Who are you?" I couldn't understand his question, so I told him I was an American soldier and I was a commander of the U.S. forces. He insisted, saying, "No. But what are you?" He said, "You are not an American." Finally, I understood the question. I told him that I was a Mexican American. I told him a little bit about my grandparents and my great-grandparents and how they'd come to the United States. And his response was, "How can this be? How is it that a minority is commanding all of U.S. forces here in my country?" He couldn't comprehend what it was to have equal opportunity.

Years later, as recently as a couple of years ago, in a conversation with a western European military leader, we started talking about the opportunity for high command and strategic leadership within their armed forces, and he stated flat out, "You would never have become a general officer in our country. Your background and ethnicity would have automatically disqualified you. You might've become a lieutenant colonel or colonel."

My country gave me great opportunities, but in the end, I was asked to retire. Now, we must be proud of being Americans. We can never forget the tremendous benefits and rights that we possess, and we must understand that we have a responsibility to serve our country. Our opportunities as minorities and specifically as Hispanics within the military are unlimited. There is no other segment of society that has embraced equal opportunity and non-discrimination to the same extent as the American military. This is what I meant earlier when I said I had lived a sheltered life.

This is not to say that there aren't problems, because as Hispanics we still have glass ceilings. We still are not represented at the strategic level of leadership, at the general officer, army general officer level, at the same rate as we are represented across the society and within the military. Over the last 40 years, we have never had more than five to seven Hispanic general officers at any given time in the American Army. Over the last 75 years or so, we have had only three active duty three-star generals that made it their life's profession to serve in uniform and only one four-star. What's the problem? We are just as capable, just as competent, just as well educated as any other segment of this society.

Furthermore, when we finally hang up our uniforms, regardless of length of service, regardless of rank, we return to a society with multiple disadvantages. Not only do we return to be in a minority but also, we carry the added burden that accrues when America has lost touch with its military, with its armed forces. Sometimes we return to the poverty and the problems that we left behind when we joined our Army. Corporate America values the traditional characteristics that have always been attributed to a warrior: courage, dedication, discipline, all of those things. But what they do not understand is a tremendously broad range of experiences and responsibilities that these warriors bring back to American society. The economic opportunity for a returning warrior is scarce, and America must re-dedicate itself to correcting this injustice.

Never forget where you came from. It will give you humility, and humility provides a window to the heart and the soul of many who would otherwise shun you. Many choose to aggrandize themselves at the expense of others by whatever means, and some do succeed, but that is not necessary to succeed. There is absolutely nothing wrong with being idealistic, aggressive, disciplined and focused and, in fact, if you are a minority, these traits are absolutely essential if you're going to have a chance at success. But you must temper these characteristics with a dose of reality, compassion, humility, moral courage and absolute integrity.

Throughout my professional career, I learned that in battle, even the simplest things are hard. The same is true in our daily lives. All the challenges that the Lord has allowed me to face have been a blessing, and He has taken me to the heights of glory and the depths of despair. But I walk away proud of having served my country and I thank Him every day. We are not guaranteed an easy life, and, in fact, what is guaranteed is that we will struggle through untold sacrifices, desperation, sadness, disappointment and injustice. But in the end, what is most important is that during the toughest of times, we never left the moral high ground and we displayed the courage to walk by faith and not by sight.

Hilda L. Solis
U.S. Secretary of Labor

November 20, 2009

Secretary Hilda L. Solis was confirmed as Secretary of Labor on February 24, 2009, becoming the first Latina to serve in a U.S. president's cabinet. Prior to confirmation as Secretary of Labor, Secretary Solis represented the 32nd Congressional District in California, a position she held from 2001 to 2009. In Congress, Solis' priorities included expanding access to affordable health care, protecting the environment and improving the lives of working families. A recognized leader on clean energy jobs, she authored the Green Jobs Act that provided funding for "green" collar job training for veterans, displaced workers, at-risk youth and individuals in families under 200 percent of the federal poverty line.

Solis experienced what many first-generation Latinas experience in this country—living with a foot in two cultures. On the one hand, there was the expectation that a girl who finished high school was expected to get married and not go to college. If she was lucky, she could study to be a secretary, but she had to live at the home while she studied and not move to a dorm. Lucky for Solis, she felt the calling to pursue an education and used that education to inspire not only her siblings, but helped many underserved communities pursue educational and employment opportunities.

I am proud to be a Latina. Yes, it's very evident; I wear it. But I also come from a small town, from humble beginnings, from a small community known as La Puente. In Spanish, that means "the bridge." Maybe in some ways it's very important to talk about that because La Puente brought me a long way. It brought me to a place like Washington, D.C. I was someone who probably growing up did not think that she would be coming back to Washington, D.C.

I worked here in the Carter administration well over twenty years ago. I was an intern working on my master's program through the University of Southern California and found my way into an office that was then represented by Esteban Torres, the representative special assistant to President Carter. I came in as a writer. That was the first real big change in my life: leaving a small-town community like La Puente, where maybe less than five people even went to college.

Some of the folks from those communities that we represent still don't have that opportunity. Some of our youth may have experienced this. But oftentimes, there are people who don't see us in these roles, don't think that we can achieve, that we can actually be successful and become more than just secretaries or office workers.

At my high school, many of the students were "tracked," as we say into vocational programs, to the military. If you were a young woman, well, if you got married you were lucky, or you went on to become a secretary or a government worker as a clerk. That's what most of the counseling staff predicted for this population, which was at that time about 85 percent Latino. Not knowing any better because I had no one else—no other siblings in my household who went to college—I believed what these counselors were telling me, until I ran into someone who actually told me, "Hilda, you can actually be something more than that. And because you care so much about your community, why don't you think about channeling that energy in a positive way by getting an education and coming back and helping to rid your community of these injustices that you see, that you grew up with?"

I thought to myself, "Wow, that's a big calling, to be able to try to do something like that." It was very enormous and very intimidating for a young Latina whose parents traditionally would say, "You can't leave home. You can't go to college and live in the dorm. And if you do, we've got to go check it out. We've got to make sure you're telling us the truth." I had to convince them about the whole culture of education. It was a long time coming, but I'm happy I went through that experience because after I went to college, thank goodness, the majority of my five younger siblings decided to do the same thing.

I'm happy to report that it does matter that someone in the family or in our culture talks about educational opportunities. It does matter that someone talks about mentoring, networking and bringing in other resources, and talks about how we can improve our communities. The way we do it is by channeling that information to our siblings and bringing them in contact with other networks. I'm happy to say that in my family, I have a sister who has a PhD in Public Health from UCLA, and I have two younger sisters who are ten years my junior, who graduated from UCLA: one is a petrochemical engineer and the other one is a communications IT engineer.

It's no secret that I've been fighting for most of my public life to try to correct some of the wrongs that I personally saw in our society. When I was elected back in 1992, I had a group of friends whom I had worked with in higher education. I had worked with them before I was elected to try to help undocumented students receive access and placement in the universities and colleges around California. I carried the first bill in the assembly during that time when there were very few Latinos, and the Speaker of the House at that time was Willie Brown. He looked at me and he said, "You've got to be crazy, girl. You think you're going to get a bill right now?"

This was pre-1994, before Proposition 187 in California. I knew very little, being naïve and thinking, "Oh no, we've got to put this issue out there. There're a lot of students who deserve to be able to be admitted to college. These are our best and brightest." Well, lo and behold, I made three attempts; all three attempts failed. I couldn't even get sixteen votes from our Democratic Caucus. It taught me a tough lesson at that time.

But the fight went on. Assemblyman Marco Firebaugh and I later worked long and hard on that bill to get it through in the California legislature. I'm just recalling how long it takes sometimes for our progress to be made and how we seed progress, how all of us here have a responsibility to take risks and to remember who brought us to the table. They were people who helped to improve our lot in life by allowing us have these positions in which we are legitimately taken seriously by corporate America and by our government. And you do it through education.

So much has happened in the last twenty years since I worked here as a student, and there are a lot of challenges. I'm coming in at a time when people ask me, "Hilda, why are you taking this position as labor secretary when you're in the worst recession that this country has seen in 30 years?" I say to myself, "You know, I didn't take it on the premise that we were in trouble. I knew we were in trouble. I served for eight years in the House of Representatives, and many of the initiatives that I'm able to now put forward are no longer blocked. We get funding for youth programs. We get funding for enforcement, for labor protections. We get funding to be able to put people into new job training opportunities that they have not received in the last decade. Finally, we have an administration that puts workers first. Now, to me, that is the underlying priority that brings us all together here as Latinos. We must not forget our community. We must not forget who brought us to the table. We must not forget the fight that we face every single day. And that's whether or not you see an increasing unemployment figure for our population, which is well above 13 percent, and for our youth, 25 percent.

In some communities, in small towns in Texas and Tennessee, it's upwards of 30 and 40 percent. And it isn't just Latinos; it's African Americans and poor whites. The literacy rate of our workforce continues to lag behind. We're talking about fifteen million people who are unemployed; a good number maybe well over half have no high school education. If you start to look in the weeds and see who those folks are in our community, many of them have not been able to achieve access to higher education or go beyond high school.

Our work is still much needed, and our efforts have to be even stronger and more forceful. We don't have time. The clock is ticking, and that's the way I see my job. We have so many things on our plate. I'm also not just entrusted with helping to take care of workers' rights and protections. I'm not sure if everyone realizes this, but we are the second largest enforcement agency in the federal government: The Department of Labor. People don't know that. And you know why? Because the previous administration did not take this seriously, and they did not stand up for a lot of the people who are in this room and who are not in this room. Now, that has changed.

Maybe it sounds funny—some people have dubbed me "the new sheriff in town"—but I will tell you that I take my job very seriously. We're going to do everything we can in moving forward to see that we protect workers in the workplace. We have a very ambitious program to hire well more than 670 investigative personnel, whether it's in the Wage and Hour Division, the Occupation Safety and Health Administration, the Employment Benefits Security Administration and all our other agencies that require assistance. But it doesn't mean that we're going to go knocking on your door, banging it down. It means we want to work with you, we want to make sure that corporations know that, yes, we're going to be there. We want to make sure that everybody abides by the rules. Because when you don't abide by the rules, then you hurt American workers and you hurt especially the most vulnerable populations, and that is our population, the Latino population.

I don't have to tell you what the statistics are in terms of fatalities in construction: they're abysmal. We have the most deaths in Texas in construction with Latino workers. In other parts of our country, it's under-reporting of injuries, death, illnesses, harassment, termination—those things have been under-reported for a decade. Now we're hoping, with the help of other groups like yours that are here, that we can work to turn that statistic around and be proud of our Hispanic community workforce and businesses. We can be partners in this venture, and I hope that we can continue to do that.

For the last seven months now, I have been visiting more than 35 cities; I've traveled more than 35,000 miles. I thought when I gave up my pin to be a member of the House that I would be able to go home more and maybe reduce my travel. Well, nothing could be further from the truth. I am actually traveling more and more and more, and I am going out to places that I have never seen with so much need and yet inspiration. Because there are a lot of people out there that are hurting, that are looking to this administration, that are looking to a few good leaders who can make something happen for them.

I feel very, very proud when I go out on an assembly line and look at workers who are getting retrained, who just got laid off from being an autoworker who are now in a training program that's offered by a union apprenticeship program, the International Brotherhood of Electrical Workers programs. They are now re-tooling these folks to become solar panel installers and learning a whole new smart grid electricity system that will reduce our dependency on foreign oil. When I see people of color engaging in these new types of job opportunities and women—underscore "women" we are looking for women to get into these non-traditional fields; that's something that the Department of Labor will put their teeth into.

I am saying that we all have to participate, that we all have to take responsibility for helping to move our economy in a positive direction, so that we can see that we're adding jobs to this economy. I feel very positive about the types of systematic changes that this president has made to our economy, financial-wise, by allowing for credit to be made available to small businesses, allowing for new incentives in the Department of Energy to re-energize and re-tool our manufacturing base, whether it's creating new electric vehicles, hybrid vehicles or lithium batteries, or targeting our efforts in taskforce mode to look at the automobile industry—that is under my jurisdiction.

We are trying to put together a BRAC team, a strike force that will go into our different communities and begin piece by piece to see how we can help put these communities back together. It may not be the automobile industry regions any longer. It may be to re-tool something entirely different. That's what the Department of Labor would like to do in coordination with all the other cabinet members of this administration. I feel very strongly about the progress that I've seen and that we're making.

So many good people have influenced my life: Bobby Kennedy, Martin Luther King, Jr., Dolores Huerta, Ted Kennedy and César Chávez. More importantly, I have to give thanks to my parents because they're really the ones who helped set me straight, who keep me honest. When I go home, they still say, "You may think you're the cabinet secretary, but you're still our daughter." So, believe me, that keeps me very humble.

I just want to say what a proud moment it is to be serving in this capacity, to be able to leverage our support, our resources, to put people back to work. I had the opportunity just yesterday to give out $55 million, which is a small amount of money, in green job training, programs aimed at youth, at dislocated workers. The places that we called were in *Tejas*, San Antonio, Phoenix, New York, East Los Angeles—we had grants going everywhere. The criteria have changed as to who receives that money, because somebody asked for an administrator, different guideline language and panelists to help us decide where the money goes. It's not relying on what was done ten years ago. It's changing the whole design and it's about moving rapidly.

We're going to be rolling out another $220 million of our $750 million that will go to healthcare careers. We are encouraged to see more of our young people getting retrained in these and IT programs. We want to see that happen.

I thank Senator Bob Menéndez, the members of the congressional Democrats and the few brave Republicans who voted for the American Recovery and Reinvestment Act, because without that, I would not have the ability to pass out these grants that we are making available to re-tool America and to re-tool the Latino workforce.

Lionel Sosa
Author, Advertising Executive & Artist

September 2, 2008

Growing up in San Antonio, Texas, the son of Mexican immigrants, Lionel Sosa was expected to vote Democratic. But he was so impressed with the message of opportunity by Dwight D. Eisenhower's televised speech at the 1952 Republican Convention that he decided he wanted to be a Republican. His mother told him that Republicans were the party of the rich and the Democrats the party of the poor. Lionel decided that rich was better than poor.

Sosa founded Sosa, Bromley, Aguilar & Associates and grew the company to become the largest Hispanic advertising agency in the United States. From 1978 on, Sosa and his team have worked diligently to elect Republicans to office, eventually working on seven presidential campaigns, from Ronald Reagan in 80 and 84, George H.W. Bush in 92 and 98, George W. Bush in 2000 and 2004 and John McCain in 2008. In addition to developing his expertise in political campaigns, he is a recognized expert in Hispanic consumer and voter behavior. He is also a portrait artist and the author of Think and Grow Rich: A Latino Choice, The Americano Dream: How Latinos Can Achieve Success in Business and in Life and Children of the Revolución: How the Mexican Revolution Changed America.

People ask me, "Lionel, why did you become a Republican? You're a Mexican, you're supposed to be a Democrat." It happened when I was thirteen years old in 1952. My parents bought our first television set, and back then, there were only three television options: ABC, CBS and NBC. It just so happened that our TV arrived about the same time the national political conventions were on the air. The only thing we could watch if we wanted to watch TV were the convention speeches because all three networks ran them simultaneously.

First, I heard Dwight Eisenhower make his speech. He talked about love of country. He talked about personal responsibility and about family values and about opportunity, that is, making one's own way without government intrusion. He sounded a lot like my dad. A couple of weeks later, I heard his opponent, Adlai Stevenson. Stevenson was different. He didn't seem quite as strong. He talked about the importance of government and how much free stuff it could offer us.

Somehow Dwight Eisenhower's words resonated with me. I went and proudly told my parents, "When I'm able to vote, I'm going to vote Republican." They said, "*Dios mío*, Lionel, how can you possibly do that?" "*Te vas al infierno*." "You're going to go to hell." "Why?" "Because you can't be a Republican, you're a Democrat," they said. "Why?" I asked. "Because we're Mexican!" I didn't get it. "We have to be Democrats because we're Mexican?" "Yes." "Any other reasons?" "Yes, because we're poor. You must understand, son, the Republicans are the party of the rich and the Democrats are the party of the poor." "OK, that settles it," I said confidently, "I want to be rich, so I guess I'm Republican." My parents never forgave me.

In 1978, I had my own business, a small ad agency in San Antonio. One day, out of the blue, we received a phone call from U.S. Senator John Tower's office: "We're looking for an advertising agency for the senator's next campaign, and we think you would be just right because two of the four agency partners are Mexican and we're going to need a lot of Spanish ads." I was stunned. We'd never done political advertising, and we'd never done Hispanic ads. "That's okay," they said, "we think you can do it."

We made a presentation and won the business. They spent $500,000 on Hispanic media, which was a lot of money back at the time. Nobody had ever spent that much on a senate race. Not any Democrat. Not any Republican. But John Tower knew that he needed to get the Latino vote because at the time, only 8 percent of Latinos voted for Republicans.

Election day came and Tower won 37 percent of the Latino vote! Overall, he won by only one-half of 1 percent of the total Texas vote. That meant the Latinos got him re-elected!

A week after the election, I was sitting in Tower's office. "Lionel, you were instrumental in helping me win and now, I want to help you." I said, "You don't have to do anything for me, Senator. You've given me the opportunity to work with you and learn. That's payment enough." "No," he replied, "I want to do more. I want to help you do more business." He picked up the phone and called his favorite reporter at the *Wall Street Journal*. "I want you to do a story about someone who helped me win this election," he commanded.

The *Journal* did a big story, complete with a small pen and ink drawing of me. The day the story was printed, my world changed. Within three months, Coca-Cola, Bacardi Rum and Coors Beer became my clients because of that article. All of a sudden, we went from being a small, unknown local business to a big, respected, nationally recognized advertising agency billing millions instead of thousands. We were now on the map because one man had opened the doors of opportunity, allowing us to walk through. No government handout needed, thank you.

A couple of months later, Tower called again. "Lionel, I want to introduce you to a fellow by the name of Ronald Reagan. He's going to be the next president of United States." At a fundraiser in Dallas a couple of months later, Tower introduced me to Ronald Reagan and suggested that I should be hired to work on his Hispanic outreach. Reagan hired me. At our first planning meeting, I understood why Reagan was known as "The Great Communicator." He summed up my assignment in a few words. "Your job's going to be easy. Latino values are the same as mine. They're conservative values—love of family, pride in good hard work, faith in God, personal responsibility, a better life for our children and a burning desire for opportunity. Latinos are Republicans, they just don't know it yet." His words took me back to the words of my dad and Eisenhower. "All you have to do," he continued, "is communicate the fact we share the same values and believe in the same things. As long as you do that, you're going to be just fine." In less than a minute, Reagan gave me the entire communications strategy needed to win over the Latino voter.

It's a strategy I've been using in every election since.

Julie Stav
Financial Expert & Best-Selling Author

November 1, 2011

Julie Stav is a financial planner, bestselling author and host of an acclaimed daily call-in radio show and podcast, Tu Dinero con Julie Stav. *Stav has dedicated her career to the education and empowerment of millions of Americans. She previously authored two New York Times bestsellers,* Get Your Share *and* Fund Your Future. *Both have been developed into successful PBS specials on personal finance.*

Through her work, Stav empowers financially underserved communities by providing them with the knowledge and tools they need to make the best financial decisions in personal banking, credit, retirement, investments, major life purchases and small business operations. Stav, who was born in Cuba and, at age fourteen, was sent to live in an orphanage in Mexico City in order to escape the Castro regime, recalls an early lesson from her father: "Power is something you take. It is not something you give."

I was born in Cuba. My mother was a stay-at-home mom and my dad was a farmer. He and five brothers grew, cultivated, refined and then exported rice. When Castro took over, my parents wanted to give my brother and me—my brother is a year older—a better future. If you were between fifteen and 27, you couldn't leave Cuba because that was military age. So, my brother

left through Spain by himself when he was fourteen. The following year when I turned fourteen, the only way that they could get
me out of the country was to send me to an orphanage in Mexico
City. I later went to Los Angeles, and my parents arrived two and
a half years later.

When I was still in Cuba, my brother asked for a job at a
cathedral high school in Los Angeles, mowing the lawn, but he
was not given the job. My dad, a farmer in Cuba, sat down and
wrote a long-hand letter in Spanish to the Pope. We thought that
he was crazy . . . but the Pope answered. Thanks to that letter, both
he and I went to Loyola Marymount University on grants, scholarships and loans, and we made it through college. My dad said,
"You know, God was busy, I went to the second guy in command,"
which really taught me a lesson right there. That is that power is
something you take; it's not something you give, and it's something that we need to learn especially in our community.

I went to Hollywood High School. I had been there for a
month and a half when I was given an IQ test. Of course, I didn't
speak any English, but I took the test. They gave their analysis: I
am down as mentally retarded in Hollywood High School. But I
knew how to swim, and in the water, we were all the same. It did-
n't matter if I spoke English or not. When you talk about sink or
swim, I swam my little heart out, and that kept me out of trouble
and on the road to college.

My job is to talk to our people. I am hopefully the first bridge
that they cross when they come to this country that helps us all
not only tackle the hurdle of learning the English language, but
also the language of money. I believe that we bring so many
myths, especially when it comes to money. But one thing that I
see, a vein that is common among all of us who are able to lead,
is the fact that we always see that glass half full. I tell my mother
. . . My mom says, "Oh, my daughter has been divorced twice."
And I say, "You know what, Ma, some women go through life and
they don't find one man to marry them. I found three. Look how

lucky I am." It doesn't matter what life you get, it's what you do with it.

During my shows, I tell the audience that there are three ways of making money. The first one is labor. One of the first words we learn in English is *part-time*. If we need more money, we go get another job, don't we? But there are only 24 hours in a day and seven days a week, so that gets old very fast.

The second one is charity. I don't care if it's the husband or the government, when you lean on somebody else and you rely on charity, you pay with the most expensive price there is, and that's your dignity, so, that's not good.

The third one is capital. That is when you're able to build that little machine that makes money for you, even when you sleep. That little machine that today you can do from your home, you can do with an individual taxpayer identification number (ITIN), you can do it whether you speak English or not, because just like that water in that swimming pool, we are all the same. You can do it if you're a man or a woman. Money is green. It's not blue, and it's not pink. And you can build that little machine.

I wrote the first book for women, because I feel that when you change a man, you change a man; but when you change a woman, you change a generation. We bring our kids in. We tell our *comadres* and our sisters and we talk to the man that served our plate and the lady in the restroom and everybody else; you gentlemen are the heads of our families, but we as Latinas know very well we are the neck, and we turn that head any which way we want.

The next glass ceiling that we really need to break is the glass ceiling of financial independence, and that is what I am using the media shamelessly to teach. To teach our kids who are born with Intel inside that it is better to own a share of Nike than a pair of Nikes, that we can't complain that they spend their time on the computer, wasting time or spending money, because we don't give them any alternative. We need to get to our kids and change the way they look at money.

A woman named María called my radio show once and said that she lived in Oxnard and picked strawberries in the field. She didn't know how to work the computer but her daughter, Denise, did. What Maria would do is take notes during the radio show, and then when Denise came home, she would tell Denise what to do. Denise opened a brokerage account for María, who only had an ITIN number. Today María has her own business. She has paid off her home and she invests in the stock market. María is not alone. The information is there. We have to put this into our heads . . . How many of you have ever heard that, "Destiny is written?" I would ask my mother, "Mommy, am I pretty?" And she would say, "You know what, it's the beauty inside that counts." I grew up thinking I was the butt-ugliest thing that was ever born. If my own mother said that to me, imagine . . . We're taught to be humble and to not make waves. My mom would say, "Some of us were born to be hammers and some were born to be nails." Really?

In interviews I am often asked, "Well, what about the economy? It's so bad." I don't know if you've ever heard or read the book by Dr. Camilo Cruz, La Vaca, a book about a man who was a farmer. This man had many sons, they were very poor and all they had was this little skinny cow that gave them a little milk hat they would sell. One day, a genie showed up and said, "I'm here to make you rich." The man replied, "Yes, I want to be rich!" The genie took out a knife and, what do you think he does? He killed the cow. This man said, "Oh, no . . . what are we going to do without the cow?" The genie went away. The genie came back in a couple of years and saw this mansion and beautifully cultivated fields. The genie knocked on the door, and the same man, dressed beautifully, answers: "You are the genie. I have to thank you because you made me rich. You killed the cow. You killed the one thing that kept my children from learning how to cultivate that land. You killed that one excuse that I had, why I didn't move on. Thank you!"

This is what I do on the radio every day. I help my listeners "kill their cows." What is your cow or what is *your* excuse? Is it that the economy is so bad? Well, what about FedEx? What about Disney? What about all those businesses that were born during recessions and depressions? You know the difference between recession and depression? Recession is when your neighbor loses his job, and depression is when you lose yours. But there is no excuse. The economy of a country begins at home. Ladies, my divas, you have a book there that is going to help you determine what kind of money personality you have. Investments are like shoes: one size doesn't fit all.

How many of us really need more sleep than anything else? We're so tired of working and we keep spending money unconsciously because we deserve it. This is why we work so hard. Isn't it? How many companies play to that, saying, "This is more expensive, but you are worth it?" I want you to bring all of this to consciousness and really see that with the help of your computer, your iPhone, your smart phone or your iPad, you have everything that you need to start making your money work for you, so you don't have to work so hard for your money.

As leaders, we need to open doors, we need to mentor and we need to bring those people along who have come after us. We all have gone through hard times; we all have very sad stories. Just give it a moment, let's blow our nose, let's wash our face and let's move on. Let's have our kids, let's have the next generation start where we ended here. This is a relay race. Let's have them begin by knowing that Wall Street can be Main Street, it can be Olvera Street, and that they have all the tools that they need to own a little piece of America.

A good education is going to get us the tools to work for the best company. I want you to own the best companies. You can do that one little piece at a time. The information is out there. For the first time, we are using the media, which is long overdue in the Hispanic community, to teach us how to invest. Listen to the following quotation. It comes from a book, A *Return to Love* by Marianne Williamson. It says, "Our deepest fear is not that we are inadequate. Our deepest fear is that we are powerful beyond measure. It is our light, not our darkness that most frightens us. We ask ourselves, 'Who am I to be brilliant, gorgeous, talented, and fabulous?' Actually, who are you *not* to be? You are a child of God. You're playing small does not serve the world. There is nothing enlightened about shrinking so that other people won't feel insecure around you. We are all meant to shine, as children do. We were born to make manifest the glory of God that is within us. It's not just in some of us; it's in everyone. And as we let our own light shine, we unconsciously give other people permission to do the same. As we are liberated from our own fears, our presence automatically liberates others." We're very familiar with failure. It's not the fear of failure that keeps many of us back. It's the fear of success.

Leticia Van de Putte
Texas State Senator

June 15, 2006

Ever since she was a young girl running around her grandfather's pharmacy in San Antonio's West Side, Leticia knew she wanted to be a pharmacist. Growing up in a nurturing atmosphere, the oldest of five children, she was always told by her parents that she could be anything she wanted to be.

Leticia Van de Putte has represented the people of San Antonio at the Texas Legislature since 1991. From 1991 to 1999, Van de Putte was a member of the Texas House of Representatives and she represented the 26th District in the Texas Senate from 1999 to 2015. In 2014, she was the Democratic nominee for lieutenant governor but lost the general election to her Republican senatorial colleague, Dan Patrick of Houston.

Leticia Van de Putte worked as a pharmacist in mental health clinics, a hospital and her grandfather's pharmacy, The Botica Guadalupana, before purchasing her own business, the Loma Park Pharmacy and Medical Clinic. She has been actively involved in the National Conference of State Legislatures, serving as the 2006-07 president. She is an active member of the National Assessment Governing Board, the American Legacy Foundation Board and the National Hispanic Caucus of State Legislators, where she served as president from 2003 to 2005.

I'm probably one of the few people that carries around a copy of the Constitution, because you never know when you might need it. I say this because there are two things in this that I love. If you ever, ever feel as Latinos, that somehow you are on the margins of discussions, take out that Constitution. In that preamble it says, "We the people of the United States, in order to form a more perfect union." Then I take the very back sentence of the Declaration of Independence, and it says, "We mutually pledge to each other our lives, our fortune, and our sacred honor." *Mis amigos*, that's what we do.

If you think about it, what is more important than something sacred, a mutual pledge to each other? No one can take that away. *Es un honor sagrado* that we owe to each other. Especially at these times in our country and considering all of the issues that are before us not only as Latinos but as Americans, we know that we must play a critical role in our national debate, particularly now, as we try to embark on a rational, comprehensive immigration reform that secures our borders and yet eliminates the inequities in the current system. You and I have to be a part of that dialogue. *Es sagrado, un honor* that we have to do. Yet, we know that I can only stand here before you, other legislators, other congressmen that are here today and my congressman who was here today, Charlie González, because of those trailblazers that came before us. They didn't just knock at the door; they kicked it open so that we could be here. They didn't do it alone.

I'm the daughter of a Korean War veteran. Because of that sacred honor, let me tell you a little bit about the Latinos who have served. We have more than 600,000 veterans right now of Mexican descent, including 39 Medal of Honor recipients who are Latinos. We have 1.1 million Latino veterans. Since 2001, we make up more than ten percent of our armed forces. If you think about it, we make up almost twenty percent of the infantry, the gun crews and the ship crews right now, the men and women who are in uniform. Let us not forget that sacred honor.

I grew up in San Antonio. I'm the oldest. I have two sisters and two brothers. I grew up in a very wonderful family in San Antonio's West Side. My grandfather, Don Daniel San Miguel, was *el boticario*. The role model that I had was my grandfather and his Botica Guadalupana. The smells were wonderful. It was a time when things were compounded. We didn't know it but we were way ahead of our time in herbal medicine. Now, everything is a natural product. They just didn't know that when we got sick, they gave us *un tesito*, tea. My grandpa used to make a wonderful cough medicine that was called *mata tos*, which was just as good as the *pomada* that I made twenty years later called *mata sizote*, fungus killer.

I grew up in that atmosphere, and I always knew that I wanted to be a pharmacist. I have parents that said, "*Mi'jita*, you can be whatever you want to be." Yes, yes, yes, you can be whatever you want to be. I wanted to be a pharmacist because even at the age of six I wanted people to look at me like they looked at my grandpa. He was a person of respect. They came to him because of his knowledge. I knew that I wanted to be a person of knowledge. We have to continue to strive in our young people that they can be a person of knowledge and of respect. But I also knew, *como mujercita*, when my father would introduce me, the first thing they'd say was, "Ay, *qué bonita la muchachita*." Oh, what a pretty little girl. And the first thing out of my dad's mouth was, "She's the smartest girl in her class." I wasn't, but because my father said so, it must have been true. Because somebody whom I love said I was. I studied because I thought I could be somebody. I was very lucky that I was pretty adept at math and science, and that enabled me to become a pharmacist.

I benefitted from a family structure in which I was loved and nurtured. I went to the best public schools and to great universities on scholarship, knowing that in some way I would be able to be like my grandfather. We need those role models.

It was in pharmacy school in Houston that I had a professor who called us up, and we would do math problems on the board.

This was before calculators. I was great with a slide rule. Today, you can see them in museums. This female professor called me up, and I got the problem wrong in front of the whole class. I was so embarrassed. Many humans who find themselves in error, they make light of it. I made a little remark, and I'll never forget what she told me. She said, "Ms. San Miguel, just because you're white for a Mexican, doesn't mean you can't make mistakes like that." I was in total awe and shock. I couldn't believe that she had said something like that to me in front of my classmates. I was hurt, and I wanted an apology. When class ended, I went up to her and said, "What you said was absolutely wrong. I was unprepared for this class. But it has nothing to do with me being of Mexican descent." And then I said, "I want an apology. And I want you to make this apology in front of class tomorrow." She told me, "You make me sick." I said, "I make you sick? Do you realize what you have just said to me?" She answers, "You think you're here for you? How many girls are in this class?" There were eight out of 65. She said, "How many Mexicans are here?" There were three of us. She said, "You've got so much potential and you are having a good time. You think you're here for you." She walked out. It was very painful because she was right. I never thought until that point that what I did as Leticia San Miguel, *hija del dueño de la Botica Guadalupana*, reflected on *mis hermanas*. I never thought that it was my duty to be so good so they'd let other women in. I never thought about myself as being doubly good so they'd let more *Raza* in. I never thought about myself in the same way. It's not about me. My friends, it's not about you. It's about us.

As it turned out, Professor Rouse did apologize during the next class. After that, we became, until her death, very good friends. Maybe for people like me who weren't the first generation to break down those doors, we needed to be reminded. I was reminded in a way that slapped me and assaulted what I thought. But she got her point across.

I went on and finished pharmacy school at the University of Texas, got married and started to work *en la botica*. My dream was to own my own pharmacy, and I did. In between, in the 1980s, I had six children. That pharmacy provided me with the opportunity to take my babies to work, something that most women can't do unless you own the joint, and I did. I got to be with my babies. And as I saw what the disease burden was for people in my community, I began to think, *who makes these laws? Who makes this policy?* You see, in 1990 in Texas, we had a comprehensive policy that made sure that every cow was going to be vaccinated. We had a registry. We didn't have a similar policy for children. But in agriculture, industry and manufacturing, cows are money, and so it was a product of our economy. My friends, in the social sector, service sector economy, my little oil wells are those little Chicanitos in third grade. We must invest in immunizations and in an immunization registry. I thought I'm going to put my name in. They don't know what they're doing. Who's making education policy? Who's making this? I got angry.

I had never held office, and I wasn't supposed to win, but I did. I've loved it ever since. I love making laws and policy at the state level. We all are leaders. I may be a leader in my community, but everyone in my community and all Latinos are leaders. We are all public servants. We are all servant leaders in our own capacities. I've loved being engaged in the legislature. If you sit here today and you're involved in education, then you are a servant leader. If you're involved in health care, you're a servant leader. Many decisions are made in boardrooms. Many decisions are made at the state legislative level and at our precious capital, very close to here. But more decisions that affect Latinos are made at a supper table, and that's where you and I need to be those servant leaders, to affect family life.

I'm always reminded of my grandmother. Whenever we get off-track, whenever something would go wrong, *Güelita* would say, "Checkpoint, checkpoint," because there were four questions that the Border Patrol asked her. If you ever get off-track a individual in your organization, whether it's a community-based organization or a governmental institution, think about the checkpoint and the questions. The first question they ask is, "¿Quién es?" Who are you? Who are we? Who are we as Latinos? What do we represent? Second question: "¿Qué traes?" What do you have? I think they were worried about vegetables and fruits and other stuff. But, ¿qué traes? What qualities, what skill sets do you possess that make you an asset to your family, to your community, to your employer? Third question: "¿Adónde vas?" Where are you going? And we know where we're going. The fourth question, probably the most difficult one that they'd ask Güela: "¿Qué vas a hacer cuando llegues allí?" What are going to do when you get there?

That's the question you and I as Latinos have to ask. We have to answer with rational thought and debate. What are we going to do when we get there? Because we are here. Be a leader. I have been given every opportunity. But I am in awe and wonder of that single mom with two kids who got pregnant, got her GED, and is at the community college and working and has this dream. That's the leader. That's the person who didn't have it easy, as I did. Or the young man who battles those demons of addiction and yet knows that he's got to finish his education; or the small business owner just barely making it—those people are courageous. They're the ones that haven't had the opportunity.

I'm lucky. I should be here. I had parents who loved me, went to the best schools and been given a great opportunity. You all have your own stories, las historias. Let's share them with our young people. And if we ever get off balance, or if you ever question ask what is our purpose, Checkpoint!

Nydia M. Velázquez

Congresswoman
U.S. House of Representatives

November 16, 2010

Congresswoman Nydia M. Velázquez is currently serving her twelfth term as the Representative for New York's 7th Congressional District. In the 114th Congress, she is the Ranking Member of the House Small Business Committee and a senior member of the Financial Services Committee.

She has made history several times during her tenure in Congress. In 1992, she was the first Puerto Rican woman elected to the U.S. House of Representative New York's 7th Congressional District, which encompasses Brooklyn, Queens and the Lower East Side of Manhattan. In February, 1998, she was named Ranking Democratic Member of the House Small Business Committee, making her the first Hispanic woman to serve as Ranking Member of a full House committee. In 2006, she was named Chairwoman of the House Small Business Committee, making her the first Latina to chair a full Congressional committee.

Born one of nine children in Yabucoa, Puerto Rico in 1953, Velázquez started school early, skipped several grades and became the first person in her family to receive a college education. After graduating magna cum laude in political science from the University of Puerto Rico in 1974, she earned a Master's degree from New York University and taught Puerto Rican studies at Hunter College.

As a fighter for equal rights of the underrepresented and a proponent of economic opportunity for the working class and poor, Congresswoman Velázquez combines sensibility and compassion as she works to encourage economic development, protect community health and the environment, combat crime and worker abuses and secure access to affordable housing, quality education and health care for all New York City families.

I love the work I do, my community and the people that I represent. It's all those beautiful children that give meaning to the work I do in Washington. I honor my father and my mother, because believe me, growing up in a rural barrio of Yabucoa with nine children, when things were really tough, my father and mother never walked away, even in the most difficult moments. Sometimes when we cried at night because we were hungry, my mother would say, "Don't worry." I would say, "Mommy, I want soda," and she would go and mix sugar and water and give it to us with some lemon juice. They were relentless; they understood their commitment to give to us a better life, a better future, and they instilled in me the value of education. That taught me that, once I'm gone or do something else in life, that commitment is the best legacy that we can leave to our young generations.

From a young age, I saw how political action could benefit people's lives. Some of my earliest memories involve talking politics at the dinner table, going to political rallies with my father or listening to him giving a speech in a flatbed truck. I came to NY at the age of nineteen to work on my master's degree at New York University. I was able to come to New York because the government of Puerto Rico gave me a full scholarship. I do know that there is a role for government to help those most vulnerable, and I will always, always fight for that.

I came to D.C., though I wasn't supposed to be here. I was supposed to be a number, a school dropout or something else, but I wasn't. Since I came to Washington, I decided. I don't know why, but I guess because I saw my father struggling to understand rules and regulations when he opened up his little brick shop—*una fábrica de cemento de bloques*—and he couldn't understand them. There I was, a sixth grader, trying to interpret for him in Spanish regulations that at an early age I didn't understand. It was very difficult for my father. So, when I came here, I knew that the most important thing to be able to provide for my community was jobs, and still today that is our biggest challenge.

I decided that I wanted to serve on the small business committee. Soon, I asked, "Where is the money, financial services? I'm going to go and I'm going to ask for financial services." I am proud of the work that I've done as chair of the small business committee, especially making sure that the tools are there to help Latinos and minorities expand economic opportunities. If there is any accomplishment, at least I can tell you that every time an agency cabinet hires a contracting officer, they call me up and let me know what they did because they know that I'm watching to see if they are accomplishing their contracting goals for small and minority businesses.

I have flown on Air Force One with multiple presidents and taught a secretary of state how to dance tango. I have had the privilege of chairing the Congressional Hispanic Caucus and the Congressional Hispanic Caucus Institute (CHCI). Not bad. Not bad for the kid from that barrio in Yabucoa. I know something about starting with little and using education to find your way in life, which is why it has been so important to me and a privilege to lead the CHCI, which helps young people pursue their dreams. As the Hispanic community's role in the United States grows, CHC and CHCI will continue working to ensure that Latinos claim their place in the American narrative.

By 2013, there will be 75 million Hispanic-Americans. That is 25 percent of the population. Hispanic entrepreneurs as a group is growing three times faster than any other group. The buying power of Latinos is approaching almost $1 trillion. My friends, if that is not power, what is? We are becoming an ever more politically robust force.

Voter turnout among Hispanics reached record levels in 2008. This year, during an otherwise very bad election for Democrats, Hispanic voters made the difference in returning Senate Majority Leader Reid, Senator Boxer and Senator Bennett to Congress and retaining the Senate. I hope that Senator Reid is listening and all those potential presidential candidates: You just can't win without at least getting 40 percent or 45 percent of Latino voters in this country.

When Sonia Sotomayor became the first Latina Supreme Court Justice, young Latinas and Latinos were immediately provided a new source of inspiration. If we are to capitalize on these strengths, there must be additional opportunities for the next generation of Latino leaders. CHCI's mission is to make sure that these young people can achieve their goals.

In the last two years, we have been changing the face of the federal government here in Washington. We have been changing the makeup of the committees in the Senate and the House. We have been changing the workforce's face throughout Washington. We doubled the students that we are serving to 1,500 students, the number of congressional interns and the number of ready-to-lead high school students. In 2010, the CHCI has awarded 150 scholarships, the most ever. So, we are very proud of that.

It is the CHC's job to ensure Latino voices are heard on policy matters. Today, we are making our presence felt on every issue, big and small. I'm proud to say that there are historic numbers of Latino appointments in the new administration. This wasn't done because of the work of the CHC. This was done in collaboration with the community-based organizations and Latino leaders.

We fought with all of you to ensure everyone is counted in the census. The CHC worked to boost the size of Pell grants. The caucus helped pass healthcare reform legislation, including $2.55 billion for minority-serving institutions and $1 billion for Hispanic-serving institutions, and we changed the face of the U.S. Supreme Court forever.

The political math may have changed in Washington, but one thing will remain constant: our commitment to justice. We will not stop fighting to make sure that we do what the American public is telling us to do. They are ahead of policymakers in Washington and political pundits. They want to reform the broken system that we call immigration. We have to do it.

This morning, I had a meeting with Speaker Pelosi. Now, I'm walking out to go and meet with President Barack Obama. Hopefully, during the week of November 29th, we will be taking a vote in the House of Representative for the first time on the DREAM Act. This is not going to be easy. We want a standalone bill without adding jobs or H-1 visas, because we cannot lose our leverage to bring about comprehensive immigration reform. If we attach any of those elements to the DREAM Act, ten million undocumented will continue to live in the shadows for years to come. I am not telling you that this is going to happen, that we are 100 percent there.

Antonio Ramón Villaraigosa

Chairman of the Democratic National
Convention & Mayor, Los Angeles

September 12, 2012

Antonio Ramón Villaraigosa served as the 41st Mayor of Los Angeles, California from 2005 to 2013. Prior to being elected mayor, he was a member of the California State Assembly from 1994 to 2000, the Democratic leader of the assembly from 1996 to 1998 and the Speaker of the California State Assembly from 1998 to 2000. After being termed out of the State Assembly, he was elected to the Los Angeles City Council (2003) and served until he was elected Mayor (2005).

Villaraigosa was born Antonio Ramón Villar Jr. on January 23, 1953 in Los Angeles. He graduated from Theodore Roosevelt High School in Boyle Heights and went on to attend East Los Angeles College and the University of California, Los Angeles (UCLA), where he graduated with a B.A. in History in 1977. He then studied at the Peoples College of Law (PCL), but did not pass the bar exam. After law school, he became an organizer and became aware of the importance of ensuring all teachers have the resources they need to be successful in their profession. He later served as president of the Los Angeles chapter of the American Civil Liberties Union and the American Federation of Government Employees. He changed his surname to Villaraigosa upon his marriage to Corina Raigosa in 1987.

Villaraigosa recalls becoming politically active at age fifteen, when he went from working at a Safeway supermarket to volunteering with the farmworkers' movement and joining the picket lines in front of the supermarket.

I knew at fifteen what my job was. I want to mention someone who I met at fifteen. She doesn't remember me back then. I think she only remembers me from around the time that I got elected as president of the American Civil Liberties Union and was a union organizer, probably for that. But at fifteen years old, I had never worked in the fields. I'll be honest: I was a city boy. I didn't speak any Spanish. My mother, Natalia was born here. My grandpa, Pete, came here a hundred years ago from León, Guanajuato, Mexico. I remember working at a Safeway, and there was a picket line in front of the Safeway on 3rd and Bonnie Brae. They were boycotting grapes. I was working inside of the Safeway. I was feeling complicit in what they were boycotting against and what they were protesting. Over time I figured out a way. I didn't want to be working there anymore because I didn't want to be the symbol of the boycott. So, I joined that picket.

I never worked for the farm workers, as some lore has said. But I did join the boycott, and I was a passionate advocate for those farm workers even though I never worked in the fields and knew no Spanish. I knew even at fifteen that I had a responsibility to stand up for what was right, to stand up against injustice. To speak up for people who can't often speak for themselves. My leader, the woman on whose shoulders I stand, the woman on whose shoulders all of us stand, is Dolores Huerta. I'm here today because there was a Dolores Huerta. I'm here today because there was a César Chávez and a farm workers' movement that opened up the country to you and me.

You know, when I hear people talking about family values, nobody has a monopoly on those values. They're neither Democrat nor Republican. Frankly, they're not uniquely American. We love our families. Our families give us strength. Our families are there when you don't have a big job anymore. When you're no longer the center of attention and when the light's not beaming bright on you, your families are there. They're your inspiration. They're your consolation. They're your rock of support. I couldn't be prouder that my kids are here with me today.

I want to say something about Janet Murguía. She's my leader, and she knows it. She's right. I am not a shrinking violet when it comes to defending our community; but particularly on this issue of immigration, an issue that I have been involved in since I was probably nineteen or twenty, when I started fighting for immigrants and the undocumented, when I began to organize them in power and worked through them. That's when I started learning a little bit of Spanish. But I'll tell you something. When I'm thinking about where we need to be, what we need to be thinking about when it comes to civil rights, when it comes to human rights, when it comes to immigration policy, when it comes to so many issues across the board, I go to my friend and leader, to the head of the preeminent Latino civil rights organization in this country, the National Council of La Raza—I go to Janet.

You know, I was listening to Secretary Solis. I'll be honest with you: I was getting upset. She introduced me as her friend and colleague. And I'm saying, friend and colleague? Twenty-five years, we have been in battle after battle after battle in the California legislature. When I was an assembly member, when she was a senator, when I was speaker, she was with me. When I was at 3 percent in the polls, if you were buying stock, my stock was selling for three cents a share; she was with me against an incumbent. She was with me for city council against an incumbent. I've been with her in every race and, yes, I was with her when she buried her dad. So, when she said 'my brother' at the end, she vindicated herself because when she got up here, and said what she did . . . I love her. I respect her so much. This is a woman with the heart of a lioness. Thank you, *hermanita*.

I want to say something about the people of L.A. When I ran for state assembly, I ran in a district where a Latino had never won. It was a civil rights created district. The outgoing assembly member was about to become a senator. It was a very, very tough race. Sacramento—the establishment was all on the other end. Everybody said it wasn't going to happen because there were multiple candidates and many Latinos, and I was running against an Anglo. They said that on just the numbers, Antonio, you can't do it. You've got all these people running. You're not going to be able to cross over. The electorate is so polarized. You're not going to be able to do it. I said, "Why not?" I believe in the great generosity of the town I grew up in. I believe the people are good and they're fair. I believe that I can knock on any door and talk to anyone and listen to him or her, and emote with him or her, and understand him or her. I knocked on those doors, and we won. And then we went on. A few weeks later, I became majority whip; two years after that, majority leader; and then speaker of the California State Assembly.

I never forgot that politics was local. I never would have gotten here if I hadn't gotten elected by the people in Boyle Heights and in Highland Park and in El Sereno; by the people in Echo Park and Silver Lake; by the people from Mount Washington and Eagle Rock; by the people that gave me a shot. My neighborhood, the people I've grown up with, the people I had gotten to know. I always thank them because I think it's important to start with where it all started.

I thank the people of L.A., too, because as I said, when Hilda Solis and many of the elected officials who are here from L.A. got on board when it was like 3 percent in the polls, he's at 45 percent. Nine percent of the people know you, 72 percent know him. He's been in public life for 25 years. You've been in public life in the city for six. Hey, brother, it ain't going to happen. Latinos won't get elected to the mayoralty until 2017, they told me because at that time, although we were 44-46 percent of the city, we were only 22 percent of the electorate. Everybody said it wouldn't happen until 2017, when we'd be about 32 percent of the electorate. I see some of the heads shaking because even then, great friends, they thought, *ay pobrecito, ¿qué está pensando?* But we persevered.

We put together a campaign that L.A. had not seen since Tom Bradley. It was a campaign of thousands of people. There were people from Texas there. There were people from Chicago. There were people from Denver. They camped out. They camped out, and they said we're going to do this. We won in the primary. We lost in the runoff. But we didn't give up. There were 6,000 people on Election Day, and I knew then that it wasn't about me. It's never been about that. It's about us. It's about our aspirations. It's about who we are. Therefore, two years later, everybody used to say, "Antonio, you're going to be mayor. Go make some money. Stay out eight years. You'll be elected mayor one day, just wait." And I was out for two years.

I decided I better run again. And we ran. We ran against an incumbent who at the time had 69 percent approval rating. We won for the first time in L.A. history, in the primary beating the incumbent. Then a year later, thinking I wasn't going to run, I went to the Boston Democratic Convention. I came back excited. I said, "You know what? I'm going to do it. I'm going to give it a try." Everybody around the table, sixteen people, everybody said, "No, please don't do it." They said, "You should wait." I said, "I really appreciate it, but you know what? We're going to do it." Every one of them—praise God and thanks for their friendship—jumped in. Now, it's been seven years.

As I leave this job, I'm focused on my job as mayor, wanting to finish everything we started. I'm not going to go through what we started, but anybody in L.A. knows what a difference we've made. We made, not me, my staff, my colleagues, the legislature helping out, the congressional members helping out, all of the folks who have done this together. I believe and believe strongly that in this last year, helping to re-elect President Obama has to be our mission. Why is that? I love the pundits and the haters. They love to say, "Oh, Villaraigosa was with Hillary in the primary, and he was crisscrossing the country. Now, he's trying to look for a job." Come on. It's the hate thing, you know.

I'm with President Obama because it matters to Los Angeles who's in the White House. I'm with President Obama because at the worst time in history, when you look at our economy, when you see that we lost 800,000 jobs last month before he took office, 3.5 million jobs in the six months before he took office—this president in the worst financial crisis since the 1930s took it head on. He reached across the aisle. He tried to work with the other side. He did everything he could. And what's happened since then? Twenty-nine straight consecutive months of growth in job creation, private sector job creation, the first time since the early 1990s; and the first time since the early 1990s that we're actually growing manufacturing jobs. What has he done? Let me answer the question. Are we better off today than we were four years ago? Absolutely, yes. Is there enthusiasm in this room? Yes. Why? Not only did he help to create through his policies 4.5 million jobs, not only are we growing this economy, but, you know, 32 million people have healthcare because of him. They're better off. Nine million of the 32 million are Latinos. They're better off. Ask the 150,000 kids who got student loans because of his policy. They're better off. Ask the Dreamers if they're better off. The Dreamers are better off.

When you look at this president, when you look at what he stands for . . . When my grandpa came from León, Guanajuato a hundred years ago, he came with the shirt on his back. He worked in the fields. He had nothing. He built a small business in the teens. A *mexicano* with a second- or third-grade education, I don't know exactly, second-, third-grade. . . . A *mexicano* with no education in the 1920s, building a business like that. By the 1930s, my mother was in the best Catholic boarding school in Los Angeles. Mother spoke five languages. My mother was a brilliant woman. My grandpa lost all his money in the Depression. He had a younger wife. She left him. He had two daughters. He worked day and night, but had to put them in a foster home and visited them on weekends. He put them in Catholic school so they could get a good education. That was the greatest generation. They were *mexicanos* who were part of the greatest generation. They sacrificed during the Depression and during World War II so that we would have a better life.

The opportunity of America that we believe in is the opportunity of America that gave us the Civil Rights Act and the Voting Rights Act. President Obama understands that as well as anyone. My grandfather left Mexico because Mexico was a place of rich and poor. Today they have 53 percent of their people in the middle class, but back then it was rich and poor. He wanted to go to a country where you could start at the bottom and go to the top. He wanted to go to a country where you reward work. He wanted to go to a country where even during the time of a virulent discrimination, you could start up your own business and make it.

We believe in that country too. This convention is a convention that's going to make crystal clear the two roads ahead. You know, there are really only two roads ahead. There could be a third road, but they've gone so far to the right that there are only two roads ahead now. According to Moody's Analytics, not the president, not the Democrats, but Moody's Analytics, if we stay the course and follow President Obama's plan to cut $4 trillion out of our deficit, and do it in a way that doesn't raise taxes on the middle class and invest in small businesses, that will create jobs. It doesn't extend the Bush tax cuts to the top 2 percent. By the way, all the talk about taxing the rich: we're just putting them back to where we were during the Clinton years. When we took Bush 41's failed policies of deficits to record surpluses and 23 million jobs, you take that path forward; it's a path that's not going to decimate education.

So yes, I'm honored to be mayor. I'm honored to be the chair, but I'm most honored to serve you. I want to thank you. I want to say that this has been a ride like no other. But I also want to say this. I don't think you have to be in public life to serve your community. I don't think you have to be in public life to advocate for what's right. I think you can do that in many different ways. I know that the people here, all of you who are here, both Latino and non-Latino, are here because you care, because you understand that this is a growing, vibrant, important community to the future of our nation.

About the Editors

MICKEY IBARRA, a graduate of the University of Utah, is president of the Ibarra Strategy Group, a government relations and public affairs firm in Washington, D.C. He is the founder and chairman of the Latino Leaders Network, a nonprofit organization dedicated to bringing leaders together.

MARÍA PÉREZ-BROWN, a television executive with extensive experience in content development, production and programming, is the author of *Mamá: Latina Daughters Celebrate Their Mothers* (Harper Collins, 2002), which was published simultaneously in English and Spanish. A graduate of Yale University and New York University Law School, she lives with her family in New York City.